IMAGES
of America

AFRICAN AMERICANS OF PORTLAND

On the Cover: Pictured are African American children riding on an automobile decorated with roses as they participate in the 1913 Portland Rose Festival Floral Parade. The "colored float" was sponsored by the Colored Women's Council, organized in 1912. Highlights of the parade were reported in the *Morning Oregonian* of June 12, 1913. The reporter commented that the float that drew much applause was that of the Colored Women's Council, which represented the Tuskegee Institute. (Courtesy of the Oregon Historical Society.)

IMAGES
of America

AFRICAN AMERICANS OF PORTLAND

Oregon Black Pioneers
Kimberly Stowers Moreland

ARCADIA
PUBLISHING

ISBN 978-0-7385-9619-8

Published by Arcadia Publishing
Charleston, South Carolina

Printed in the United States of America

Library of Congress Control Number: 2012941001

For all general information, please contact Arcadia Publishing:
Telephone 843-853-2070
Fax 843-853-0044
E-mail sales@arcadiapublishing.com
For customer service and orders:
Toll-Free 1-888-313-2665

Visit us on the Internet at www.arcadiapublishing.com

This book is dedicated to Portland's African American pioneers. Your courage, perseverance, and self-determination will be forever remembered, honored, and deeply etched in our hearts.

Contents

Acknowledgments

This book would not be possible without the support and encouragement of several people who unselfishly gave their time, energy, expertise, and resources. First, I would like to thank my loving husband, Mike, and my children, Katie, Mike, Kristen, and Karina, for their loving support and unyielding patience as I devoted my time to completing this project. I would also like to thank dear friend, fellow breast cancer survivor, and Arcadia author Kimberli Fitzgerald for her encouragement and friendship and Willie B. Richardson, president of the Oregon Black Pioneers (OBP); Gwen Carr, chair, OBP Research/Education Committee; and fellow members of the OBP Board of Directors for deciding to move forward with the project.

Special thanks go to former OBP board member Mary Oberst and to Cathy Galbraith, executive director of the Architectural Heritage Center, for their editing skills. The OBP is indebted to board member Charlotte Rutherford, retired administrative judge, and Cris Paschild, archivist and head of Special Collections, Portland State University Library, for the generous use of the Verdell Burdine and Otto G. Rutherford Family Collections. The inclusion of Ed Washington's, Avel Gordly's, Elva Poole Belcher's, Ella Crumble's, and the Maney family's collections added a special touch. Elder Ed and Gen Robinson are much appreciated for their assistance with the Mount Olivet Baptist Church's collection. The book was enhanced by the generous access to the City of Portland Archives, the University of Oregon Special Collections, and the Oregon State University Libraries Special Collections and Archive Research Center. Oregon archivists Carolee Harris (Portland State University), Brian Johnson (City of Portland), Mary Hansen (City of Portland), Lesli Larson (University of Oregon), and Tiah Edmunson-Morton (Oregon State University) provided invaluable assistance. Much gratitude is extended to those who have paved the way for this book through their research, writings, and enthusiasm for black history. We hope that readers will find this photographic journey a worthy source of information and an inspiration to better understand the people, institutions, and community of African Americans of Portland, Oregon.

The terms *African American* and *black* are used interchangeably throughout the document. The terms *Negro*, *colored*, *Afro-American*, *Kanakas*, *Orientals*, and *Chinamen* have been used within their historical context.

INTRODUCTION

The first black of record to set foot in what is now Oregon was Marcus Lopius (or Lopez), an African from the Cape Verde Islands. He was a cabin boy and cook aboard Capt. Robert Gray's ship, which landed at Tillamook in 1788. Seventeen years later, York, a member of the historic Lewis and Clark Corps of Discovery, became the second African American man to come to Oregon and the first African American man to explore what would become Portland. African American settlers also traveled the historical 2,000-mile wagon route known as the Oregon Trail beginning in 1840. They served as guides for missionaries and wagon trains and were employed as fur trappers and traders for the Hudson's Bay Company. Many were slaves who arrived with their owners and a promise of their freedom upon their arrival.

Before Oregon's provisional government was established in 1843, a small population of African Americans was scattered throughout Oregon's rural areas; however, Oregon declared its prejudice against black people by passing the territory's first exclusion law in 1844. Between 1844 and 1866, Oregon's territorial and constitutional governments passed a series of exclusion laws designed to ban free African Americans from the territory and protect white settlers from the perceived threat of combined African and Native American hostilities. Delegates at Oregon's Constitutional Convention in 1857 overwhelmingly outlawed slavery but also banned free African Americans from settling in Oregon. When Oregon gained statehood on February 14, 1859, it became the first state admitted to the Union with an exclusion law written in the state constitution. The Oregon Donation Land Act of 1850 was passed with promises of free land for white settlers only. In 1862, the Oregon legislative session adopted a law requiring an annual poll tax of $5 to be paid by "every Negro, Chinaman, Kanakas (Hawaiian) and Mulatto residing within the limits of the state."

Oregon's exclusion laws, although not enforced vigorously, were successful in practice. Blacks residing in Oregon between 1844 and 1865 lived with the possibility they might be expelled at any time. Anti-black laws were successful in deterring early black migration and residence in the Oregon Territory. By the end of the 19th century, new employment opportunities in Portland and growing anti-black sentiment elsewhere spurred the growth of Portland's African American community. By 1867, a total of 147 African Americans resided in Portland. The Colored School was established in 1867, and 21 boys and 5 girls were enrolled at the close of the first quarter for the school year of 1867–1968. By 1872, the Colored School was closed, and African American children entered the regular schools.

The opening of the Portland Hotel and the completion of the transcontinental railroad system were two catalysts for the growth of Portland's African American population. The completion of transcontinental rail lines brought African American railroad workers to Portland. By 1909, five transcontinental rail lines ran through the heart of Northeast Portland. In 1890, approximately 75 African American men from South Carolina and Georgia were recruited to work in the Portland Hotel as waiters and barbers. Many of these men eventually settled in Portland with their families.

By 1890, the majority of Oregon's black population resided in Multnomah County, and the small African American community began to form a geographic center on Portland's west side near Union Station and the Portland Hotel. Four early black churches and the Golden West Hotel provided gathering places for the black community. By 1910, the west side had two-thirds of Portland's 1,045 blacks and almost all of its Asian Americans. The opening of the Morrison, Steel, and Broadway Bridges and the extension of the railway system spurred the growth of Portland's new middle-class neighborhoods on the east side of the Willamette River. Several black families were among those early residents of Portland's growing east side. In 1919, the realty board adopted a policy where "Negroes and Orientals" could buy homes within the area between Broadway and the Steel Bridge in inner Northeast Portland.

At the beginning of the 20th century, political, spiritual, and social institutions that promoted civil and political rights, education, high morals, and social regeneration were established. This era incubated many firsts in Oregon: the first black doctor, dentist, attorney, and police officer, as well as the first black person admitted to the bar. In 1896, Portland's first black-owned newspaper, the *New Age*, was published by A.D. Griffin. A second black-owned newspaper, the *Advocate*, was founded by several black entrepreneurs and began publication in 1903. A third black-owned newspaper, the *Portland Times*, was established in 1918. As the backbone of the community, black women advanced the betterment of the community through their active participation in local churches and civic organizations such as the Colored Women's Council. Blacks began to organize politically. In 1895, the Lincoln Colored Republican Club merged with the Bed Rock Republican Club. The McKinley and Hobart Colored League was organized in October 1896 with a membership of 33. The Portland Chapter of the National Association for the Advancement of Colored People (NAACP) was established in 1913, and a Colored Women's Republican Club was established in 1914. The first civil rights bill to be presented to the state legislature was drafted by the Portland Chapter of the Afro-American League in 1919.

By 1940, Portland's small, industrious African American community consisted of roughly 2,500 people. The World War II shipbuilding industry recruited several thousand blacks, and the respective population increased nearly tenfold. The Kaiser Shipyard provided employment for black workers from 1941 to 1945. This influx of defense workers intensified Portland's housing crisis. In response, the Housing Authority of Portland and Henry J. Kaiser built wartime housing in Vancouver, Washington, and on the muddy flats of Vanport, named for its location between Portland and Vancouver. Vanport became the largest wartime housing project in the nation and the second largest city in Oregon. After the war, due to the housing shortage and racial segregation practices, most black defense workers were confined to the "temporary" Vanport housing project; however, that all changed on Memorial Day in 1948, when Vanport experienced a devastating flood that wiped out the entire city. The City of Portland scrambled to address the resettlement of Vanport families who were left homeless.

Faced with limited housing choices, truncated civil rights, and restricted employment opportunities, Portland's new black community rose to the challenge with the enduring efforts of community leaders and long-standing institutions, such as the local churches, the Urban League of Portland, and the Portland Branch of the NAACP. Segregated housing practices and displacement caused by the construction of Memorial Coliseum and Interstate 5 forced the concentration of African Americans into inner North/Northeast Portland. A thriving black-owned business and entertainment district emerged on North Williams Avenue. National and local musicians performed at the Dude Ranch, a premier jazz venue at 240 North Broadway in the 1940s. The postwar era birthed a new generation of community activists and organizers who became the bedrock of black political leadership.

As you turn the pages of this photographic journey, you will find that the once "unwelcomed settlers" indeed found a home in Oregon, raised their families, fulfilled their dreams, and contributed to the overall wellbeing of our great city of Portland, Oregon.

One

The Prolific Journey Begins

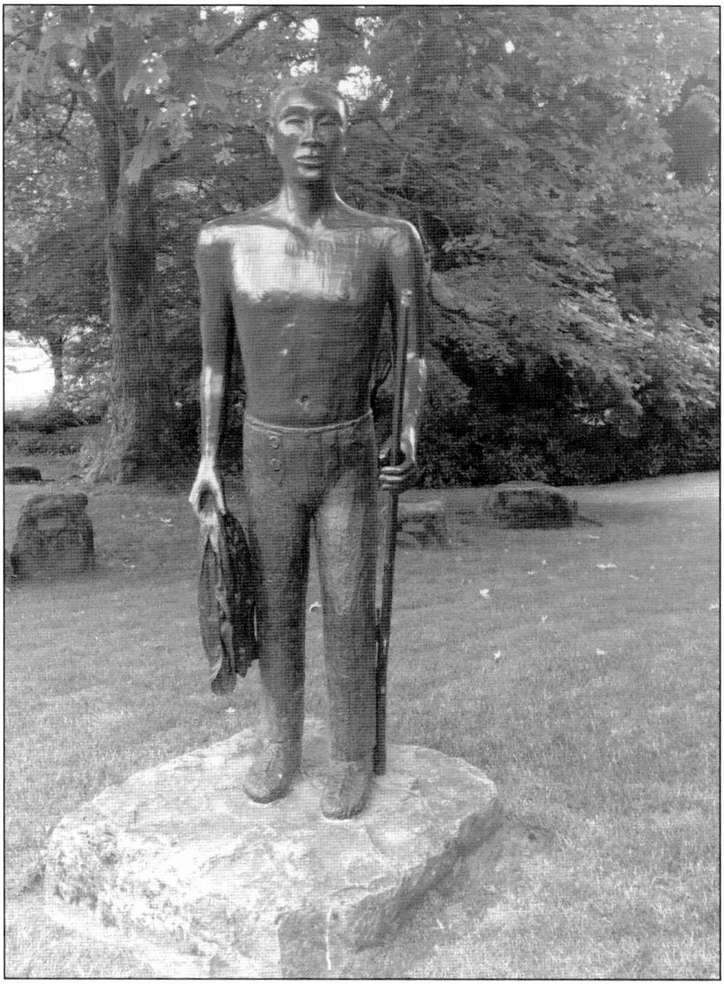

York: Terra Incognita, a sculpture by Alison Saar, represents Lewis & Clark College's permanent memorial to York, a key contributor to the Lewis and Clark expedition. York, Clark's slave, was the first documented black man to explore the Willamette River and visit the future site of Portland, Oregon. York participated fully in the Corps of Discovery, and his bravery, strength, and skills contributed to the success of the expedition. (Photograph taken by Kimberly Moreland.)

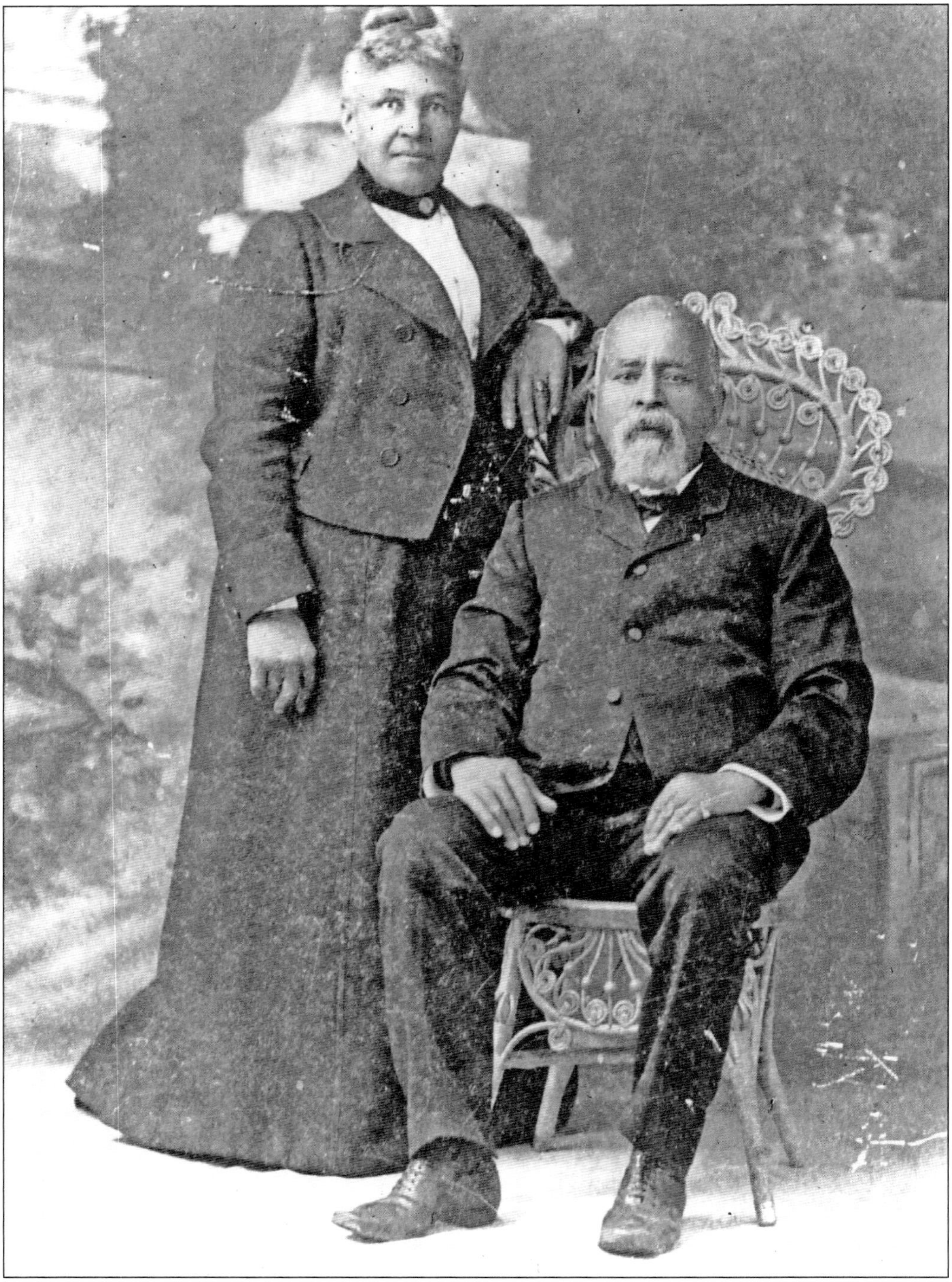

America Waldo was born in Missouri in 1844 and arrived in Oregon in 1846. Waldo married Jamaican-born Richard Arthur Bogle on January 1, 1863, the same day Pres. Abraham Lincoln signed the Emancipation Proclamation. Due to racial barriers and black exclusion laws, the Bogles settled in eastern Washington, purchased a 200-acre farm, and cofounded Walla Walla Savings and Loan Association. One of their children, Waldo Bogle, moved to Portland in 1913 and operated Waldo Bogle's Barbershop in the Golden West Hotel. (Courtesy of the Oregon Historical Society.)

Pictured here are Earl W. and Margaret Burdine and their children. From left to right, the children are Alfred, Verdell (on lap), and Delores. The Burdines came to Bend, Oregon, from Muskogee, Oklahoma, in 1913. After a few months, the Burdines moved to Marshfield, Oregon, and they later settled in Yakima, Washington, in 1920. (Courtesy of the Rutherford Family Collection and PSU Library.)

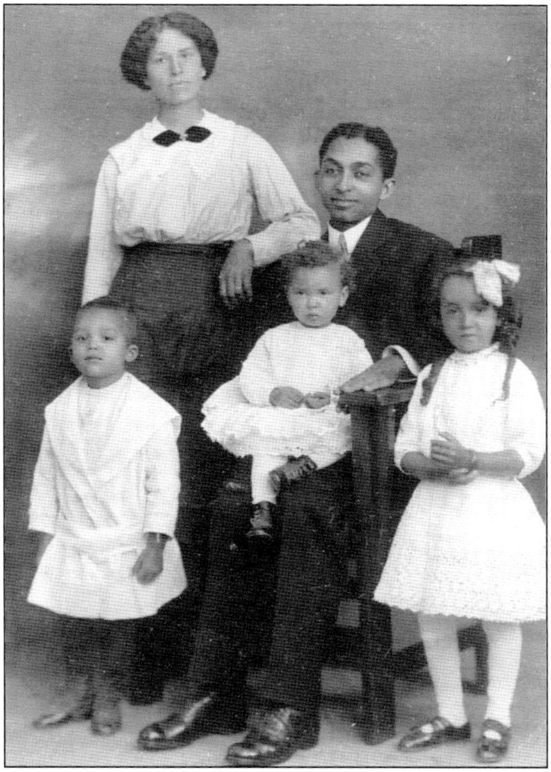

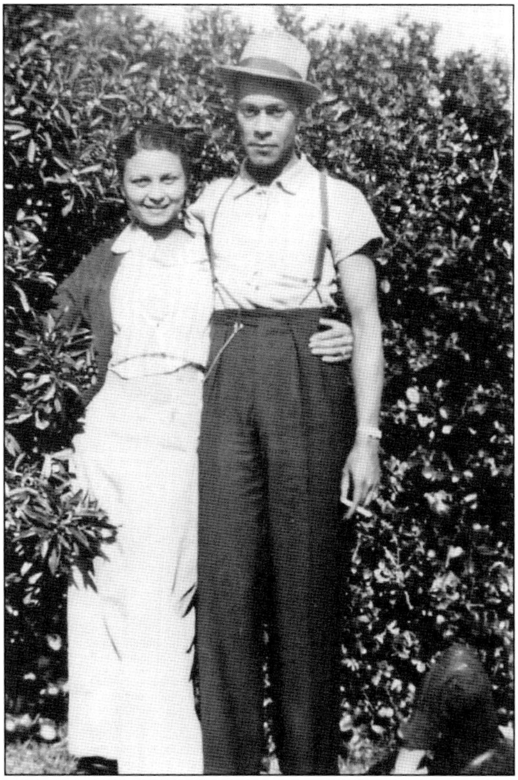

The Burdine daughter, Verdell, and Portland native Otto Rutherford met when he was eight and she was six while the Burdine family traveled from Marshfield to Yakima and stopped in Portland to worship at Bethel African Methodist Episcopal (AME) Church. They continued to meet through church activities, and Verdell married Otto G. Rutherford in 1936. The couple's activism led to the passage of the Public Accommodation Acts by the legislature in 1953, ending Oregon's long history of segregation at lodging, restaurants, and recreational facilities. (Courtesy of the Rutherford Family Collection and PSU Library.)

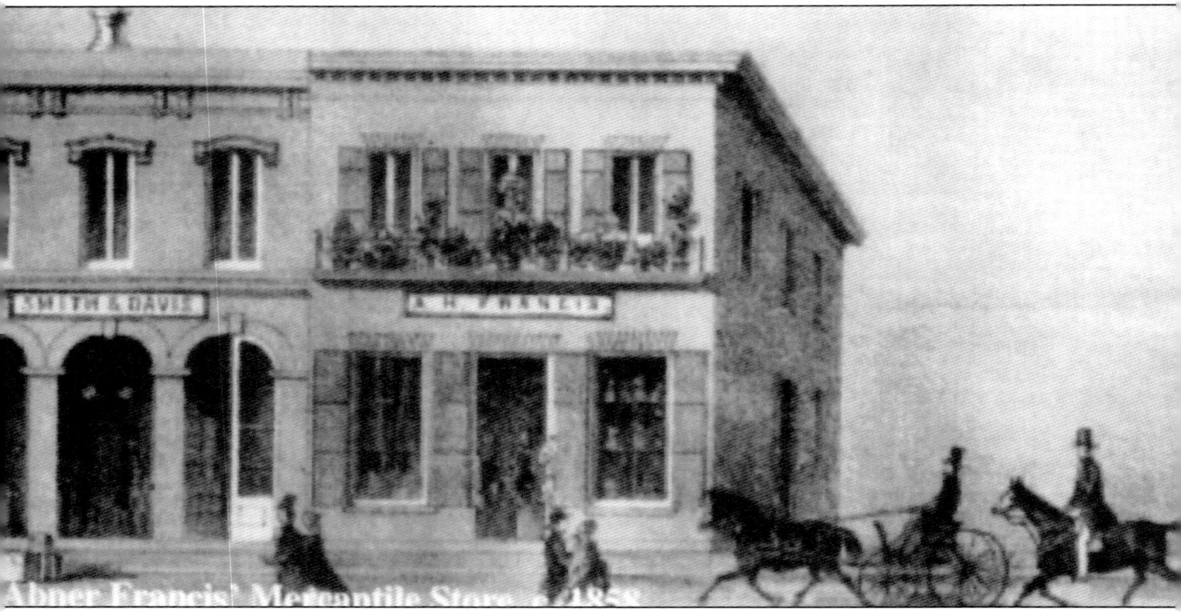

Abner Hunt Francis and his wife, Lynda Francis, and brother, O.B. Francis, arrived in Portland and opened a mercantile store. Abner was born on a farm near Flexington, New Jersey, and became a leader and entrepreneur wherever he resided. Prior to coming to Oregon he opened a clothing store in Buffalo, New York, and was a leading member of the Buffalo Anti-Slavery Society. Upon arriving in Oregon, the Francises soon became the target of judicial expulsion based on the territorial exclusion law adopted in 1849. A petition signed by 211 people convinced the legislature to allow an exemption. Before voluntarily leaving Portland for Victoria, British Columbia, in 1860, the Francises amassed real and personal properties valued at $36,000. In 1865, Abner Hunt Francis became the first black person elected to the city council of Victoria, Vancouver Island, Canada. (Courtesy of the City of Portland.)

African American pioneers' experience as seamen was their first point of contact with Portland, Oregon. Many arrived in Oregon as crew members aboard ships traveling to Oregon for many reasons. Pictured here is a crew member at the Portland Harbor in 1919. (Courtesy of Alex Blendl, Historical Photos.)

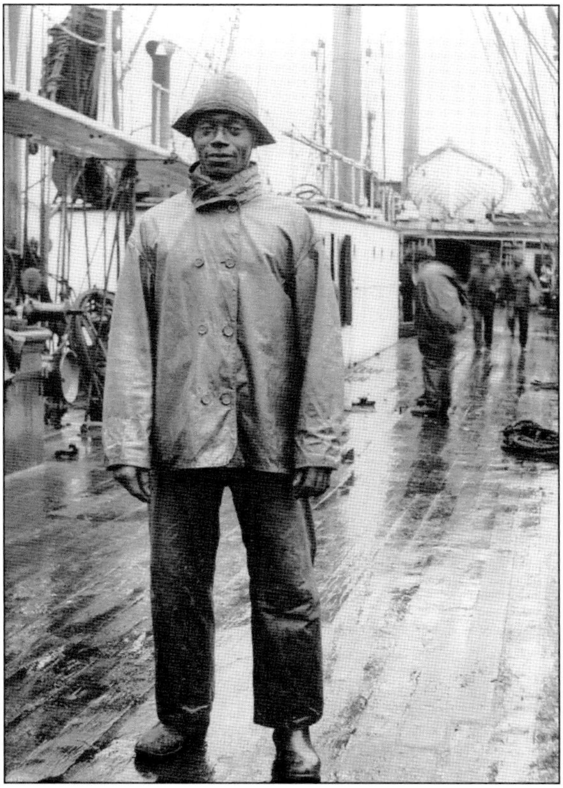

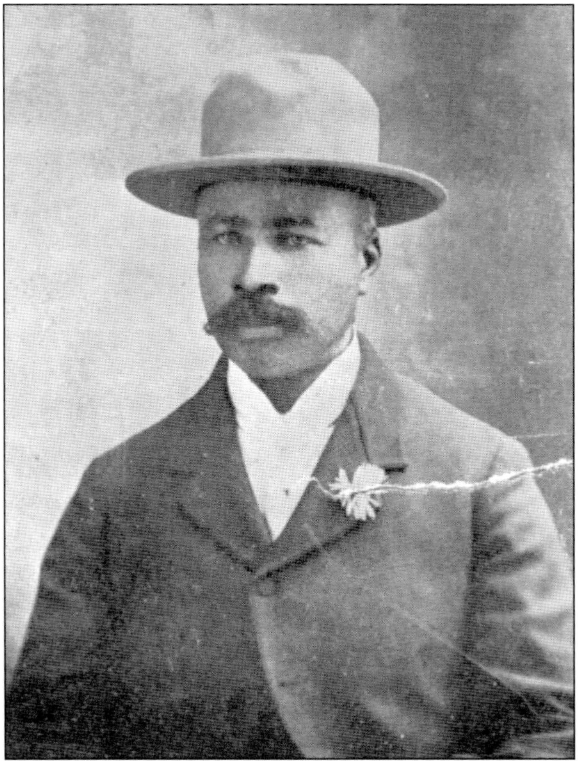

George Singleton, a Portland pioneer, lived in the area beginning in 1879. An article dated August 2, 1919, in the *Portland Times*, an early black newspaper, claims that Singleton "has lived in this city since the time it was a one-street road along the river until the present-time metropolitan city of many. He can rightfully be called a landmark because he has knowledge of every improvement in Portland during the last 40 years." (Courtesy of the Oregon Historical Society.)

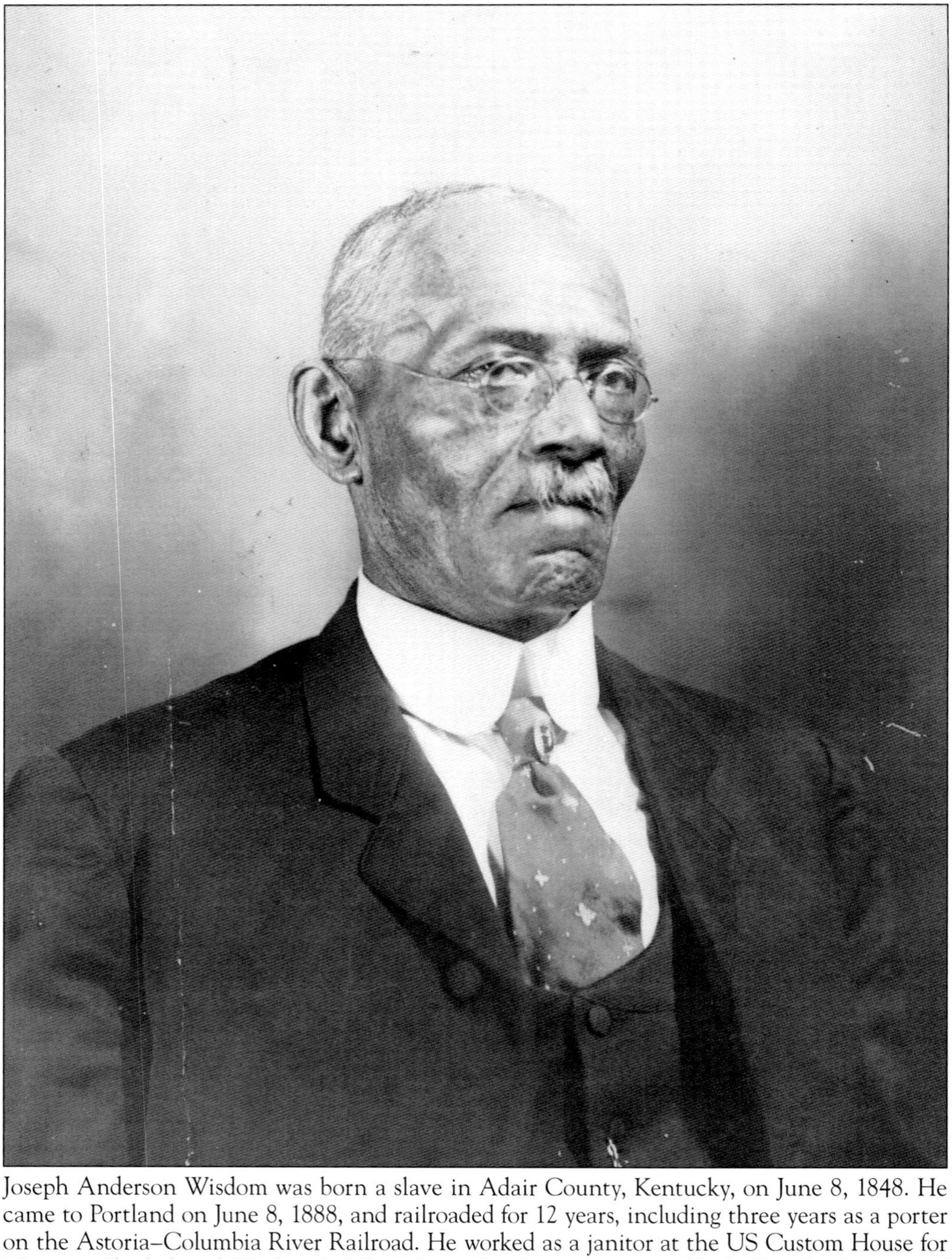

Joseph Anderson Wisdom was born a slave in Adair County, Kentucky, on June 8, 1848. He came to Portland on June 8, 1888, and railroaded for 12 years, including three years as a porter on the Astoria–Columbia River Railroad. He worked as a janitor at the US Custom House for 25 years. The beloved Wisdom led the Liberty Bond parade during World War I. (Courtesy of the Oregon Historical Society.)

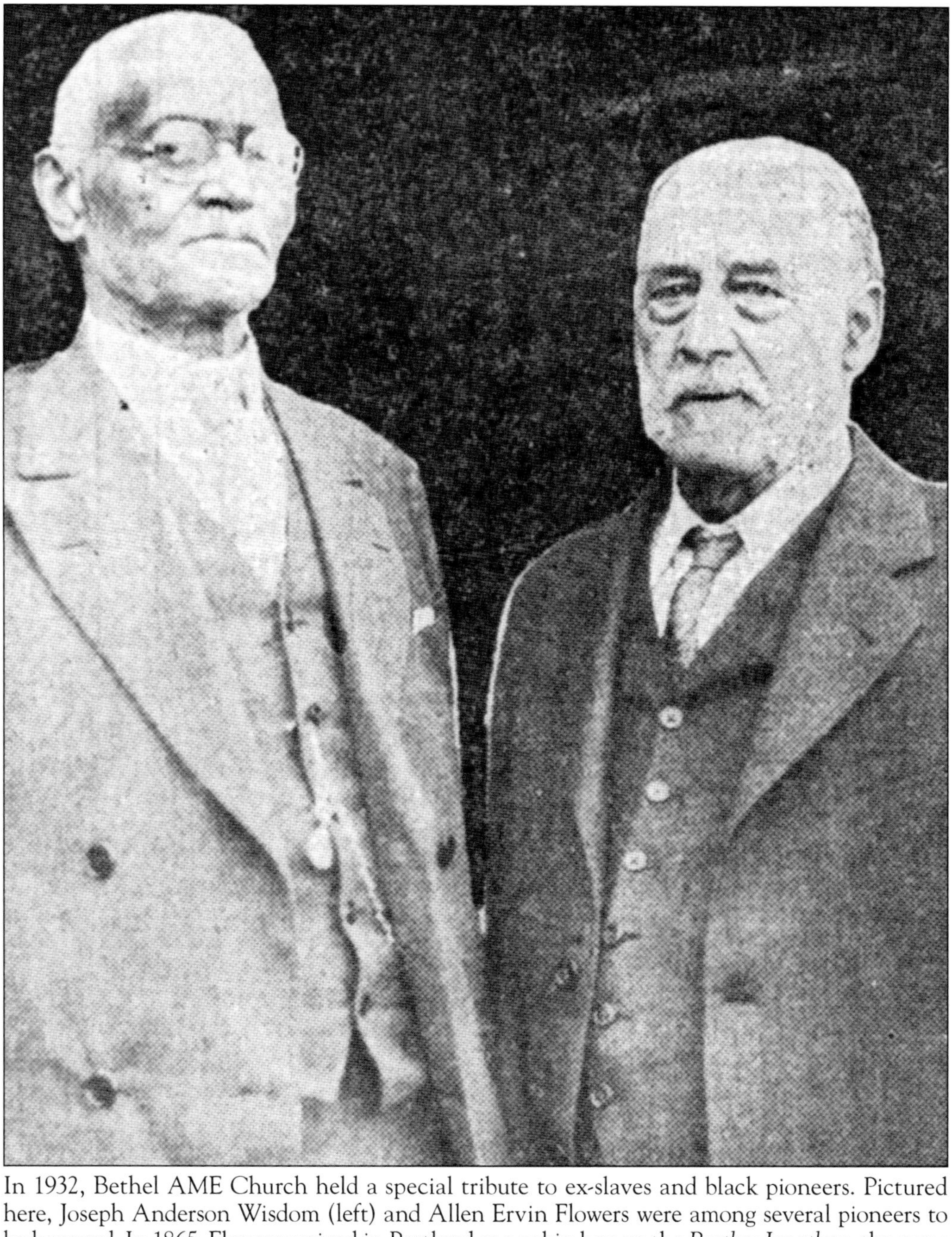

In 1932, Bethel AME Church held a special tribute to ex-slaves and black pioneers. Pictured here, Joseph Anderson Wisdom (left) and Allen Ervin Flowers were among several pioneers to be honored. In 1865, Flowers arrived in Portland as a cabin boy on the *Brother Jonathon*, the same ship that brought Oregon the official statehood announcement. When Flowers jumped ship that year, he unknowingly saved his own life, because three trips later, the *Brother Jonathon*, on its return to Portland, sank off the coast near Crescent City, California. Flowers's first job in Portland was as a waiter in the Lincoln Hotel. Later, he worked for the US Custom House and Northern Pacific Railroad as porter-in-charge between Portland and Seattle. He married Canadian-born Louisa Thacker in 1882, and their family consisted of four boys: Lloyd, Ervin, Elmer, and Ralph. (Courtesy of the Oregon Historical Society.)

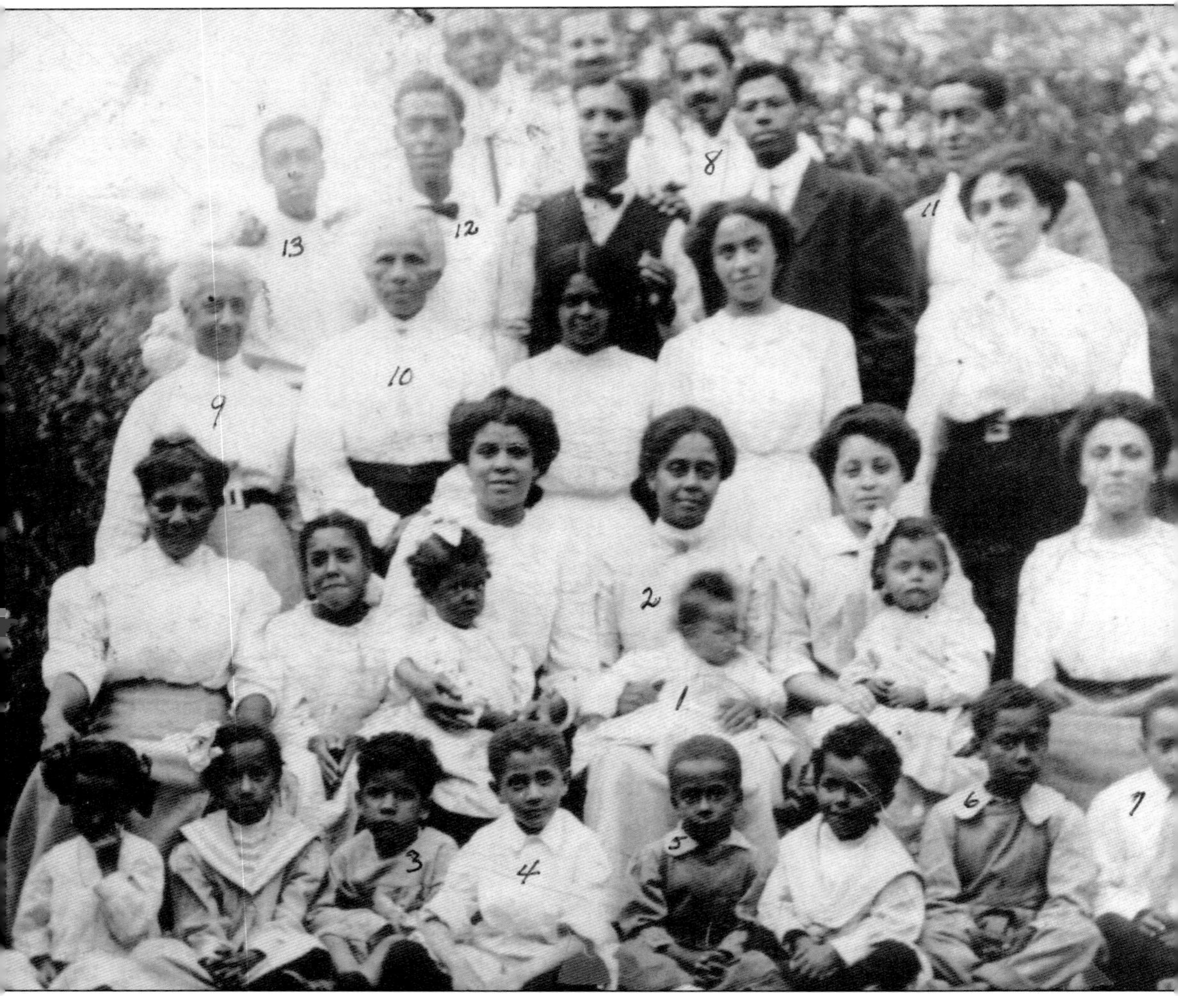

In 1901, Allen E. and Louisa M. Flowers and their four sons moved to a 20-acre farm on the north slope of Mount Scott. The Flowers family planted crops and raised cattle, sheep, and wild horses. Years later, Lincoln Memorial Cemetery purchased part of the property. The Flowerses also owned land in northeast Portland, and Allen constructed a road on Schuyler Street so that his wife could wheel her baby carriage to Union Avenue. The Flowerses were members of Bethel AME Church, and Louisa was a member of the Rosebud Club and charter member of the Williams Avenue YWCA. The 1911 photograph of a family picnic at the Flowerses' farm includes, from left to right, (first row) two unidentified children, Duncan Allen, Richard Bogle, Allen Rutherford, unidentified, William Rutherford III and Bennie Rutherford; (second row) two unidentified women, unidentified mother and child, Lottie Rutherford, Otto Rutherford (on lap), unidentified mother and child, and unidentified; (third row) Louisa Flowers; grandmother Walter, and three unidentified women; (fourth row) Ivy and Elmer Flowers, two unidentified men, and Ralph Flowers; (fifth row) two unidentified men and William H. Rutherford II. (Courtesy of the Rutherford Family Collection and PSU Library.)

After the Emancipation Proclamation, Oregon's black citizens organized an annual celebration to mark their freedom. Pictured here is an ornate announcement of the Grand Emancipation Celebration that was held in Portland at the Multnomah County Court House on January 1, 1869. The African American Methodist Episcopal Zion congregation was an early organizer and host of Portland's Emancipation Celebrations. (Courtesy of the Oregon Historical Society.)

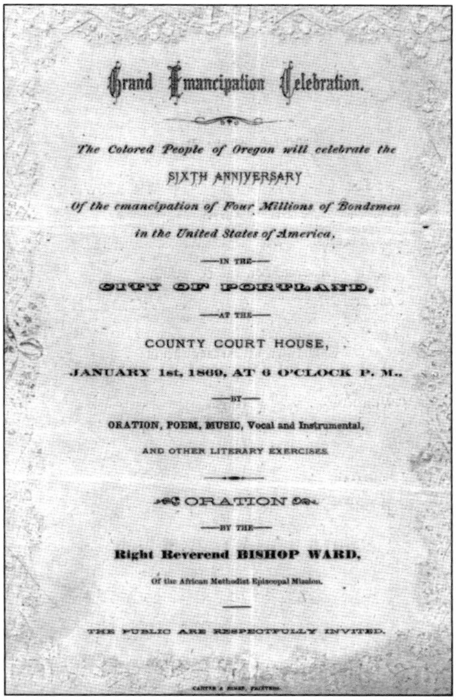

Grand Emancipation Celebration.

The Colored People of Oregon will celebrate the

SIXTH ANNIVERSARY

Of the emancipation of Four Millions of Bondsmen

in the United States of America,

—IN THE—

CITY OF PORTLAND,

—AT THE—

COUNTY COURT HOUSE,

JANUARY 1st, 1869, AT 6 O'CLOCK P. M.,

—BY—

ORATION, POEM, MUSIC, Vocal and Instrumental,

AND OTHER LITERARY EXERCISES.

ORATION

—BY THE—

Right Reverend BISHOP WARD,

Of the African Methodist Episcopal Mission.

THE PUBLIC ARE RESPECTFULLY INVITED.

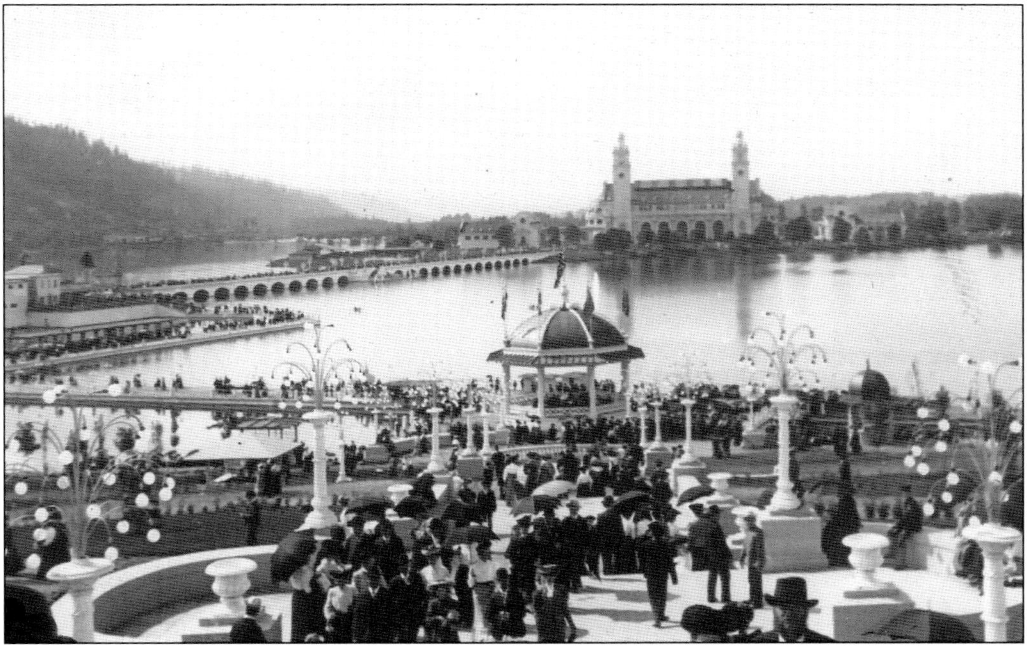

In September 1906, the Emancipation Celebration was held on the grounds of the 1905 Lewis and Clark Exposition. An organization known as the Emancipation Celebration Association was formed to organize the festivities. John Cassius Logan was the president, and prominent attorney McCants Stewart served as the secretary. A parade of politicians was present, including Judge John F. Caples, who, with the exception of his absence while serving as consul at Valparaiso, Chile, had attended the celebrations since 1865. (Courtesy of Special Collections and University Archives, UO Libraries.)

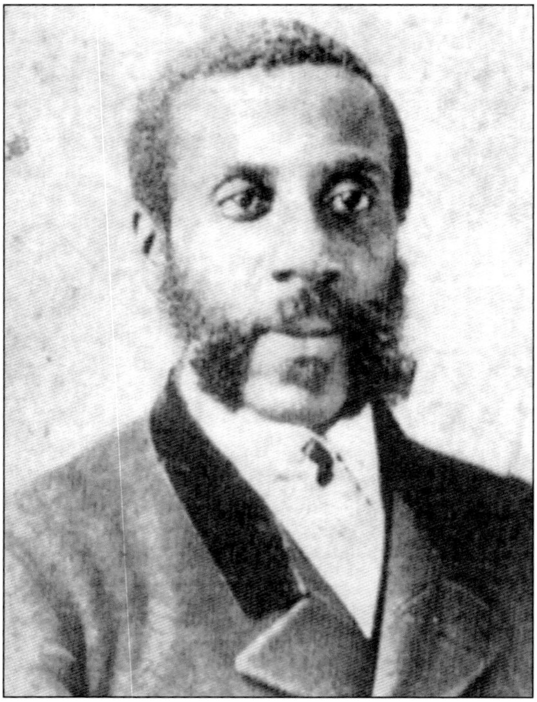

George Putnam Riley, a Boston native, participated in both the California and Canadian Northwest Territory Gold Rushes. In 1869, Riley, along with 14 other Portland residents, formed the Workingmen's Joint Stock Association (WJSA) and pooled funds to purchase real estate that was divided proportionately. The association purchased acres of land in Seattle and Tacoma, Washington. Riley died in Tacoma, Washington, in 1905 at the age of 72. (Courtesy of Blackpast.org.)

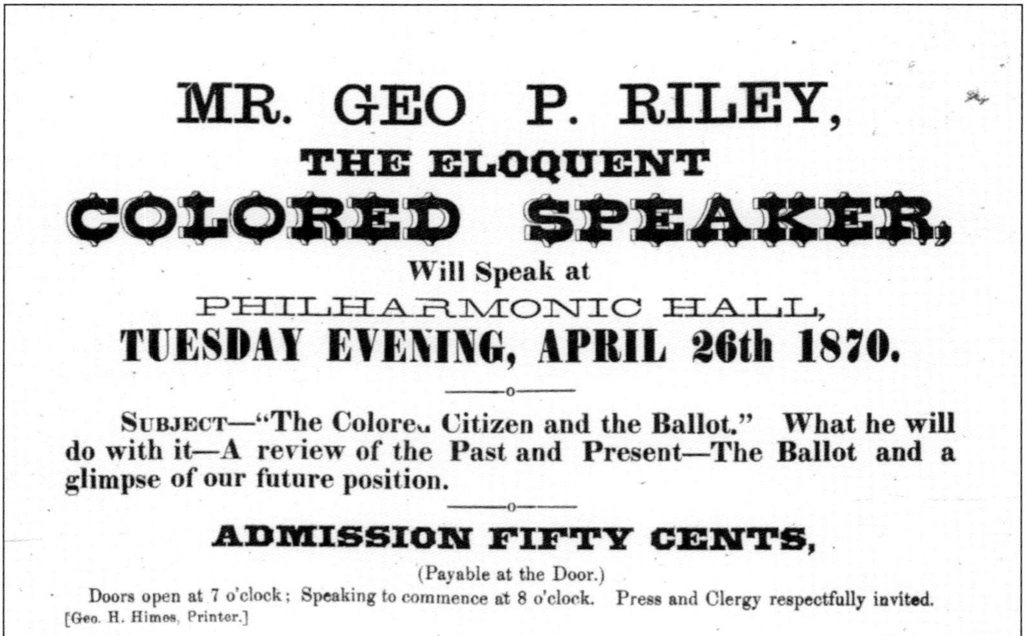

MR. GEO P. RILEY,

THE ELOQUENT

COLORED SPEAKER,

Will Speak at

PHILHARMONIC HALL,

TUESDAY EVENING, APRIL 26th 1870.

SUBJECT—"The Colore‹ Citizen and the Ballot." What he will do with it—A review of the Past and Present—The Ballot and a glimpse of our future position.

ADMISSION FIFTY CENTS,

(Payable at the Door.)

Doors open at 7 o'clock; Speaking to commence at 8 o'clock. Press and Clergy respectfully invited.

[Geo. H. Himes, Printer.]

Local printer George H. Himes produced this poster announcing an upcoming lecture by Portland resident George P. Riley. Riley's lecture was intended to draw attention to important milestones in African American history. He delivered his lecture a few weeks after Portland's Ratification Jubilee, which celebrated the passage of the 15th Amendment that extended voting rights to black men in the United States. (Courtesy of the Oregon Historical Society.)

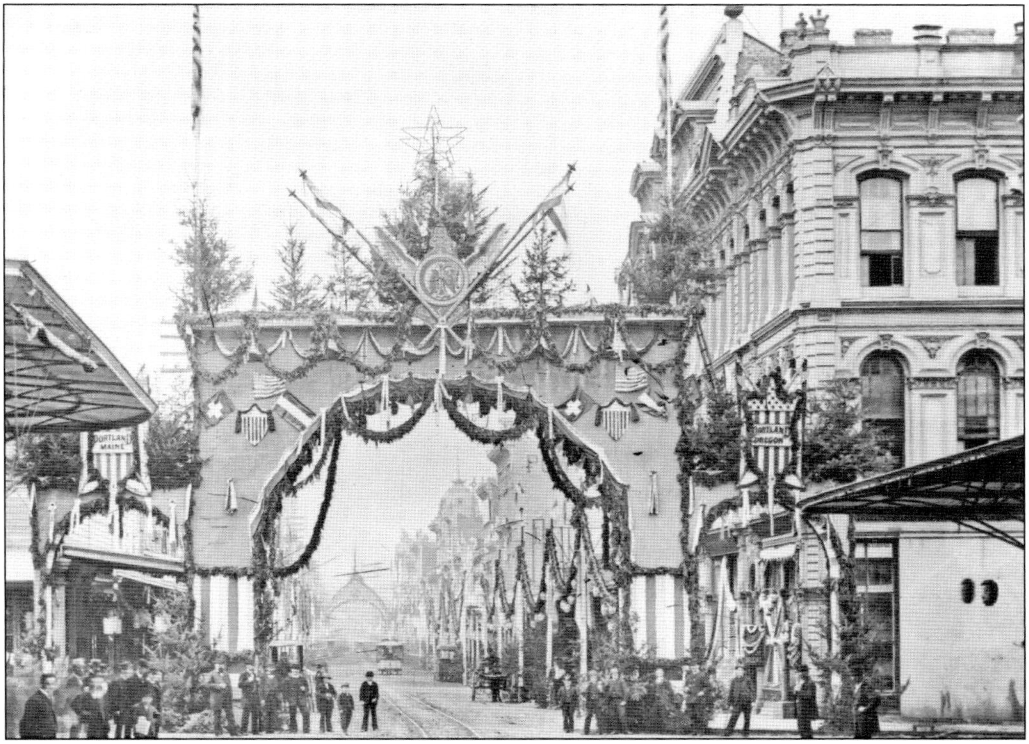

In September 1883, Portlanders organized a parade to welcome Henry Villard, German-born newspaperman and owner of the Oregon & California Railroad Company, and celebrate the completion of the city of Portland's Northern Pacific Railroad link with the eastern United States. According to an article published in the *Morning Oregonian*, dated September 12, 1883, a body of colored benevolent societies numbering around 20 people marched in the second division of the parade. Portlanders erected three ceremonial arches over First Avenue in 1883 and decorated many of the buildings along the street. (Courtesy of Alex Blendl, Historical Photos.)

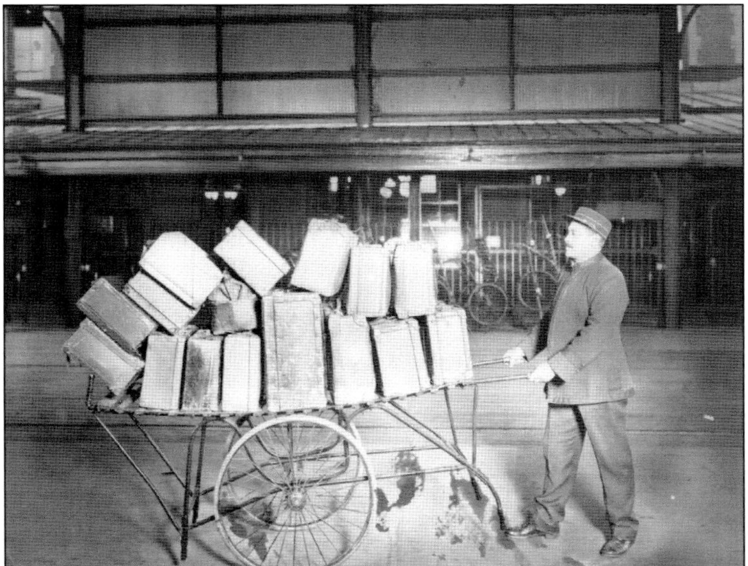

Pictured here is a railway porter pushing a metal baggage cart on the platform of Union Station in Portland. He is dressed in a uniform that consists of a short hat with brim; zip-up, long-sleeved jacket with the word "station" on the collar, and trousers. (Courtesy of Special Collections and University Archives, UO Libraries.)

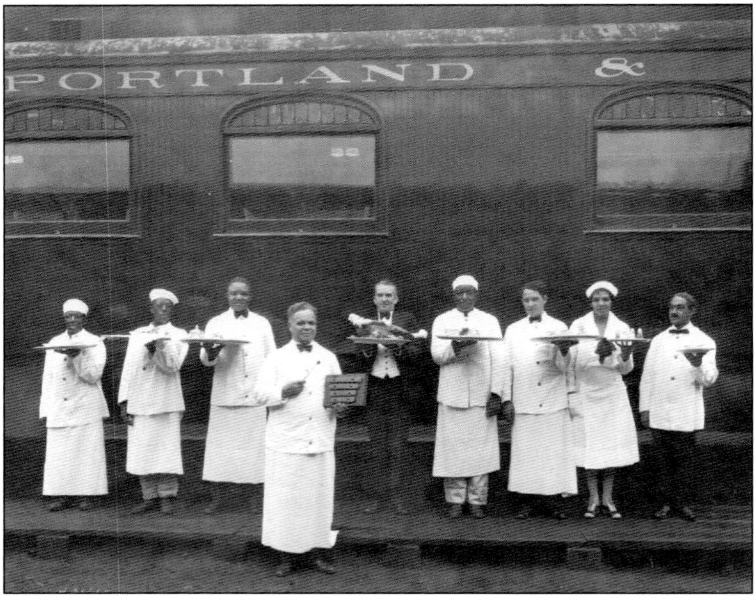

Pictured here are waiters posing in front of the Northern Pacific's Spokane-Portland-Seattle run in 1915. William H. Rutherford (far right) was recruited by the Portland Hotel from Columbia, South Carolina, in 1897. (Courtesy of the Oregon Historical Society.)

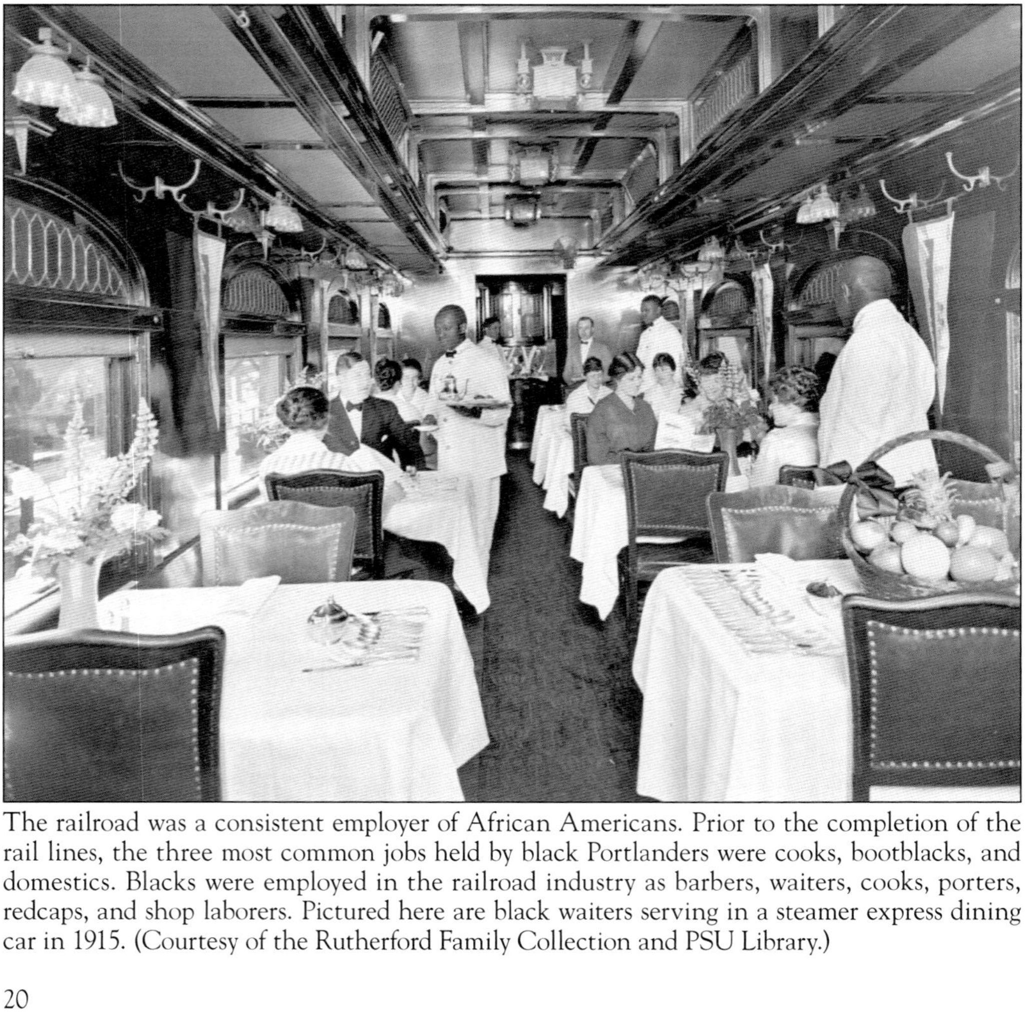

The railroad was a consistent employer of African Americans. Prior to the completion of the rail lines, the three most common jobs held by black Portlanders were cooks, bootblacks, and domestics. Blacks were employed in the railroad industry as barbers, waiters, cooks, porters, redcaps, and shop laborers. Pictured here are black waiters serving in a steamer express dining car in 1915. (Courtesy of the Rutherford Family Collection and PSU Library.)

J.C. Baker was born in Olathe, Kansas, in 1882. He started working for the Union Pacific in 1919 and was vice president and chairman of the Portland District, Local No. 465, Protective Order of Dining Car Waiters. He recruited and trained waiters for Union Pacific. Baker lived in Portland for 45 years and was a member of Bethel AME Church and the NAACP. He retired from the Union Pacific in 1946 and became president of the Retired Pensioners Association. (Courtesy of the Oregon Historical Society.)

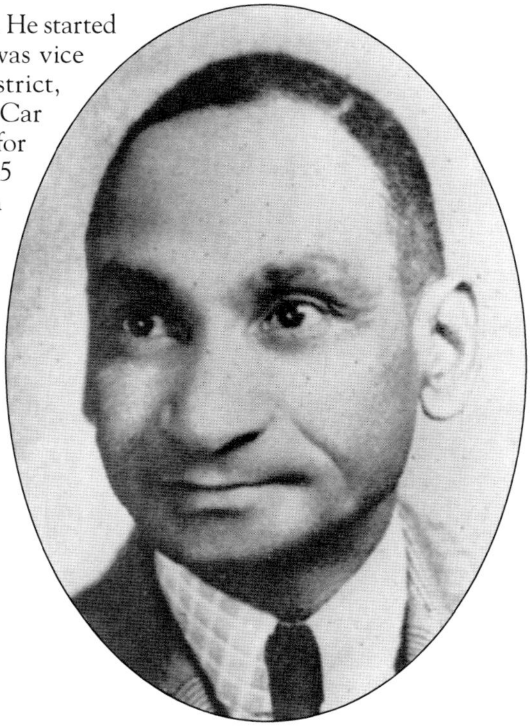

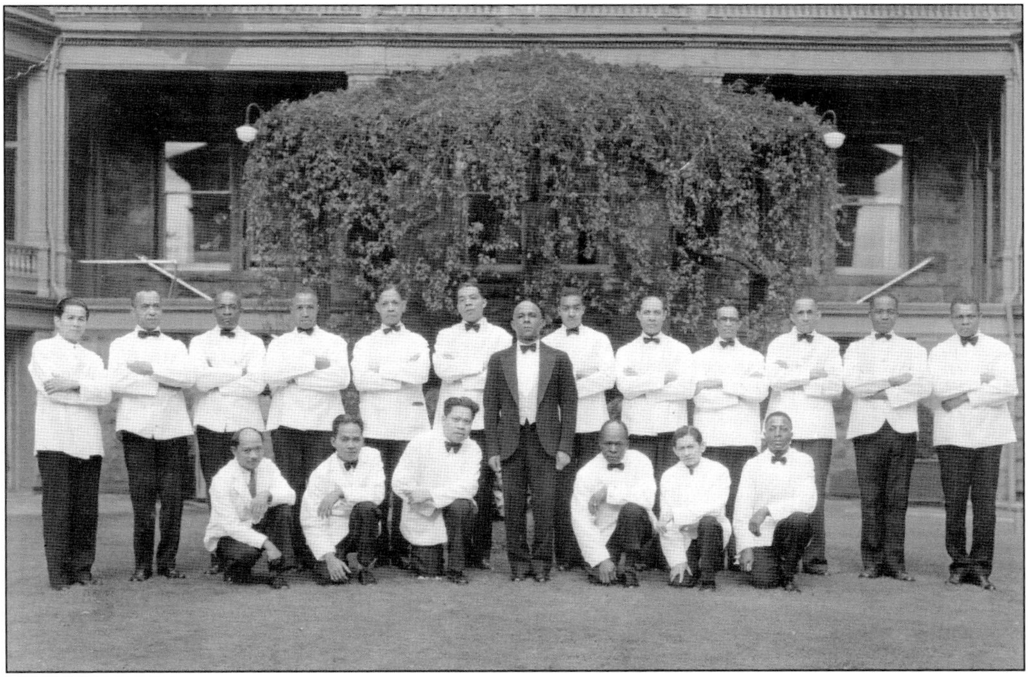

In 1890, approximately 75 black waiters and barbers were recruited from South Carolina and Georgia as employees for the lavish new Portland Hotel. They formed the nucleus of Portland's black community and eventually owned homes and raised their families. Headwaiter Albert Morton (center) is seen here with staff in front of the Portland Hotel. (Courtesy of the Oregon Historical Society.)

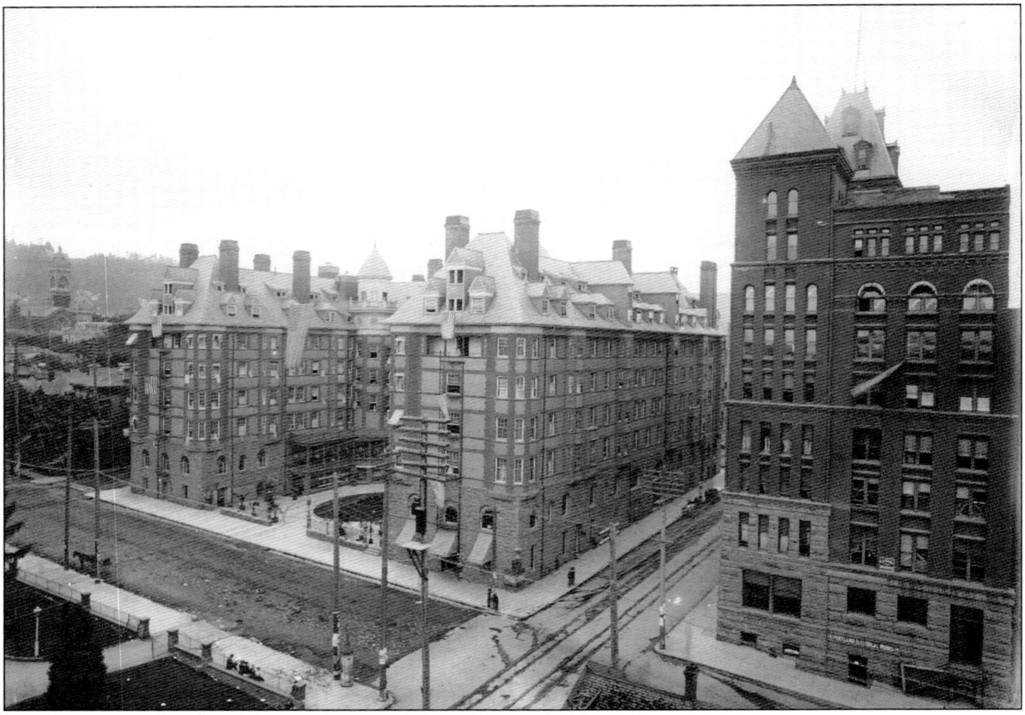

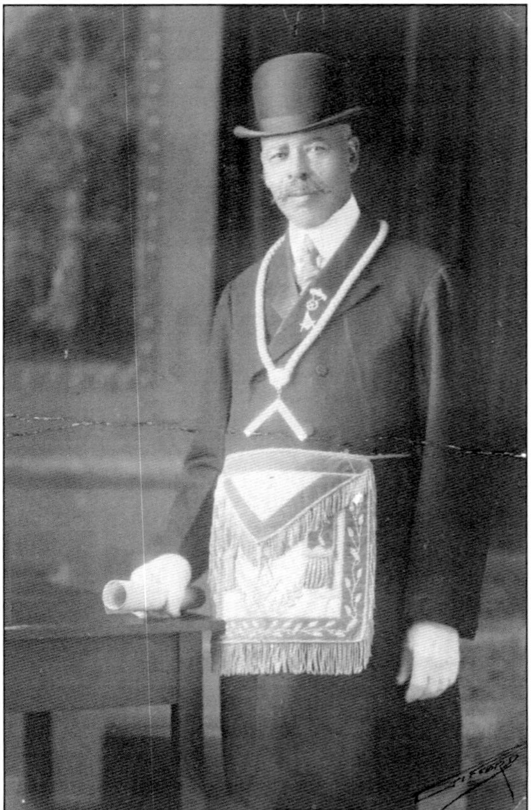

The Portland Hotel had been established and then abandoned in the 1880s. When it was completed in 1890, over $1 million had been spent to complete the eight-floor, 326-room hotel. For three decades, it was the center of business and social life in the city. (Courtesy of Special Collections and University Archives, UO Libraries.)

In an article entitled "Family Album Northwest," written by the late Kathryn Bogle, J.C. Logan was allegedly drawn to Portland from Spokane, Washington, by a Portland Hotel promoter who saw his excellent work as a waiter at a premier hotel in Spokane. He went back to his hometown in Columbia, South Carolina, to entice the best waiters he could find to join him in Portland. (Courtesy of the Oregon Historical Society.)

Two

FAITHFUL JOURNEY

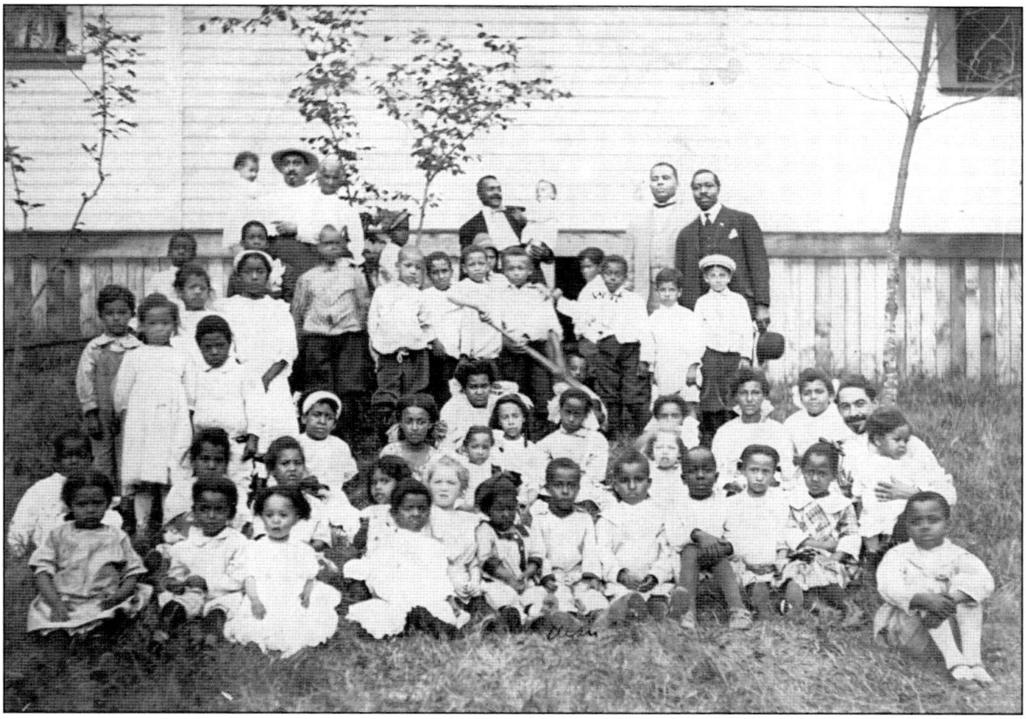

Since 1862, black churches in Oregon have played a vital role in ministering to the spiritual, social, economic, and political realities of Portland's black community. The first black church in Portland was the People's Church, founded in 1862 and later incorporated as the First African Methodist Episcopal Zion Church in 1869. These African American churches were originally established on Portland's west side near the Portland Hotel and Union Station. The early black churches were a social center for the small African American community. In 1923, there were four churches and two missions, including Shiloh Baptist Church, Mount Olivet Baptist Church, Bethel AME, First AME Zion Church, St. Philip Mission, and the Pentecostal Mission of the Church of God in Christ. An annual combined Sunday school picnic was a big affair attended by members of the black churches. The 1912 picnic included members of the Bethel African Methodist Episcopal, First African Methodist Episcopal Zion Church, and Mount Olivet Baptist Church. (Courtesy of the Rutherford Family Collection and PSU Library.)

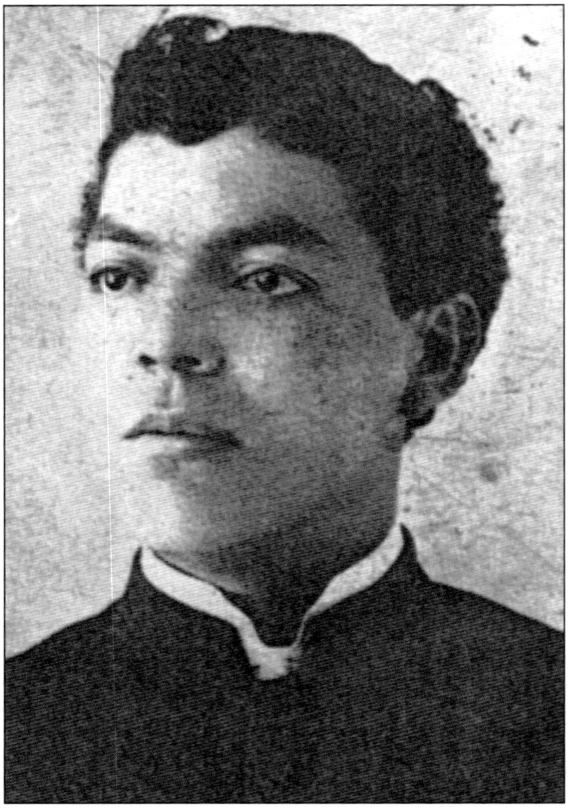

In 1889, a small group met in Phillip Jenkins's home and organized the Bethel AME Church, the second oldest black church in Portland. S.S. Freeman was the pastor appointed to Bethel AME. Freeman and his wife, Lenora, operated a successful boardinghouse for railway workers. Profit from the boardinghouse helped finance the purchase of Bethel's first church building, a former Japanese mission. His daughter, Clifford (Freeman) Dixon, shares that additional funds were raised by a cakewalk. S.S. Freeman, pictured here, left the ministry in 1899 and opened the city's first black-owned butcher shop and grocery store at Northwest Seventh (now Broadway) and Davis Streets in 1900. (Courtesy of the Rutherford Family Collection and PSU Library.)

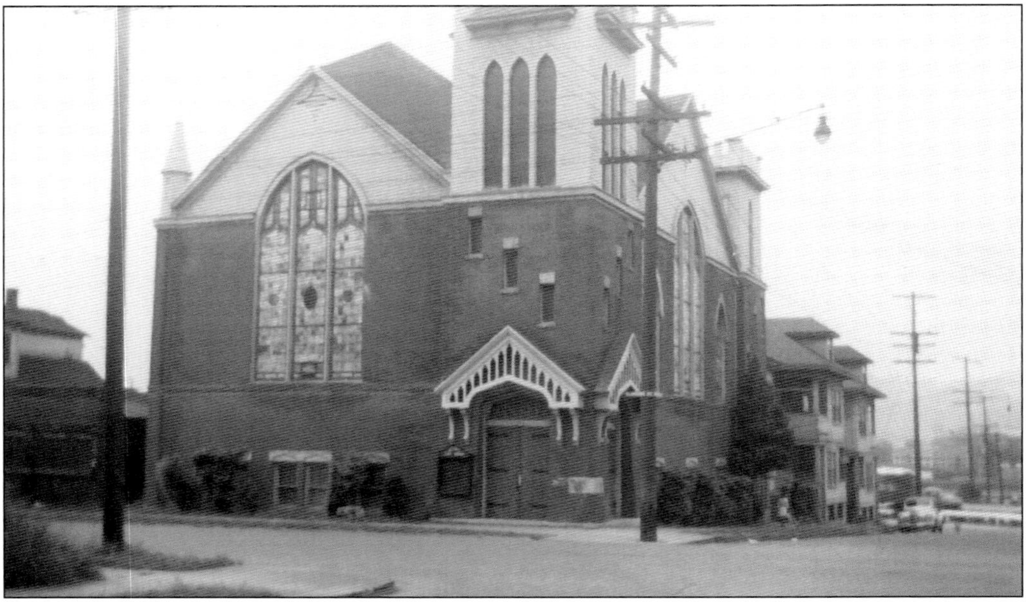

The congregation of Bethel AME remained in the former Japanese mission until 1916. It then moved to North Larrabee and McMillen Streets and worshipped in the basement until the second-floor sanctuary was added in 1922. In 1958, the church was forced to sell the property to the City of Portland for the construction of the new Memorial Coliseum and relocated to Eighth and Jarrett Streets. (Courtesy of the Rutherford Family Collection and PSU Library.)

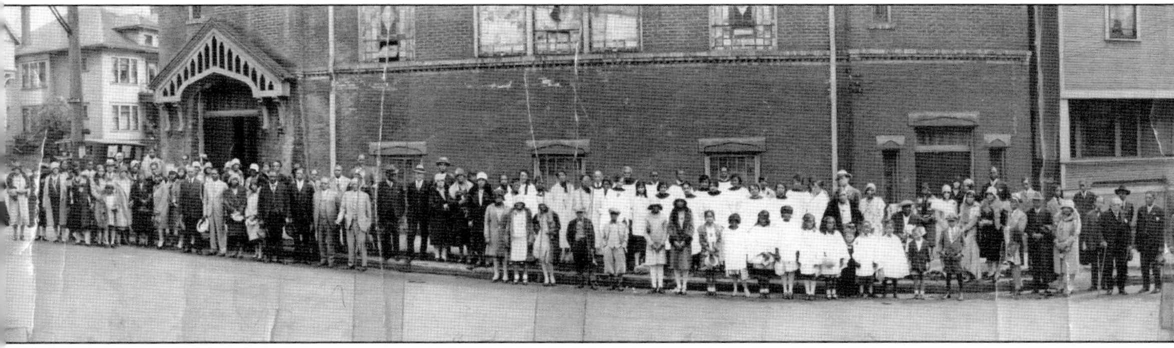

This 1930 panoramic photograph was taken on Easter Sunday in front of the historic Bethel AME Church. A similar image was captured in 1949. (Courtesy of the Rutherford Family Collection and PSU Library.)

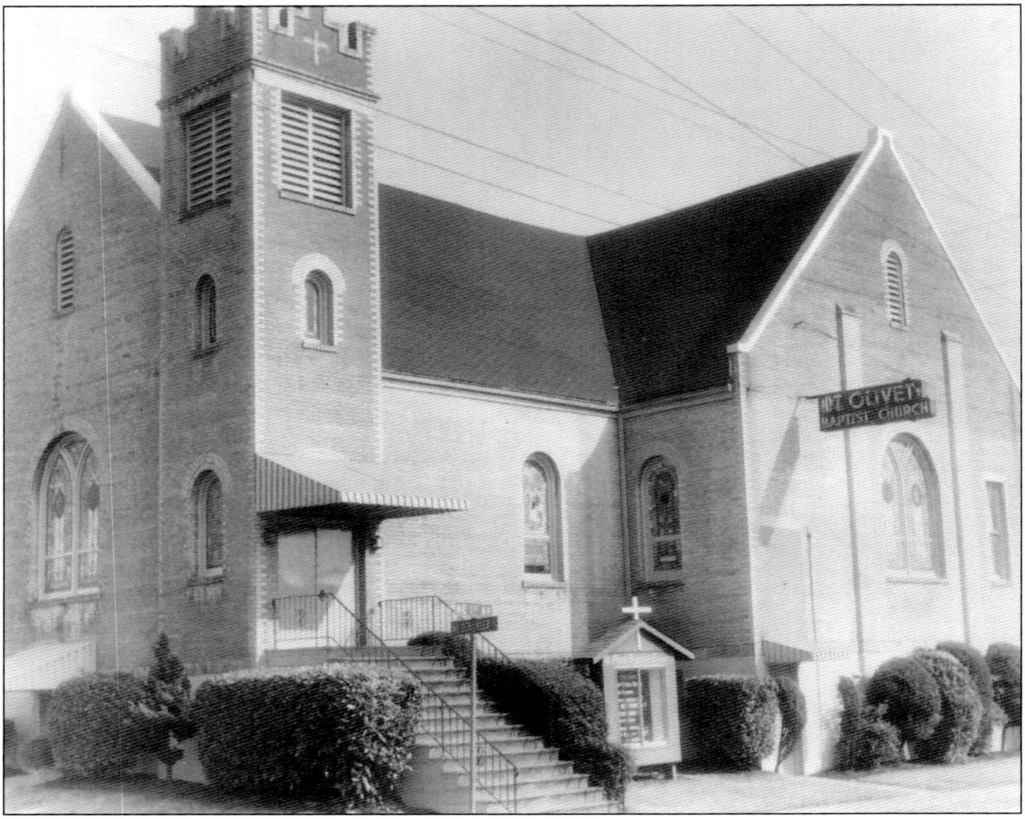

Mount Olivet Baptist Church was organized in 1897, when a small group of African Americans were successful in persuading the American Baptist Home Mission Society to grant them a contract of organization. Mount Olivet is the third oldest African American church in Portland and the first African American Baptist church in the state of Oregon. In 1900, the church was located in Northwest Portland at 85 North Seventh (now Broadway) and Everett Streets. In 1921, to get the church on the "proper side of town," the Ku Klux Klan donated some lumber to help the church relocate to Northeast Portland at Northeast Schuyler Street and First Avenue. (Courtesy of Mount Olivet Baptist Church.)

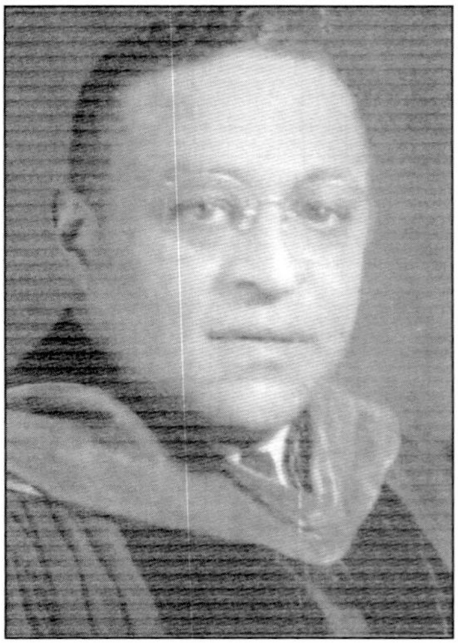

Dr. Jonathon L. Caston was formally installed as pastor of Mount Olivet Baptist Church in 1928. An advocate for racial tolerance within the church community, Dr. Caston was often asked to preach about social justice in white churches. He organized a joint service with Sunnyside Methodist and presented a speech on Abraham Lincoln and slavery. Methodist pastor Dr. Louis Magin spoke about Abraham Lincoln and manhood. In 1931, Reverend Caston was the first African American to deliver the invocation at the opening of the Oregon Legislature. (Courtesy of Mount Olivet Baptist Church.)

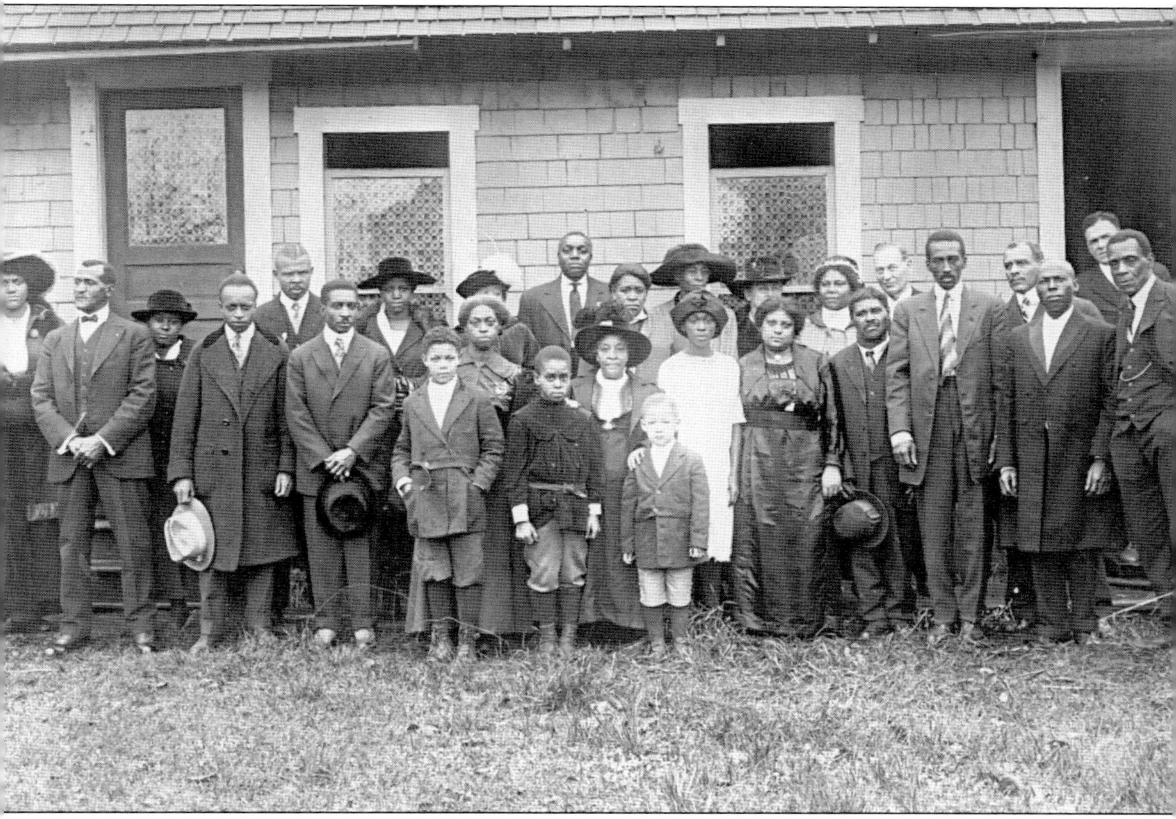

Another early African American church, Shiloh Baptist Church, was founded in 1915 and re-opened in 1924. The Shiloh Baptist Church building was located at Northeast Seventy-fifth and Northeast Everett Streets. In 1928, the *Advocate* reported that Mayor Baker was to deliver the welcome for the Washington, Oregon, Idaho, and Utah General Baptist Convention that was held at the church. This photograph, taken in 1917, was originally part of the Marie B. Smith collection. (Courtesy of the Oregon Historical Society.)

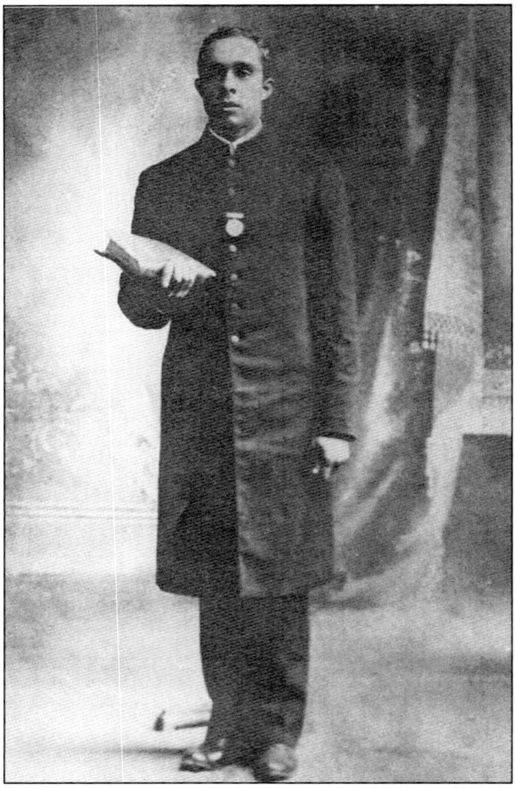

Bishop Robert Lincoln Searcie was the founder and pastor of the House of Prayer of All Nations for 57 years. He was born in 1881 in Topeka, Kansas, and began his ministry in 1902 in Oklahoma. He came to Oregon as an evangelist and met and married Rosa Marie Britton, the daughter of Lewis L. and Hattie Britton. In 1912, he traveled to California and became part of the Azusa movement, which birthed the Pentecostal movement. Shortly after his return from California, Minister Searcie established the House of Prayer for All Nations, and he later served as bishop until his death in 1968 at the age of 87. Inspired by their grandfather's spiritual legacy, several of Searcie's grandchildren through his daughter, Grace (Searcie) Probasco became pastors of local churches in the Portland area. (Both, courtesy of Carolyn Leonard.)

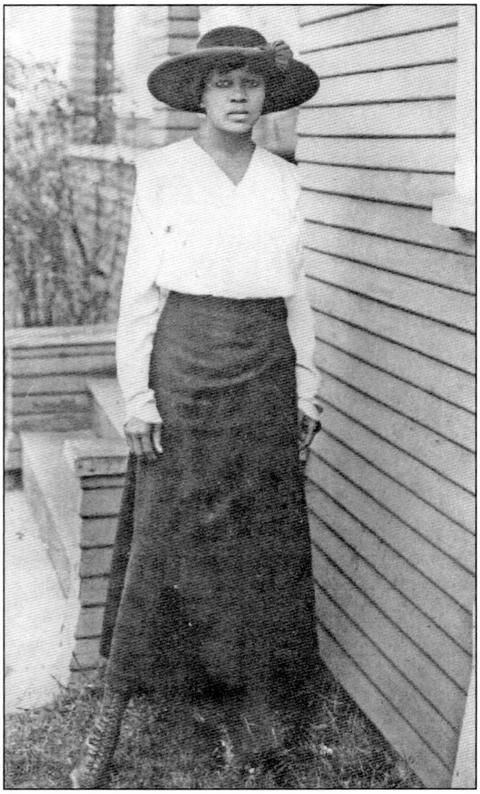

Three

Self-Determination Prevails

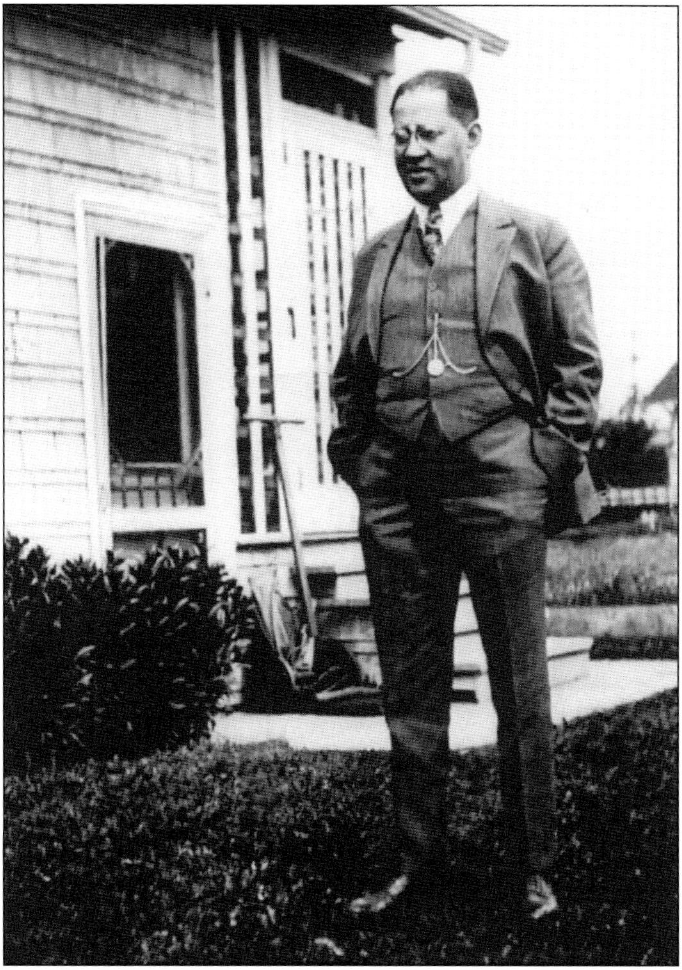

Entrepreneur William D. Allen, a native of Nashville, Tennessee, arrived in Portland in 1901. In 1905, he married Lillian Medley of Montreal, and in that same year, he purchased property at Everett Street and Broadway; the Golden West Hotel began operation in 1906. Prior to 1920, most blacks resided near Union Station and the Portland Hotel. The Golden West Hotel provided accommodation for black workers recruited by the major railroads and the Portland Hotel. (Courtesy of the Oregon Historical Society.)

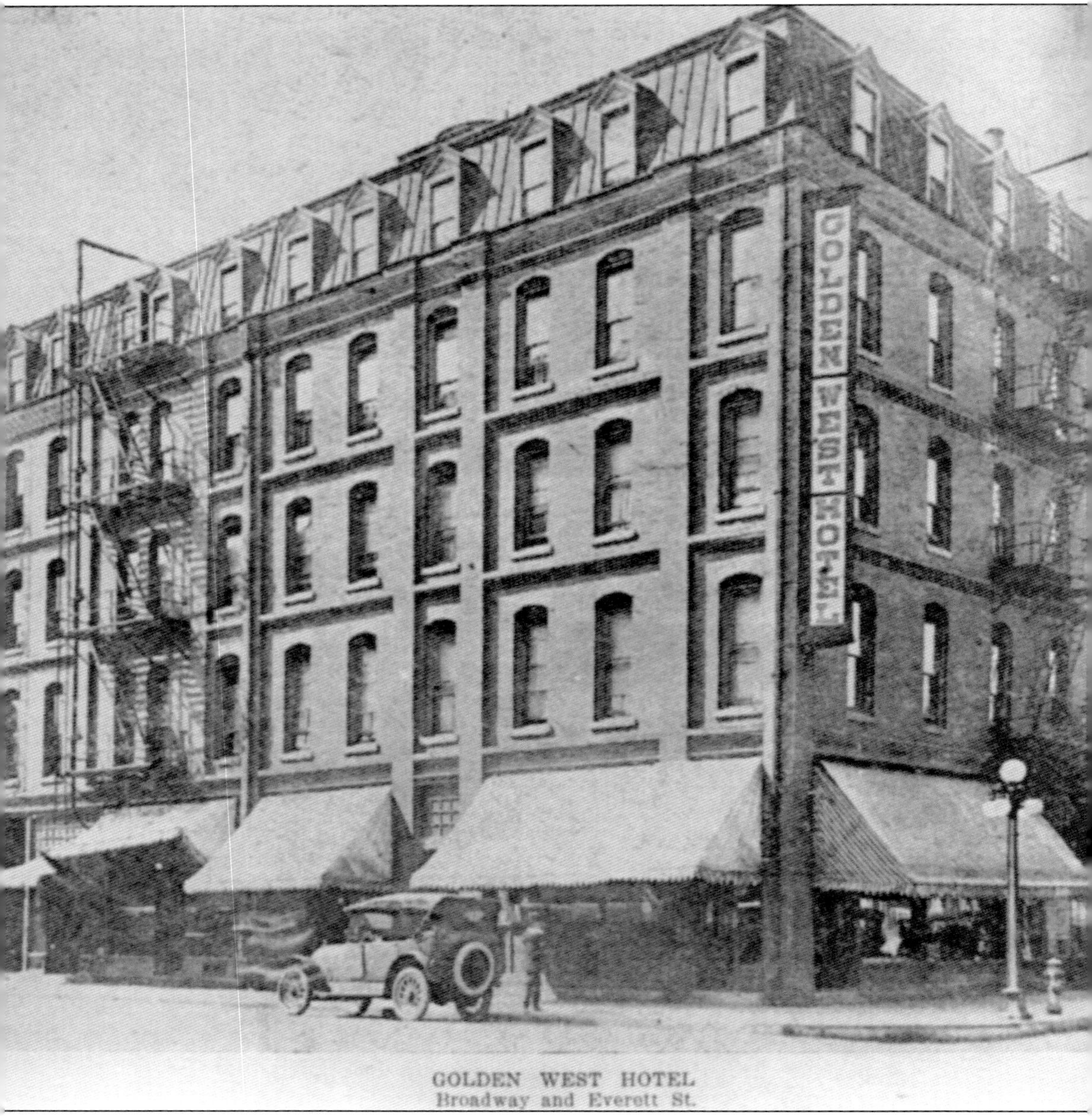

The Golden West Hotel provided space for several black-owned businesses, including A.G. Green confectionery, a barbershop owned by Waldo Bogle, and a saloon and restaurant. Golden West Cabaret was a jazz venue for local musicians. Allen's brother-in-law operated George Moore's Golden West Athletic Club, featuring a Turkish bath and gymnasium and a gambling operation in the basement. An article in the *Advocate* dated June 9, 1928, informed the readers that W.D. Allen completed the remodeling of the hotel and declared the Golden West Hotel the "largest and best equipped hostelry for colored people west of Chicago." Located close to two early black churches, the Golden West Hotel became a haven for Portland's small black community. The Colored Women's Council held meetings at the hotel. Prominent entertainers, athletes, and civic leaders, such as Illinois congressman Oscar Depriest and labor organizer A. Philip Randolph, were overnight guests. (Courtesy of the Oregon Historical Society.)

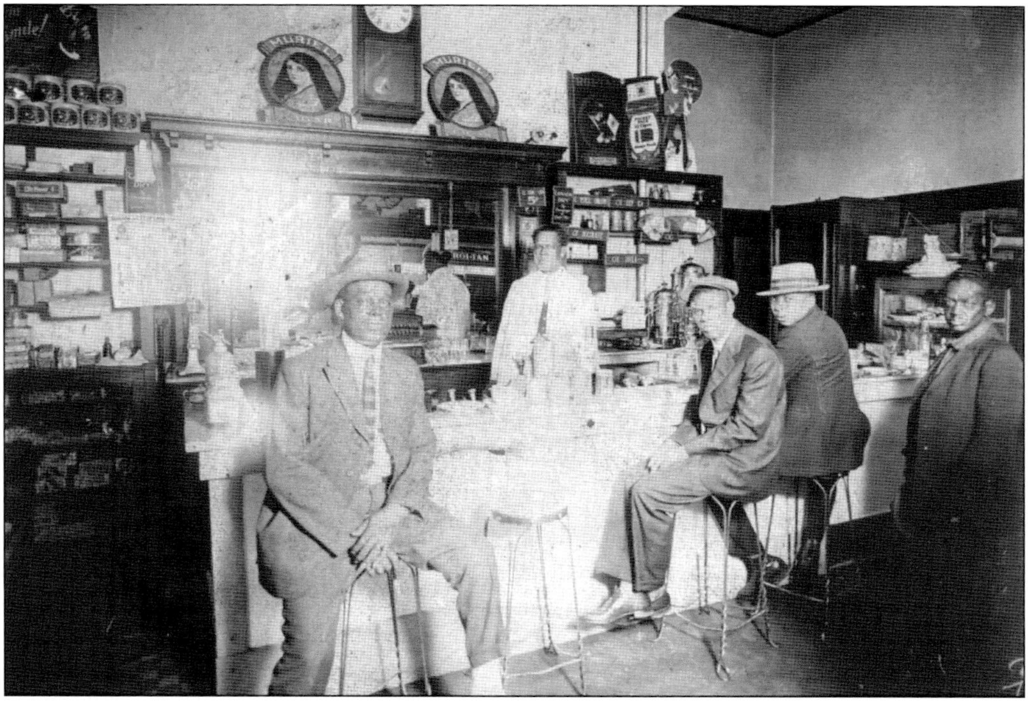

This photograph was taken inside the Golden West Hotel Saloon. (Courtesy of the Rutherford Family Collection and PSU Library.)

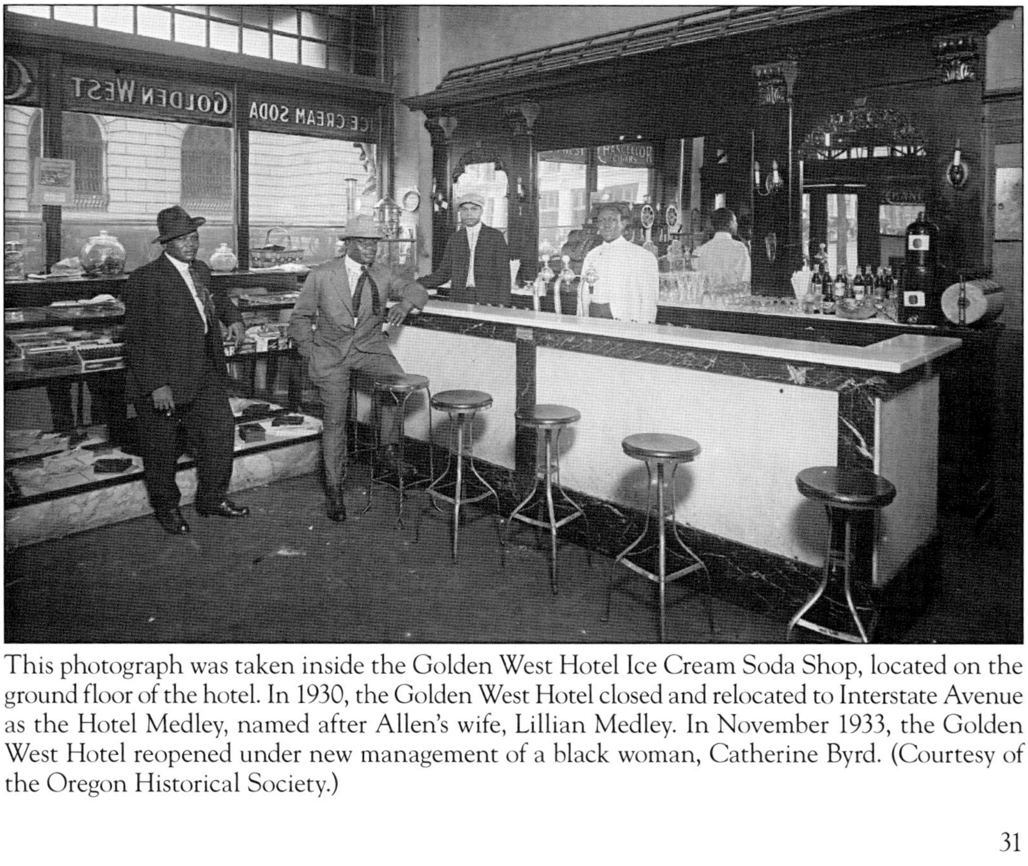

This photograph was taken inside the Golden West Hotel Ice Cream Soda Shop, located on the ground floor of the hotel. In 1930, the Golden West Hotel closed and relocated to Interstate Avenue as the Hotel Medley, named after Allen's wife, Lillian Medley. In November 1933, the Golden West Hotel reopened under new management of a black woman, Catherine Byrd. (Courtesy of the Oregon Historical Society.)

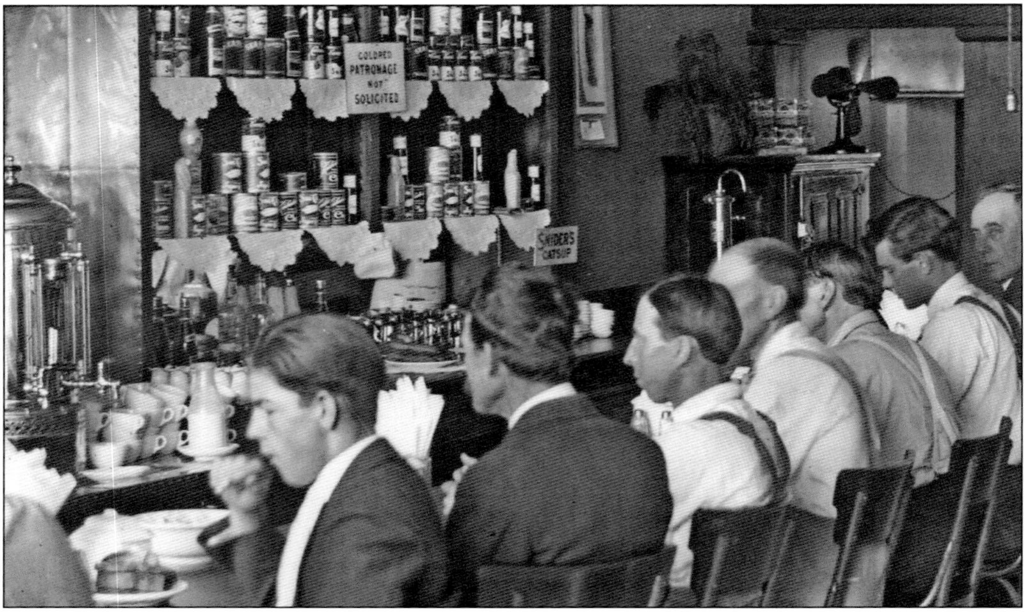

Due to overt discriminatory practices, African Americans were not able to patronize local white businesses in Portland. The Golden West Hotel and other black businesses provided much-needed services to the small but growing black community. This 1910 photograph displays a sign in a saloon that says "Colored Patronage Not Solicited." (Alex Blendl, Historical Photos.)

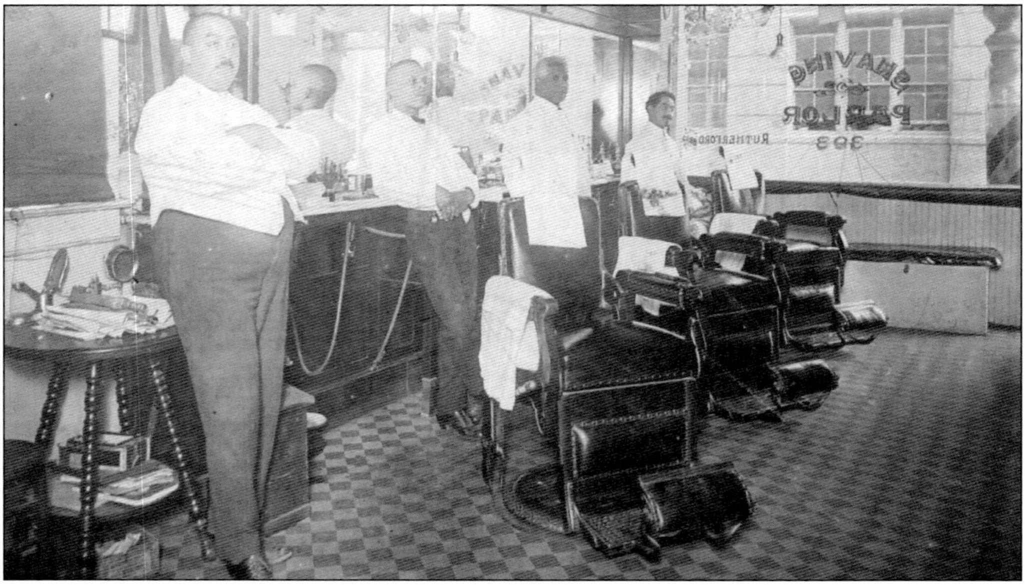

William H. Rutherford and his brother, Edward, came to Portland in 1897, recruited to work in the newly constructed Portland Hotel as house barbers. The Rutherfords provided barbering services to the wealthy and famous patrons of the Portland Hotel who did not care to be served in the more public shop. After several years of living in Portland and having established their families in this city, William and Edward Rutherford decided to open their own business. In 1907, the Rutherford brothers operated their first shop, the Club Café Shaving Parlor at Northwest Third and Flanders Streets. This 1910 photograph shows Edward Rutherford in the foreground; William Rutherford is in the background. (Courtesy of the Rutherford Family Collection and PSU Library.)

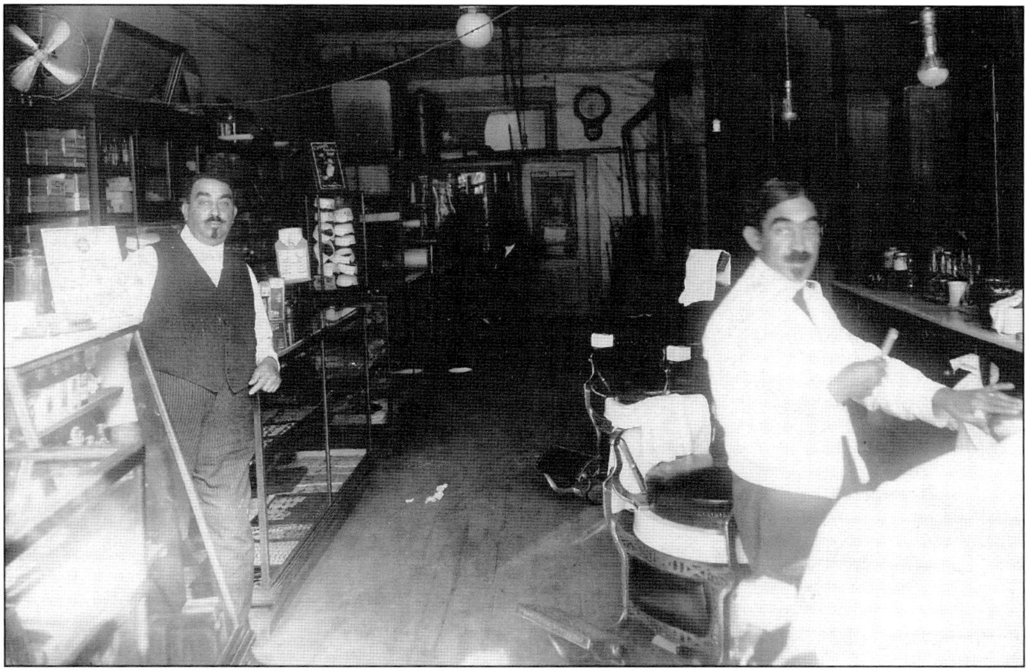

About 1911, the Rutherford brothers opened their second shop, installed a couple of showcases, and added a line of haberdashery items. In this 1912 photograph, Edward is standing next to one of the showcases in the haberdashery, and William is shown to the right within the barbershop section of the shop. (Courtesy of the Rutherford Family Collection and PSU Library.)

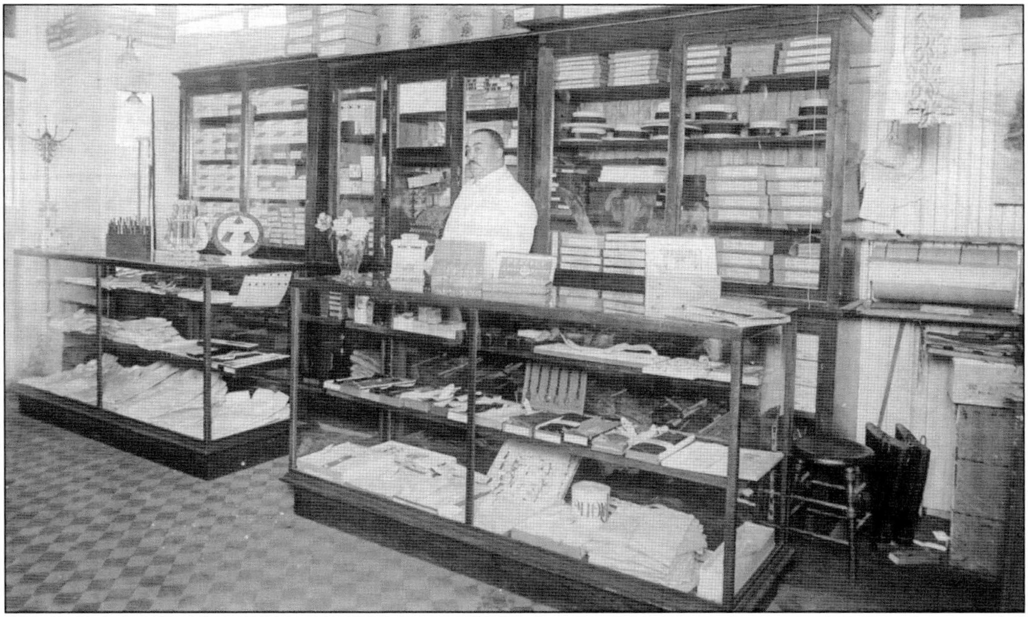

In 1914, the Rutherford brothers moved to a corner location at Northwest Broadway and Flanders Street and opened the Rutherford Brothers Haberdashery. The location provided a separate entrance to the barbershop on the Broadway side, while customers wanting haberdashery items entered through the Flanders Street side. (Courtesy of the Rutherford Family Collection and PSU Library.)

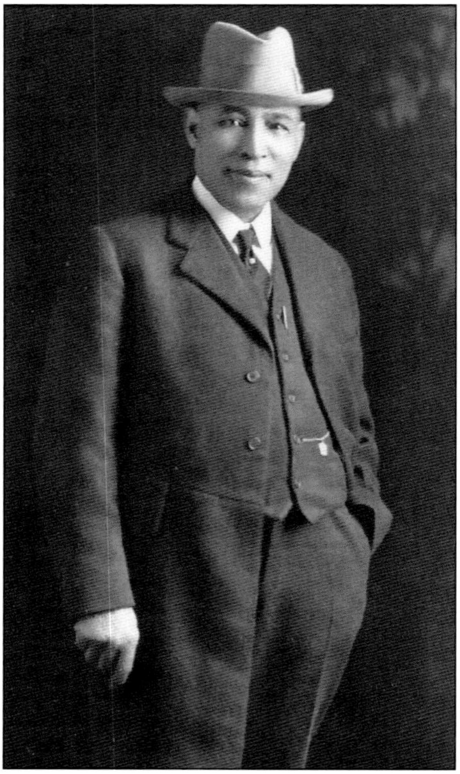

In the early 1900s, blacks began to migrate from the North to Northeast Portland, and black businesses and churches followed. Pictured here is Fred Thomas of Fred D. Thomas Catering Services. Thomas and his wife, Molly, operated the catering business for many years in their home, located at 312 Northeast Shaver Avenue. (Courtesy of the Rutherford Family Collection and PSU Library.)

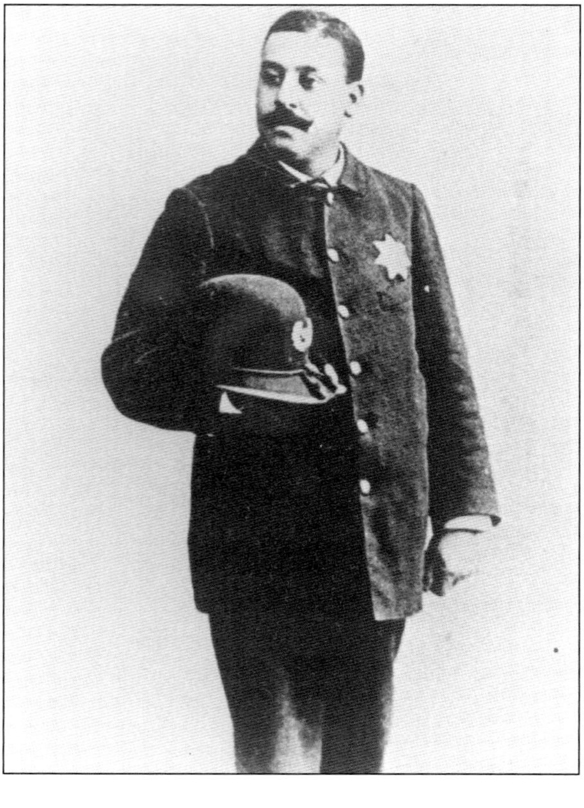

In the late 1800s, the waiters at the Portland Hotel organized the New Port Republican Club and had a membership of 80. In 1894, the club was able to secure the employment of George Hardin, Portland's first black police officer. In 1915, he was appointed deputy sheriff of Multnomah County, and he served in that role until his death in 1938 at the age of 78 years. (Courtesy of the Rutherford Family Collection and PSU Library.)

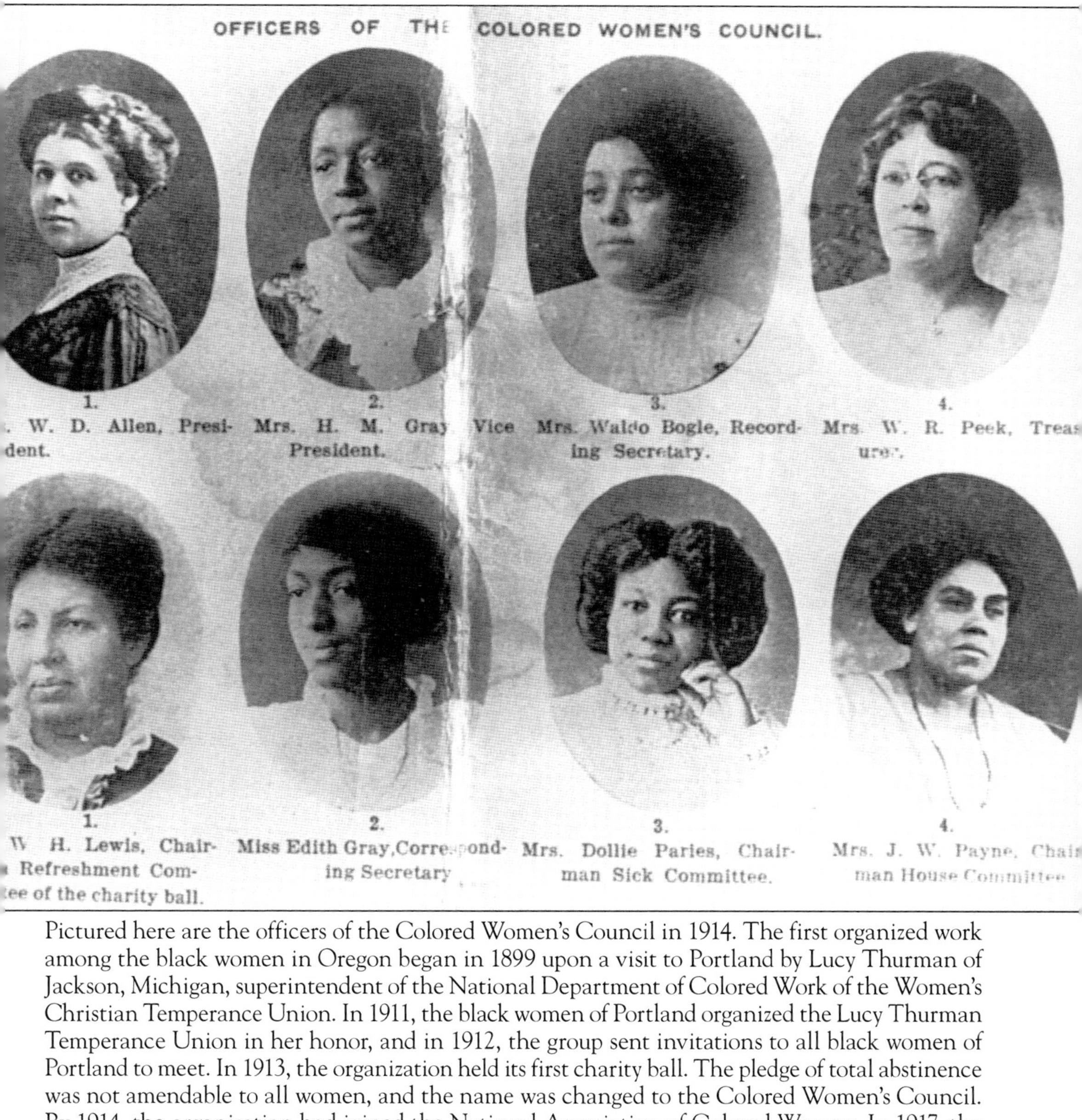

Pictured here are the officers of the Colored Women's Council in 1914. The first organized work among the black women in Oregon began in 1899 upon a visit to Portland by Lucy Thurman of Jackson, Michigan, superintendent of the National Department of Colored Work of the Women's Christian Temperance Union. In 1911, the black women of Portland organized the Lucy Thurman Temperance Union in her honor, and in 1912, the group sent invitations to all black women of Portland to meet. In 1913, the organization held its first charity ball. The pledge of total abstinence was not amendable to all women, and the name was changed to the Colored Women's Council. By 1914, the organization had joined the National Association of Colored Women. In 1917, the group merged with nine others to form the Oregon Federation of Colored Women's Clubs. Today, the group operates as the Oregon Association of Colored Women's Clubs (OACW). (Courtesy of the Oregon Historical Society.)

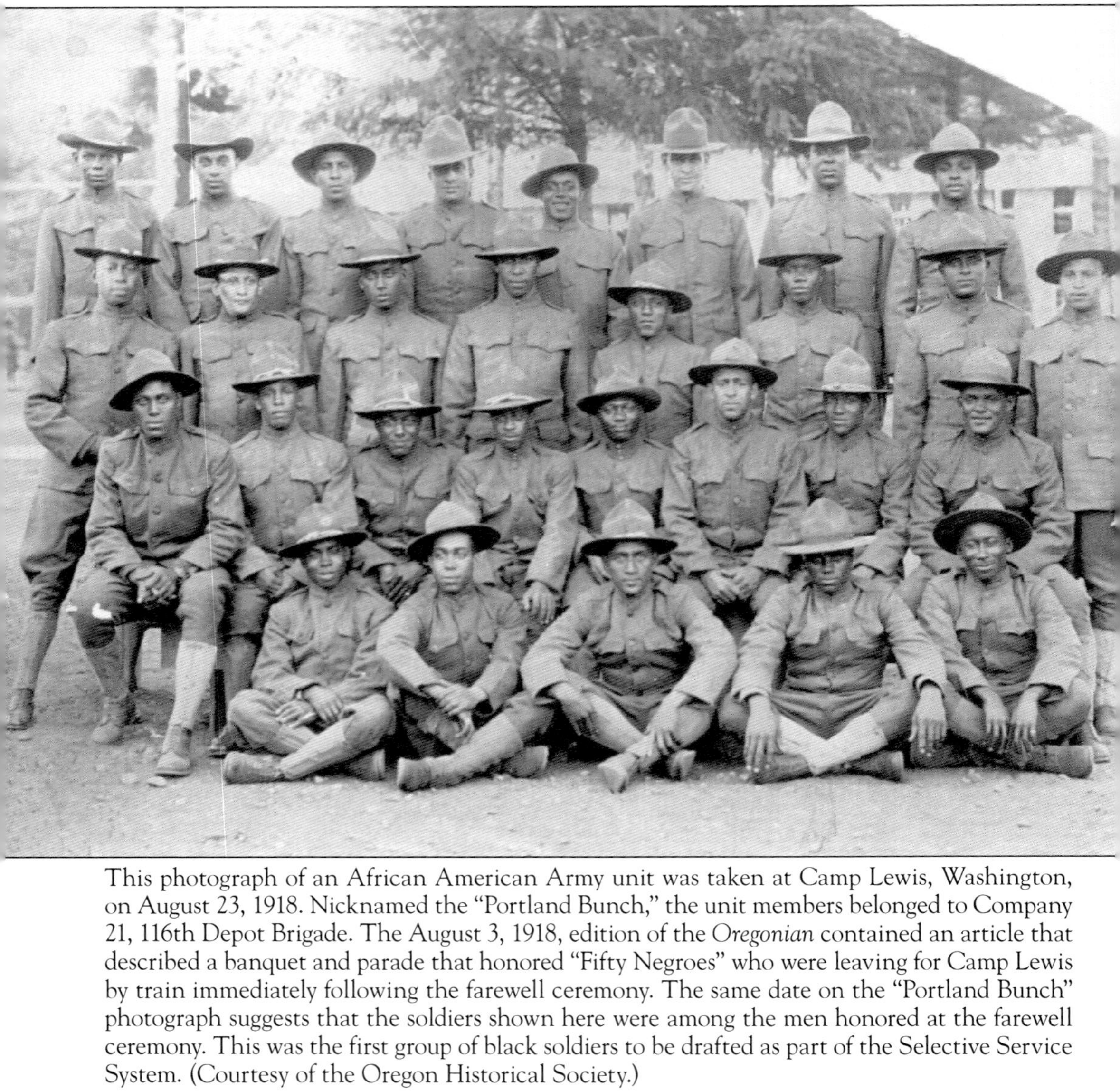

This photograph of an African American Army unit was taken at Camp Lewis, Washington, on August 23, 1918. Nicknamed the "Portland Bunch," the unit members belonged to Company 21, 116th Depot Brigade. The August 3, 1918, edition of the *Oregonian* contained an article that described a banquet and parade that honored "Fifty Negroes" who were leaving for Camp Lewis by train immediately following the farewell ceremony. The same date on the "Portland Bunch" photograph suggests that the soldiers shown here were among the men honored at the farewell ceremony. This was the first group of black soldiers to be drafted as part of the Selective Service System. (Courtesy of the Oregon Historical Society.)

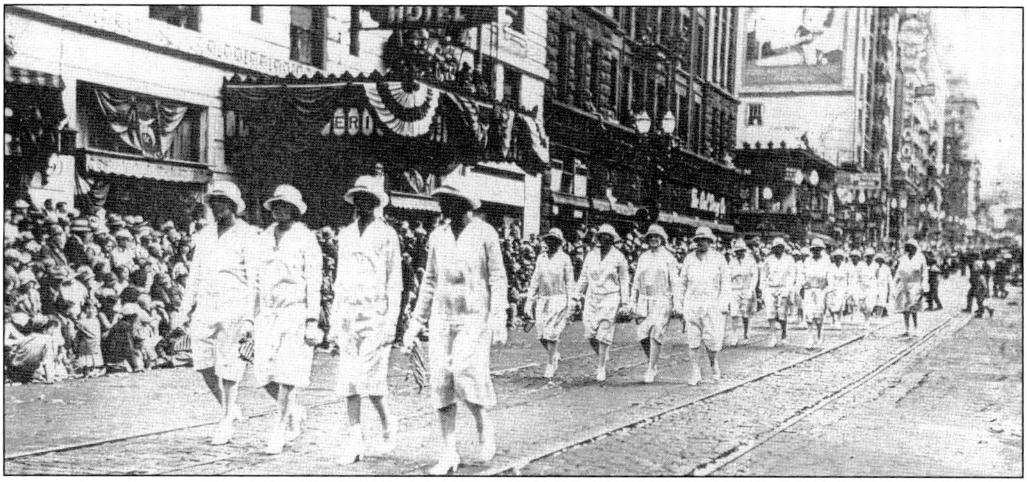

According to an August 3, 1918, article in the *Oregonian*, 30 young women comprising the Rosebud Study Club, a service group, aided in the celebration and reception for the "Portland Bunch." They served the food that was prepared by the Colored Women's Council, distributed flowers and cigars to the men, and marched with them to Union Station. Rev. J.B. Isaacs of Bethel AME provided an enthusiastic address, telling the fighting men that their conduct on the battle line of France and their behavior would reflect on the 12 million colored residents of the United States, whose hearts throbbed for their men in the service. (Courtesy of the Rutherford Family Collection and PSU Library.)

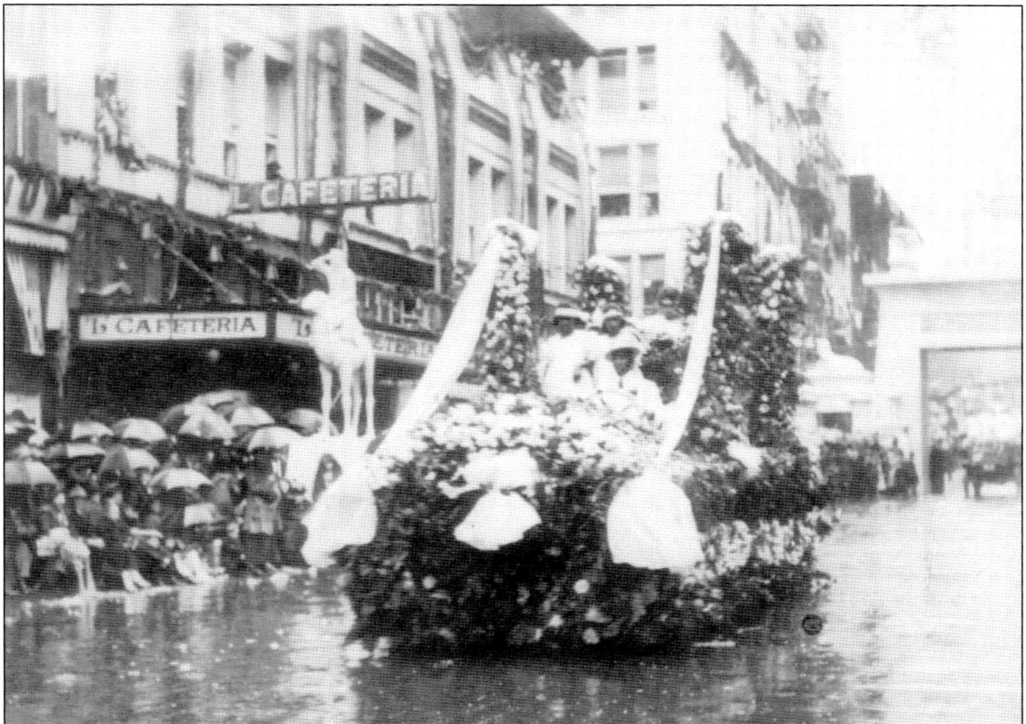

This picture includes African American women riding a float in a parade organized by Albina residents for African American soldiers departing to Camp Lewis. The date of the parade is unknown. (Courtesy of the Rutherford Family Collection and PSU Library.)

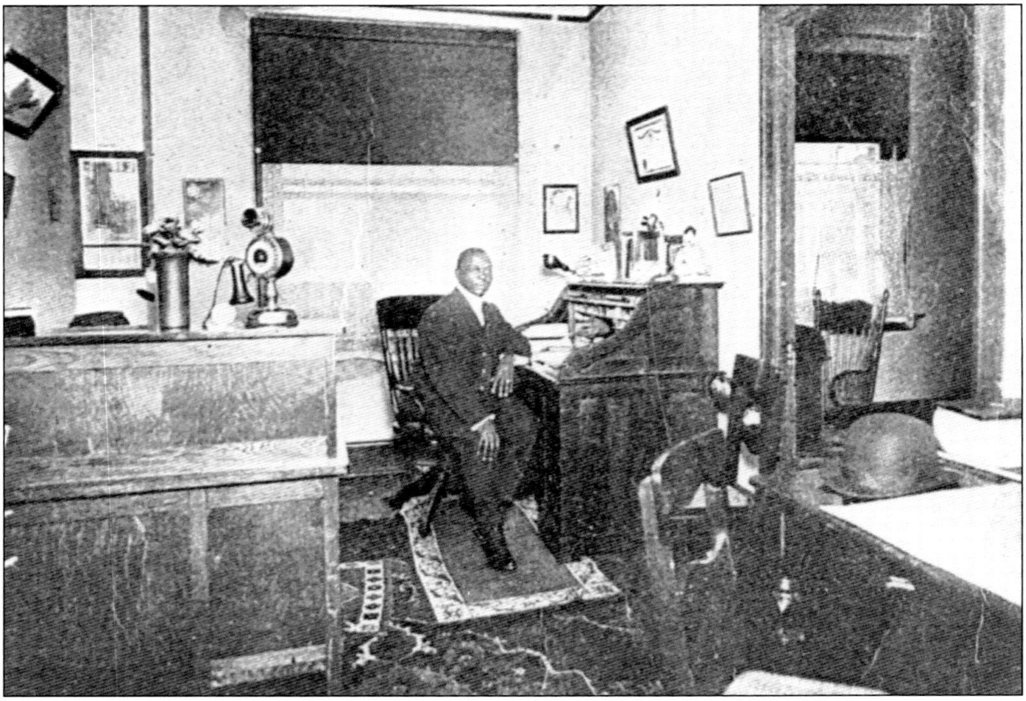

Edward Daniel Cannady was a waiter at the Portland Hotel and cofounder and editor of the *Advocate*, Portland's second black-owned newspaper. Established in 1903, the *Advocate* was founded by several local black men. Cannady married Beatrice Morrow in 1912, and she became assistant editor. The *Advocate* was a four-page weekly that informed readers about national and local black news, black advertisements, entertainment events, and society, hotel, and church happenings. (Courtesy of the Oregon Historical Society.)

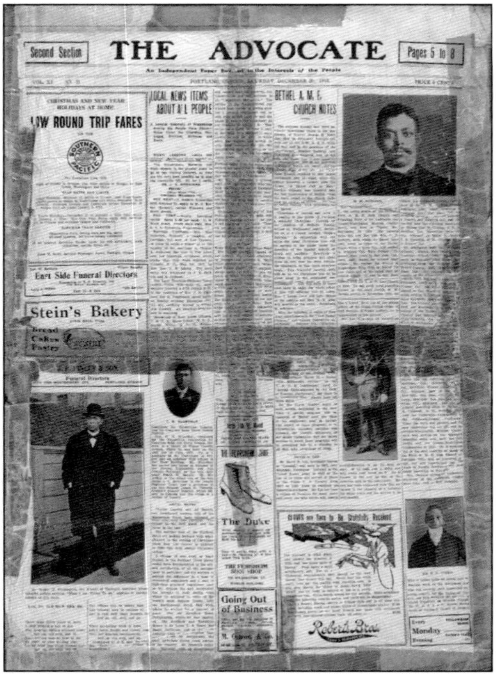

Second Section THE ADVOCATE Pages 5 to 8

LOW ROUND TRIP FARES

LOCAL NEWS ITEMS ABOUT A. L. PEOPLE

BETHEL A. M. E. CHURCH NOTES

East Side Funeral Directors

Stein's Bakery

The Duke

Going Out of Business

Shown here is a photograph of an issue of the *Advocate* dated December 20, 1913. The Verdell Burdine and Otto Rutherford Family Collection, under the care of PSU Special Collections and Archive Library, holds the most extensive, if not the only, collection of the historical newspaper. It was preserved over the years by the late Verdell Burdine and Otto G. Rutherford. (Courtesy of the Rutherford Family Collections and PSU Library.)

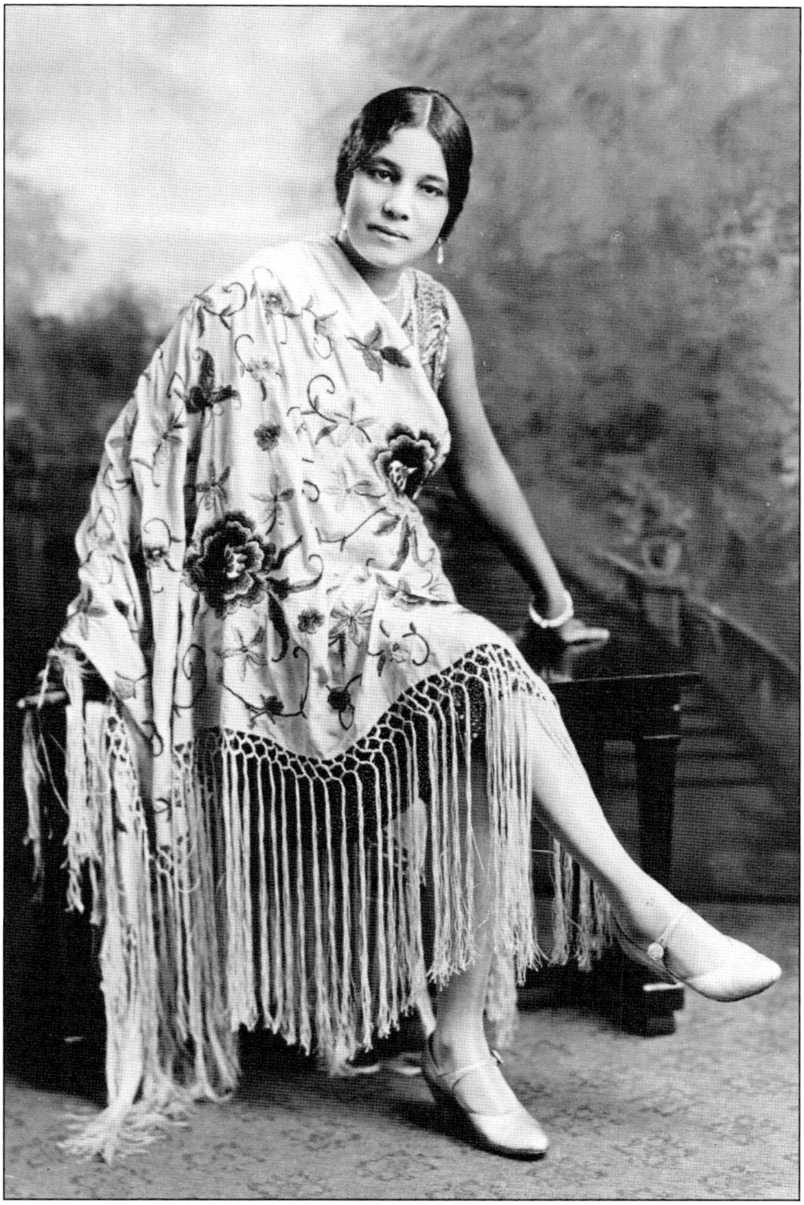

Beatrice Morrow Cannady was the most noted Oregon civil rights activist in the early 20th century. Born in 1889 in Littig, Texas, she moved to Portland in 1912 when she married Edward Cannady and became assistant editor of the *Advocate*. She launched numerous efforts to defend the civil rights of blacks and regularly challenged racial discrimination in her public talks and in the pages of the newspaper. Beatrice helped found the Portland chapter of the NAACP, and she quickly became one of the state's most outspoken civil rights activists. In 1922, at the age of 33, she became the first black woman to graduate from the Northwestern School of Law. She helped craft the state's first civil rights legislation that would have mandated full access to public accommodations without regard to race. Although the legislation failed, in 1925, Cannady worked on a successful campaign to repeal Oregon's notorious black laws. In 1932, she ran unsuccessfully for the office of state representative from District No. 5, Multnomah County. (Courtesy of the Oregon Historical Society.)

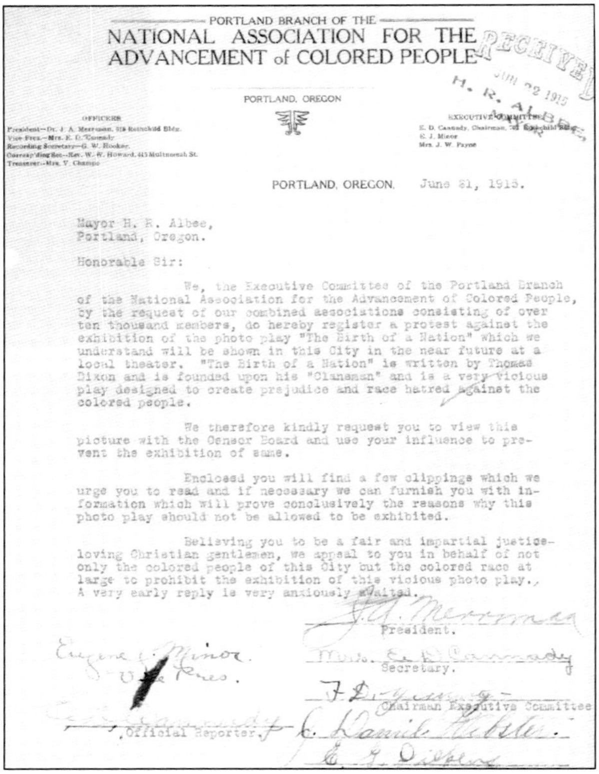

PORTLAND BRANCH OF THE
NATIONAL ASSOCIATION FOR THE ADVANCEMENT of COLORED PEOPLE

PORTLAND, OREGON

OFFICERS
President—Dr. J. A. Merriman, 315 Rothchild Bldg.
Vice Pres.—Mrs. E. D. Cannady
Recording Secretary—G. W. Hooker.
Corresp'ding Sec.—Rev. W. W. Howard, 415 Multnomah St.
Treasurer—Mrs. V. Champo

EXECUTIVE COMMITTEE
E. D. Cannady, Chairman
E. J. Minor
Mrs. J. W. Payne

RECEIVED JUN 22 1915 H. R. ALBEE, MAYOR

PORTLAND, OREGON, June 21, 1915.

Mayor H. R. Albee,
Portland, Oregon.

Honorable Sir:

We, the Executive Committee of the Portland Branch of the National Association for the Advancement of Colored People, by the request of our combined associations consisting of over ten thousand members, do hereby register a protest against the exhibition of the photo play "The Birth of a Nation" which we understand will be shown in this City in the near future at a local theater. "The Birth of a Nation" is written by Thomas Dixon and is founded upon his "Clansman" and is a very vicious play designed to create prejudice and race hatred against the colored people.

We therefore kindly request you to view this picture with the Censor Board and use your influence to prevent the exhibition of same.

Enclosed you will find a few clippings which we urge you to read and if necessary we can furnish you with information which will prove conclusively the reasons why this photo play should not be allowed to be exhibited.

Believing you to be a fair and impartial justice-loving Christian gentlemen, we appeal to you in behalf of not only the colored people of this City but the colored race at large to prohibit the exhibition of this vicious photo play.,
A very early reply is very anxiously awaited.

J. A. Merriman
President.

Eugene J. Minor
Vice Pres.

Mrs. E. D. Cannady
Secretary.

Chairman Executive Committee

Official Reporter.

The Portland Branch of the NAACP was organized in December 1913 and formally recognized by the national association on September 14, 1914, with 165 members. On June 31, 1915, on behalf of the NAACP and the Portland branch, Beatrice Cannady and other community leaders urged Mayor H.R. Albee to ban the showing of the film *The Birth of a Nation*. After viewing the film, the city council passed an ordinance that banned the showing of any film that promoted racial hatred. The letter shown here was written to Mayor Albee and signed by Dr. J.A. Merriman on behalf of the Portland Branch of the NAACP. (Courtesy of City of Portland Archives.)

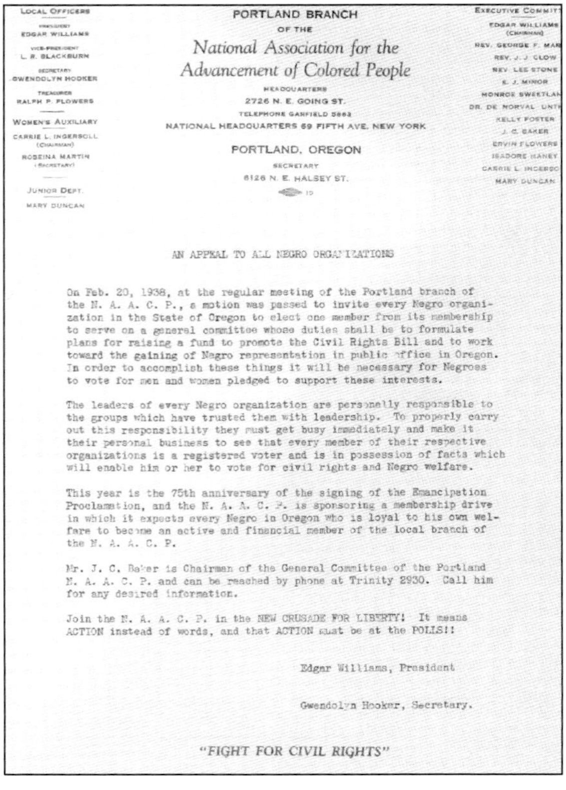

LOCAL OFFICERS
PRESIDENT EDGAR WILLIAMS
VICE-PRESIDENT L. R. BLACKBURN
SECRETARY GWENDOLYN HOOKER
TREASURER RALPH P. FLOWERS

WOMEN'S AUXILIARY
CARRIE L. INGERSOLL (CHAIRMAN)
ROSEINA MARTIN (SECRETARY)

JUNIOR DEPT.
MARY DUNCAN

PORTLAND BRANCH
OF THE
National Association for the Advancement of Colored People
HEADQUARTERS
2726 N. E. GOING ST.
TELEPHONE GARFIELD 5863
NATIONAL HEADQUARTERS 69 FIFTH AVE. NEW YORK
PORTLAND, OREGON
SECRETARY
6126 N. E. HALSEY ST.

EXECUTIVE COMMITTEE
EDGAR WILLIAMS (CHAIRMAN)
REV. GEORGE F. MAR
REV. J. J. CLOW
REV. LEE STONE
E. J. MINOR
MONROE SWEETLAN
DR. DE NORVAL UNTH
KELLY FOSTER
J. C. BAKER
ERVIN FLOWERS
ISADORE HANEY
CARRIE L. INGERSO
MARY DUNCAN

AN APPEAL TO ALL NEGRO ORGANIZATIONS

On Feb. 20, 1938, at the regular meeting of the Portland branch of the N. A. A. C. P., a motion was passed to invite every Negro organization in the State of Oregon to elect one member from its membership to serve on a general committee whose duties shall be to formulate plans for raising a fund to promote the Civil Rights Bill and to work toward the gaining of Negro representation in public office in Oregon. In order to accomplish these things it will be necessary for Negroes to vote for men and women pledged to support these interests.

The leaders of every Negro organization are personally responsible to the groups which have trusted them with leadership. To properly carry out this responsibility they must get busy immediately and make it their personal business to see that every member of their respective organizations is a registered voter and is in possession of facts which will enable him or her to vote for civil rights and Negro welfare.

This year is the 75th anniversary of the signing of the Emancipation Proclamation, and the N. A. A. C. P. is sponsoring a membership drive in which it expects every Negro in Oregon who is loyal to his own welfare to become an active and financial member of the local branch of the N. A. A. C. P.

Mr. J. C. Baker is Chairman of the General Committee of the Portland N. A. A. C. P. and can be reached by phone at Trinity 2930. Call him for any desired information.

Join the N. A. A. C. P. in the NEW CRUSADE FOR LIBERTY! It means ACTION instead of words, and that ACTION must be at the POLLS!!

Edgar Williams, President

Gwendolyn Hooker, Secretary.

"FIGHT FOR CIVIL RIGHTS"

Since its inception, the Portland Branch of the NAACP worked tirelessly to pass civil rights bills that would eliminate discriminatory practices in Oregon hotels and restaurants. This letter, written in 1938 and signed by Edgar Williams, urged Portland's black citizens to join the NAACP, promote a civil rights bill, and support black representation in public office. (Courtesy of City of Portland Archives.)

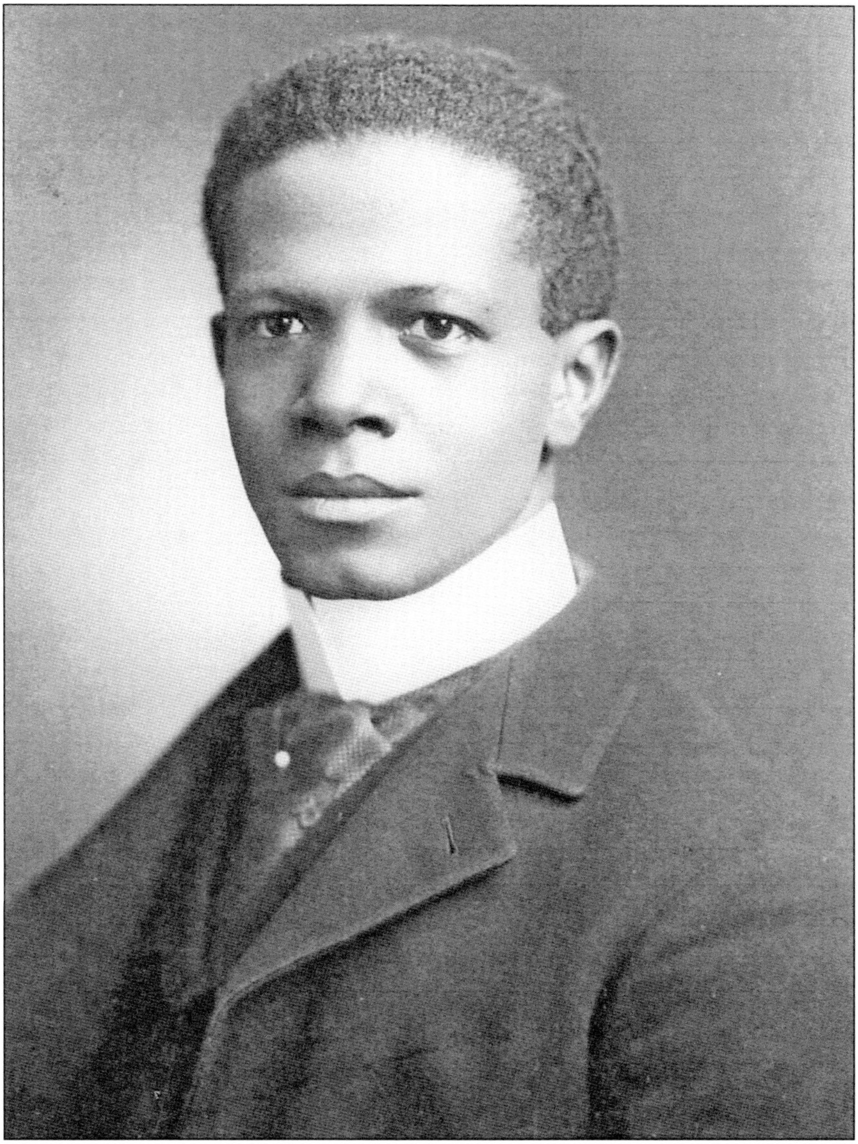

McCants Stewart arrived in Oregon in 1902 after receiving a bachelor's degree (in 1899) and a master of law degree (in 1901) from the University of Minnesota. He was admitted to the bar in St. Paul, Minnesota, in 1899 and the bar of Oregon in 1903. McCants and his wife, Mary D. (Weir), resided at 513 North Union Street (now Martin Luther King Boulevard), and his office was located on the east side of Third Avenue between Washington and Stark Streets. In 1906, Stewart successfully defended Oliver Taylor, a Pullman Porter who sued the owner of Star Theater of Portland after management denied him seating because of his race. Stewart argued before the court that the government should ensure black rights and combat discrimination. The Oregon Supreme Court agreed and ruled in his favor. Stewart was the only African American profiled in the *History of the Bench and Bar of Oregon*, published in 1910. McCants Stewart relocated to San Francisco in 1917, and after a series of health problems resulting from a streetcar accident and personal misfortunes, he committed suicide in 1919. McCants Stewart is pictured here in his 1899 law school class photograph. (Courtesy of the University of Minnesota Archives, University of Minnesota–Twin Cities.)

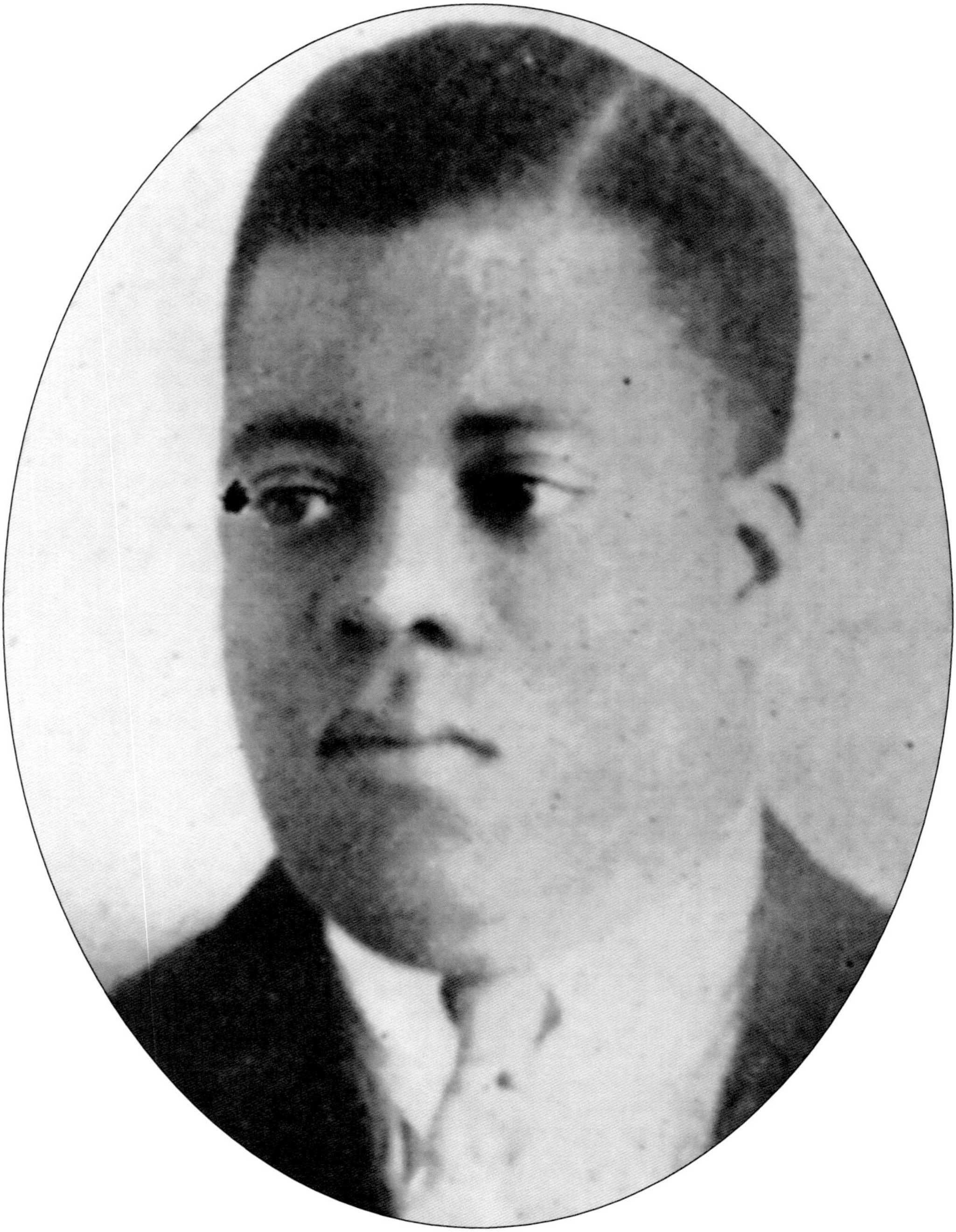

Wyatt Williams worked as a bellboy before earning a law degree from Northwestern College in 1926. He was admitted to the Oregon State Bar in 1927 and served as legal assistant in the office of Julius Silverstone. As president of the Portland Negro Progressive League, Williams worked with the NAACP and labor council to draft the 1937 civil rights bill, which failed in the Oregon Legislature. He became president of the Portland Branch of the NAACP in 1941. (Courtesy of the Oregon Historical Society.)

Formal social gatherings, such as the one pictured here, provided an opportunity for Portland's African Americans to wear their finest and enjoy an evening of live music and dancing. The location and organizers of this affair are unknown. (Courtesy of the Rutherford Family Collection and PSU Library.)

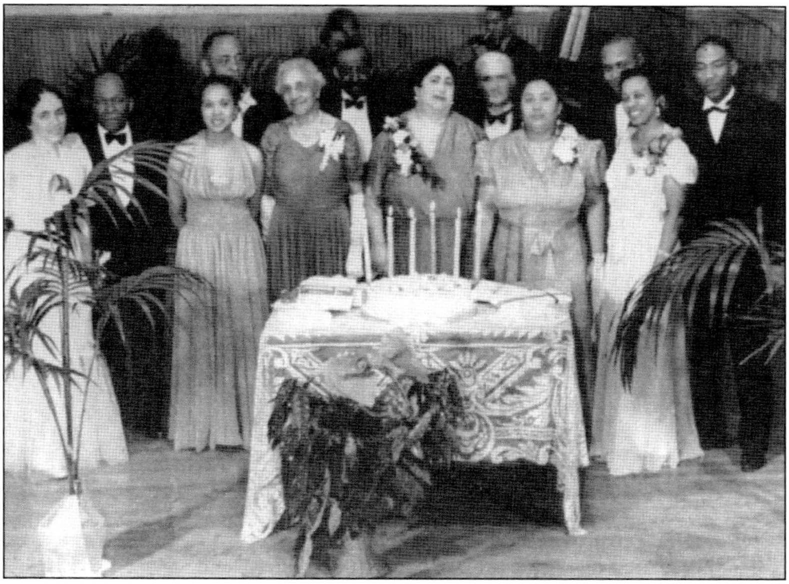

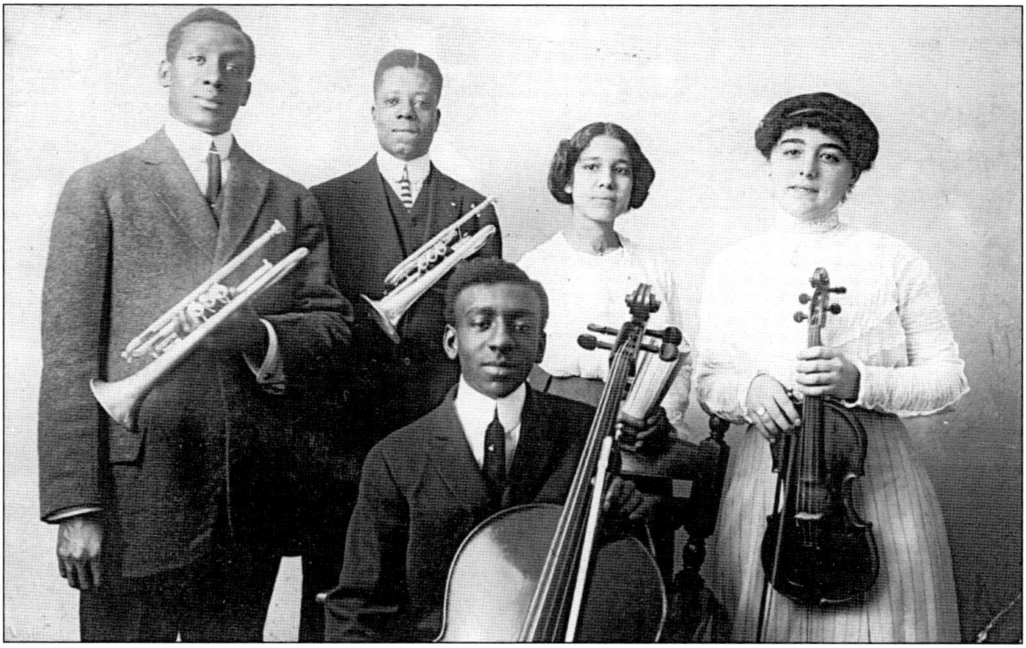

The Willamette Orchestra was composed of seven pieces around 1919. Pictured here are five of the seven members. From left to right are George Morgan, cornet; attorney Wyatt Williams, trumpet; coeditor of the black newspaper the *Advocate* Beatrice Cannady, piano; a Miss Holbert, first violin and director; and Raymond Cage, second violin. Those who do not appear are J. Jones, drum, and Edward Carr, trombone. (Courtesy of the Oregon Historical Society.)

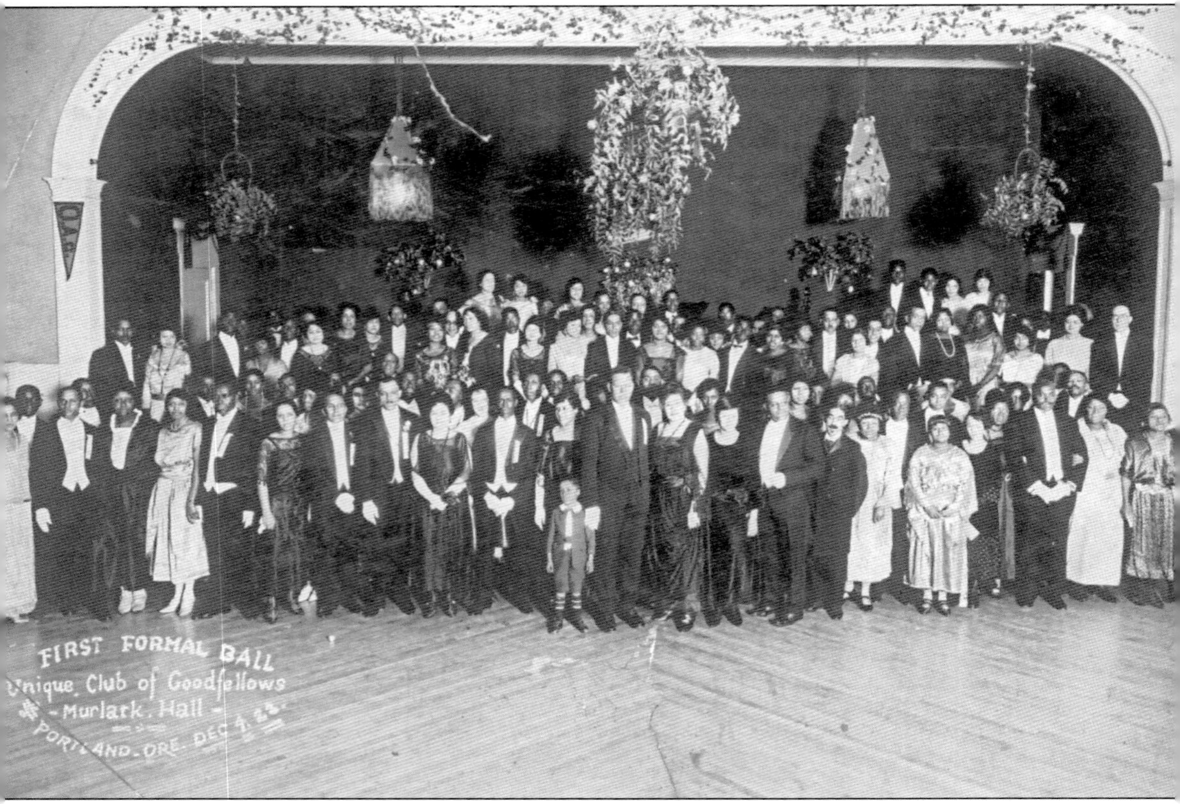

Pictured here is the first formal charity ball of the Unique Club of Goodfellows, which was held on December 4, 1922, at the Murlark Hall in Northwest Portland. The Unique Club of Goodfellows was possibly inspired by the Good Fellow movement, which was initiated by a letter written in 1909 in the *Chicago Tribune* that encouraged Christmas charity benefitting the poor. (Courtesy of the Oregon Historical Society.)

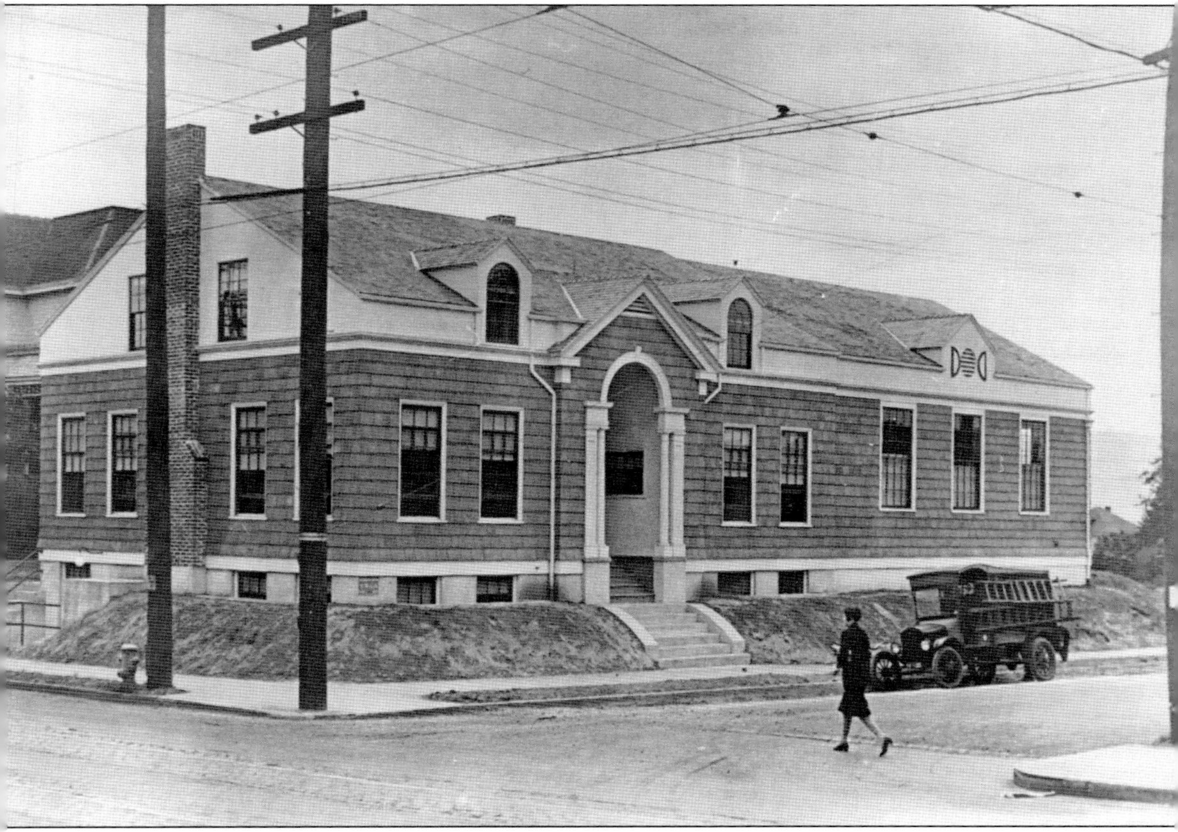

In 1921, a branch of the YWCA was established in a portable structure on the corner of North Williams Avenue and Tillamook Street. Five years later, the Williams Avenue YWCA was dedicated and opened with the generous gift of $12,000 from Mary Laffey Collins, a philanthropist, YWCA supporter, and wife of wealthy lumberman Everell Stanton Collins. The segregated Williams Avenue YWCA was managed by black women and became an active community center. During World War II, a portion of the YWCA operated as a USO for black servicemen and their families. In 1959, the Williams Avenue YWCA became the Billy Webb Elks Lodge BPOE, and it continues as such today. (Courtesy of the Oregon Historical Society.)

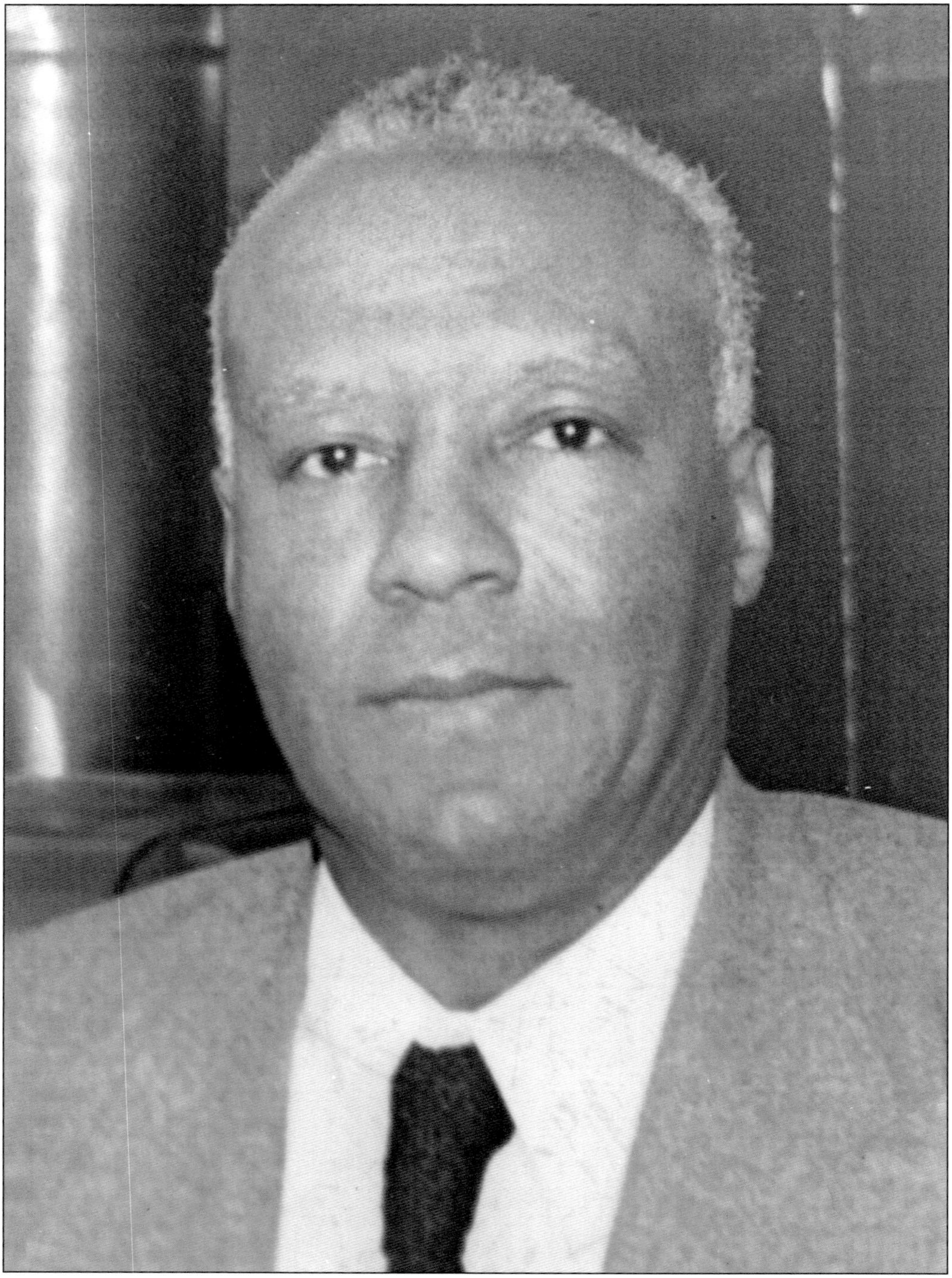

A. Philip Randolph, a general organizer of the Brotherhood of Sleeping Car Porters and editor of the *Messenger*, visited Mount Olivet Baptist Church in 1927 and spoke about the Pullman Porters' fight for economic freedom and the future of the Negro. He returned to Portland in 1929 and addressed several groups, including the students at Reed College and Willamette University and the meeting of the porters held at Bethel AME. He was also the speaker at Oregon Council for the Prevention of War held at the Portland YMCA. (Courtesy of the Oregon Historical Society.)

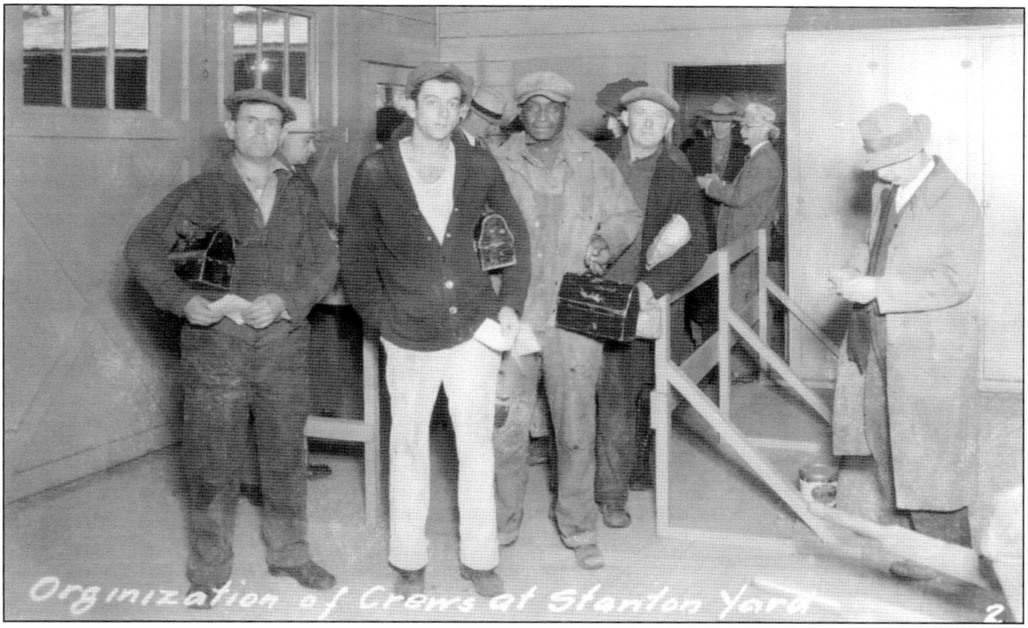

By 1909, five transcontinental rail lines (Southern Pacific, Santa Fe, Union Pacific, Northern Pacific, and Great Northern) ran through the heart of inner Northeast Portland and were serviced by rail yards. Semiskilled labor in the Albina rail yard was typically reserved for European immigrants living in Albina near the railroads. Pictured in this rare 1931 image is an unidentified crew at the Stanton Yard in North Portland that includes an African American man. (Courtesy of City of Portland Archives.)

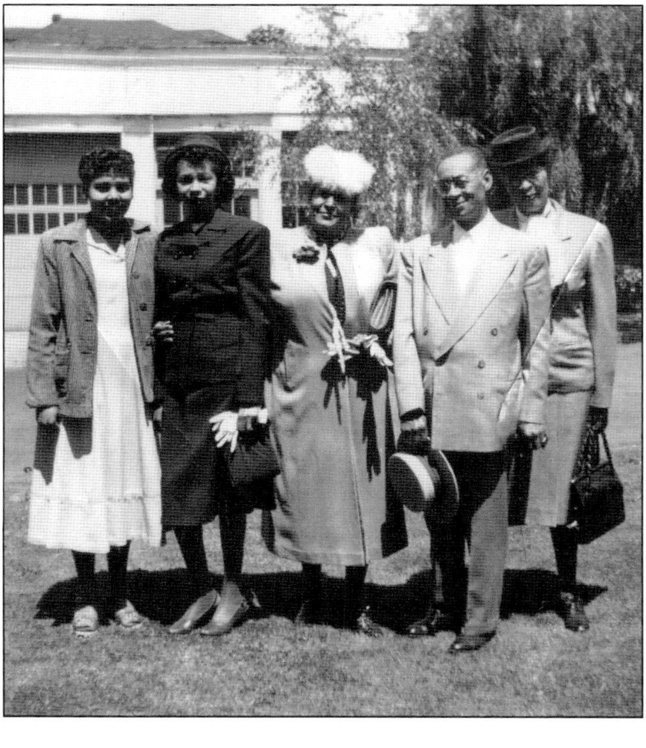

Isadore Maney Sr. and his wife, Elsie, came to Portland in 1926. In 1941, Elsie became the first black woman to be elected president of a parent-teacher association (PTA). Isadore, a mail clerk for the Union Pacific and a NAACP member, testified before the Oregon State Senate on behalf of the 1939 civil rights bills. He shared that he was denied hotel accommodation in Bend, Oregon, while on an assigned run and had to sleep in sidetracked Pullman car. A delegation of the Oregon Association of Colored Women's Clubs had a similar experience. From left to right are Cornelia Banks, Constance Maney, Elonorah Banks, Isadore, and Elsie. (Courtesy of Ella Crumble and Lauretta Moreland.)

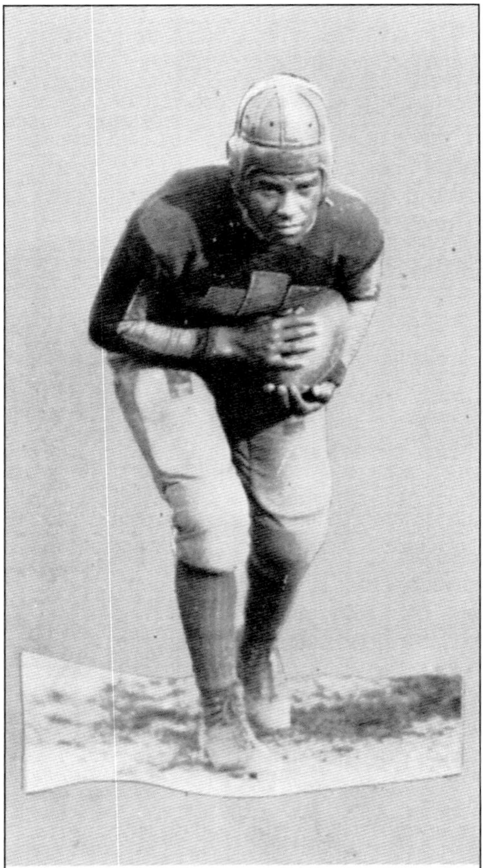

Charles Williams
Fullback

In 1926, Robert "Bob" S. Robinson (below) and Charles "Chuck" Edward Williams (left) enrolled at the University of Oregon and became Oregon's first African American collegiate athletes of record. Robinson also became the first African American to play quarterback for a major white college. Robinson was born in Temple, Texas, moved to Portland in 1922, and attended Jefferson High School. A multisport athlete, he was selected first team All-City in football. Williams, born in Kansas City, Kansas, moved to Portland with his mother and sister and attended Washington High School in 1925. He was an exceptional basketball and football player, and in his final year of high school, he was selected first team All-City in football. Due to the strong anti-black sentiment of the day, the star athletes were not allowed to live in university housing, and they missed the final game of their careers, in Miami, because the University of Florida refused to compete against black athletes. Despite outrage, the University of Oregon's administration succumbed to the racist pressure and left Robinson and Williams at home. (Both, courtesy of Special Collections and University Archives, UO Libraries.)

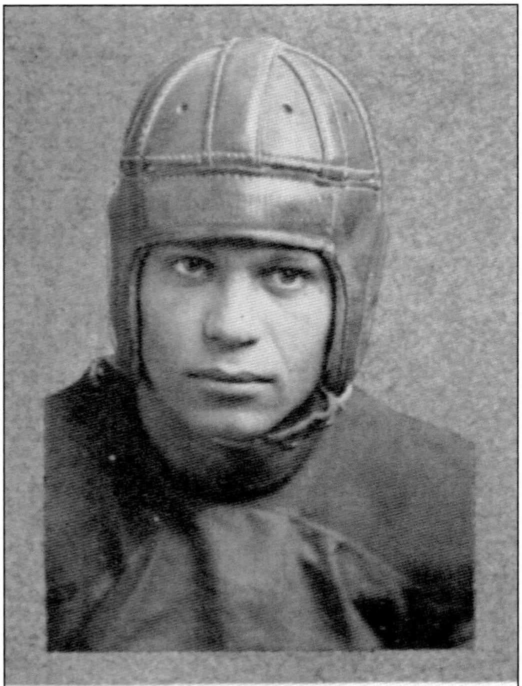

Rob Robinson

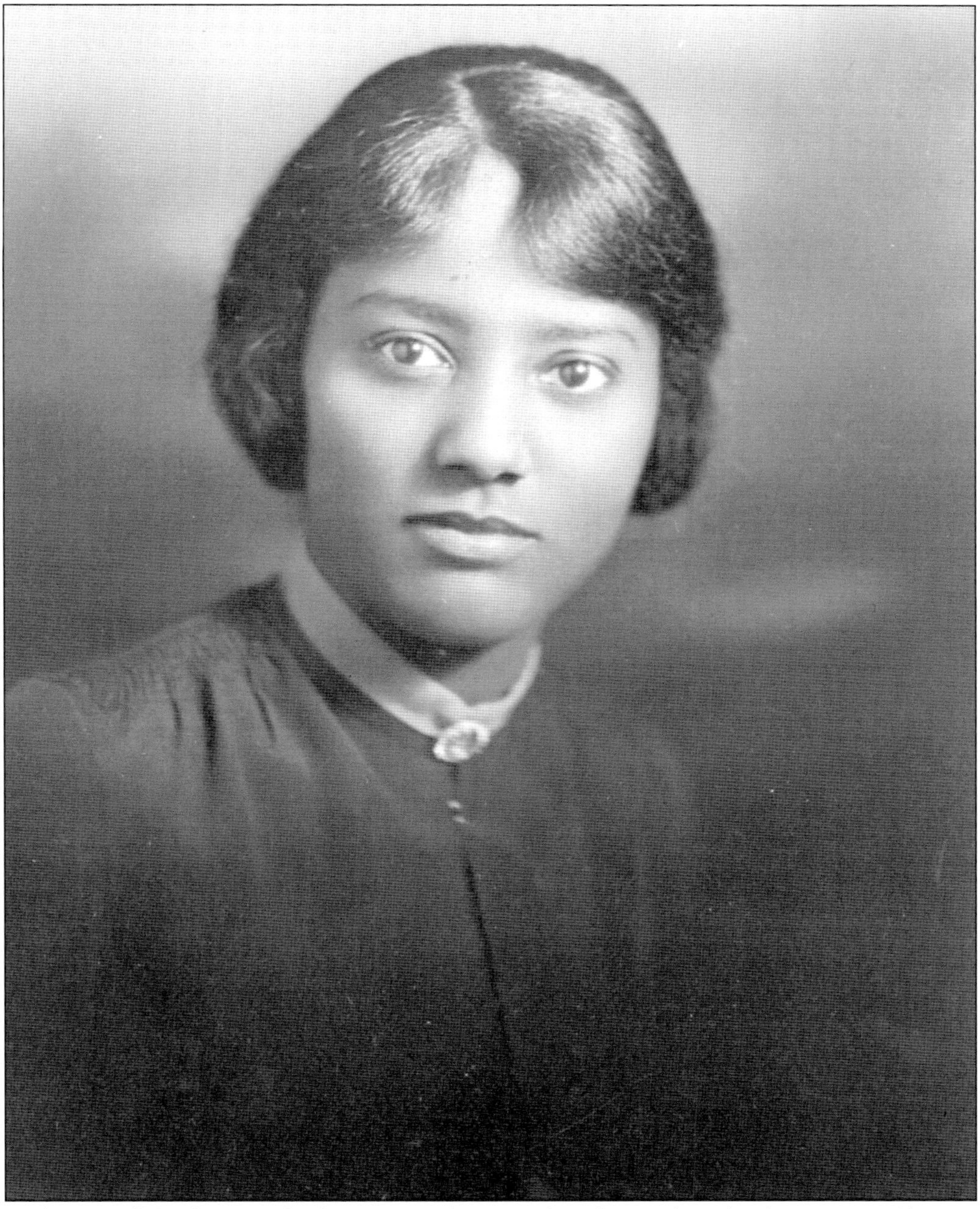

Kathryn Hall Bogle was a freelance journalist, social worker, and civil rights activist. She was a devoted member of St. Philip the Deacon Episcopal Church. Her articles appeared in several black newspapers, including the *Portland Observer.* She may be best known for "An American Negro Speaks of Color," a 2,000-word article she sold to the *Oregonian* in 1937 that described the realities of being black in Portland. It was the first time the newspaper paid an African American for a story. In 1941, she became the second African American to hold an office position with the federal government, working for the US Employment Service in Portland. In 1927, she was married to Richard Bogle, a student at the Oregon Agricultural College (now Oregon State University) studying pharmacy. The couple raised their children Richard and Linda in Southeast Portland. (Courtesy of the Oregon Historical Society.)

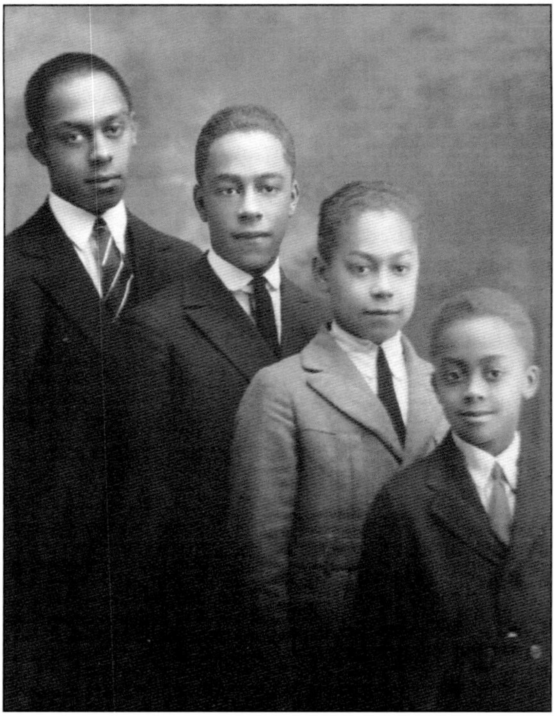

Pictured here are sons of William H. and Lottie D. Rutherford. Their oldest son, William (left), died of pneumonia in Philadelphia in 1927. The youngest brother, T. Donald (right), became an aeronautical engineer and helped build Howard Hughes's "Spruce Goose" airplane at the end of World War II and taught engineering in Los Angeles. The second-oldest son, Allen (second from left), retired as an assistant superintendent of schools in North Carolina. Otto was the only son to remain in Portland, and he became the director of the Urban League Senior Citizen Services. (Courtesy of the Rutherford Family Collection and PSU Library.)

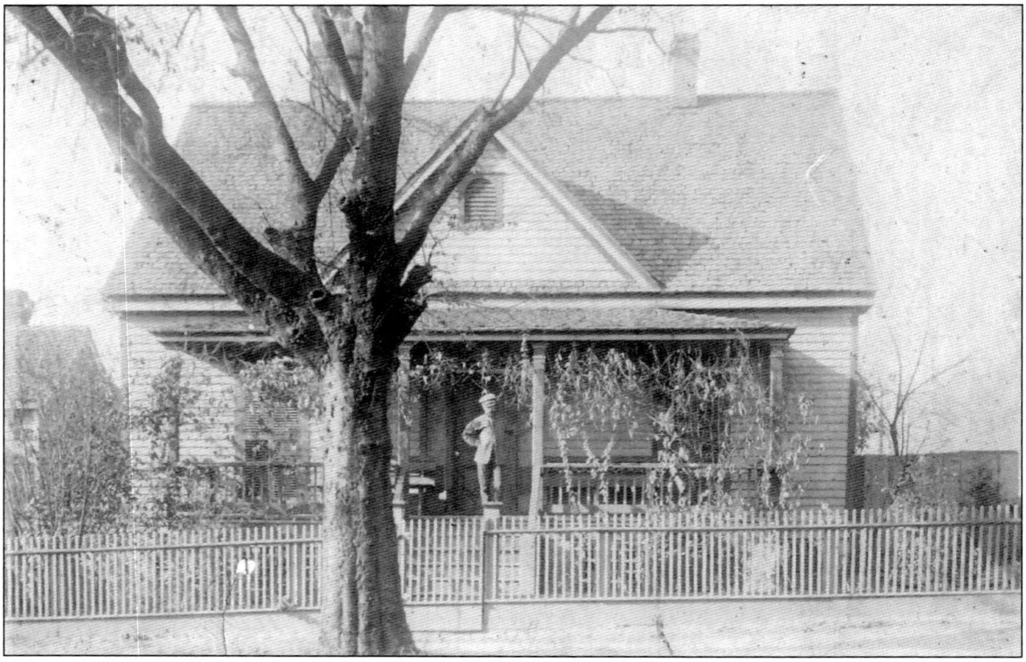

When refused the opportunity to purchase their rental home (pictured above), William and Lottie Rutherford moved to Ninth Avenue and Shaver Street and became the only black family in a neighborhood of mostly Germans. Their son and civil rights activist Otto lived there since the age of 11, and he and his wife, Verdell, lived there for 64 years of marriage. Based on the couple's role in Oregon's history, the house is listed in the National Register of Historic Places. (Courtesy of the Rutherford Family Collection and PSU Library.)

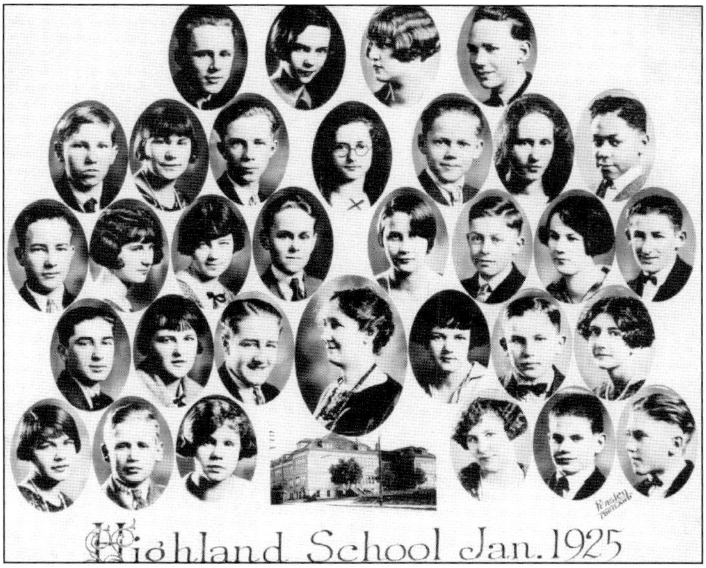

Otto Rutherford is shown here at the age of 14 with his classmates from Highland School in 1925. As one of four boys, Otto learned to fight early. He reminisced with historian Kathryn Hall Bogle that "it was eighter' fleet of foot or fast with the fist." When they moved to Shaver Street, he had trouble until the local boys realized he could fight, and then he was welcomed into their group. (Courtesy of the Rutherford Family Collection and PSU Library.)

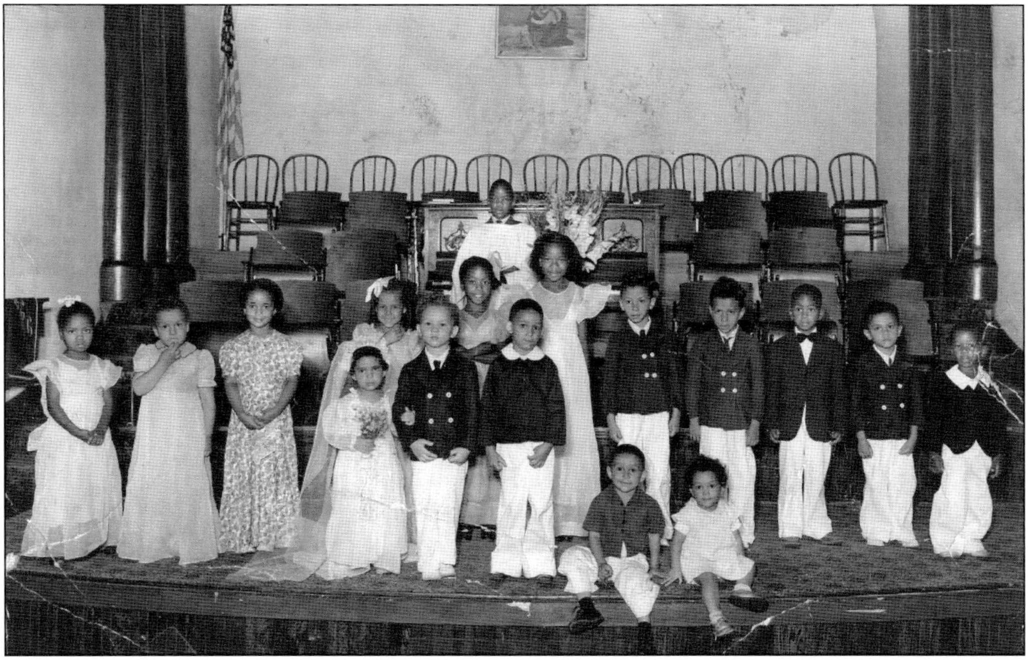

Pictured here is a Tom Thumb wedding ceremony. A Tom Thumb wedding was an opportunity for children ages 1 to 13 to participate in a pretend wedding ceremony, and they were often held as youth activities and church fundraisers. The term *Tom Thumb wedding* comes from an actual wedding: the marriage of the famous little person Gen. Tom Thumb (born Charles Stratton) to Lavinia Warren, another little person. In the spring of 1940, under the direction of Lula Gragg, Bethel AME presented a Tom Thumb wedding. From left to right are (seated) Jimmy Unthank and Thelma Unthank; (first row) bride Sonya Brooks, groom Billy Rutherford, and best man Tommie Unthank; (second row) Jennie Powell, Marianne Fuller, Adelen Olden, Janet Fuller, Margaret Powell, Ethel Harris, Edwin Washington, Ronnie Washington, Morgan Jones, Warren Washington, and Lawrence Harris; (third row) minister Lonnie Harris. (Courtesy of the Rutherford Family Collection and PSU Library.)

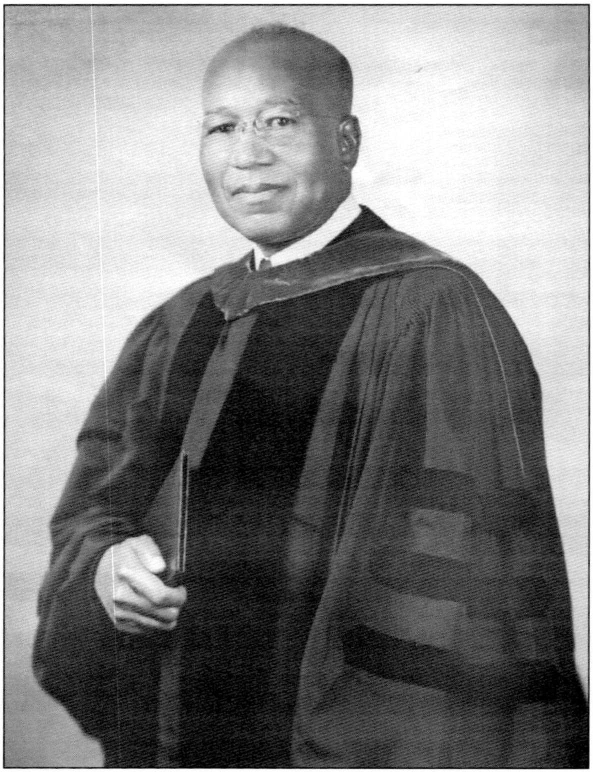

The late Rev. J. James Clow (left), a Texas native, was the pastor of Mount Olivet Baptist Church from 1936 to 1962. He was educated at the Tuskegee Institute and the University of Oregon, and in 1950, he received a doctor of divinity degree from Virginia Union University. Dr. Clow was a charter member of the Urban League and served as president of the Portland Branch of the NAACP for three years. He was an outspoken opponent of Portland's segregated housing practices, particularly in the postwar era. (Courtesy of Mount Olivet Baptist Church.)

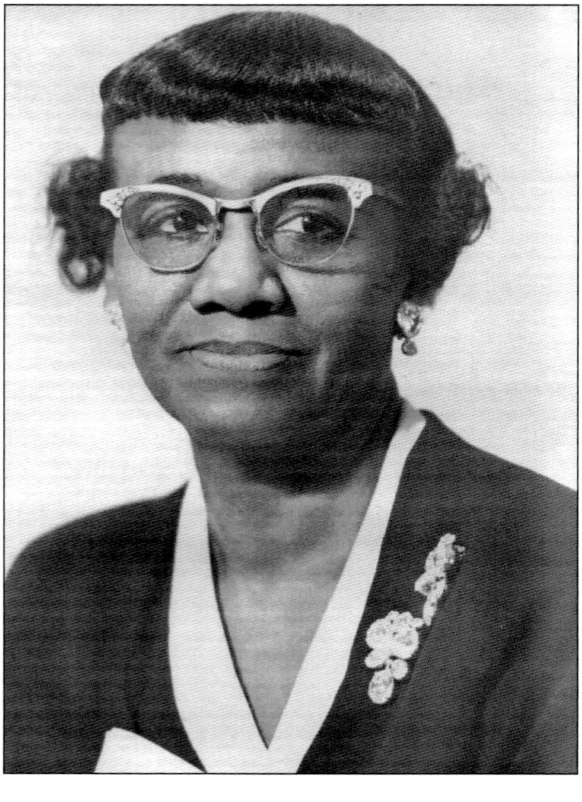

For over 25 years, Dr. Clow and his wife, Pearl Clark Clow, dedicated their life to Mount Olivet Baptist Church and were champions for social justice. A souvenir booklet created for the 25th anniversary of the Clows' ministry describes Pearl Clark Clow as "a devoted wife, and a gracious and gifted woman in her own right. She represented womanhood at its finest and best." In 1948, Pearl Clow was the president of the Oregon Association of Colored Women's Clubs and urged women to assume responsibility for political action by using the ballot box. (Courtesy of Mount Olivet Baptist Church.)

Four

THE WAR YEARS

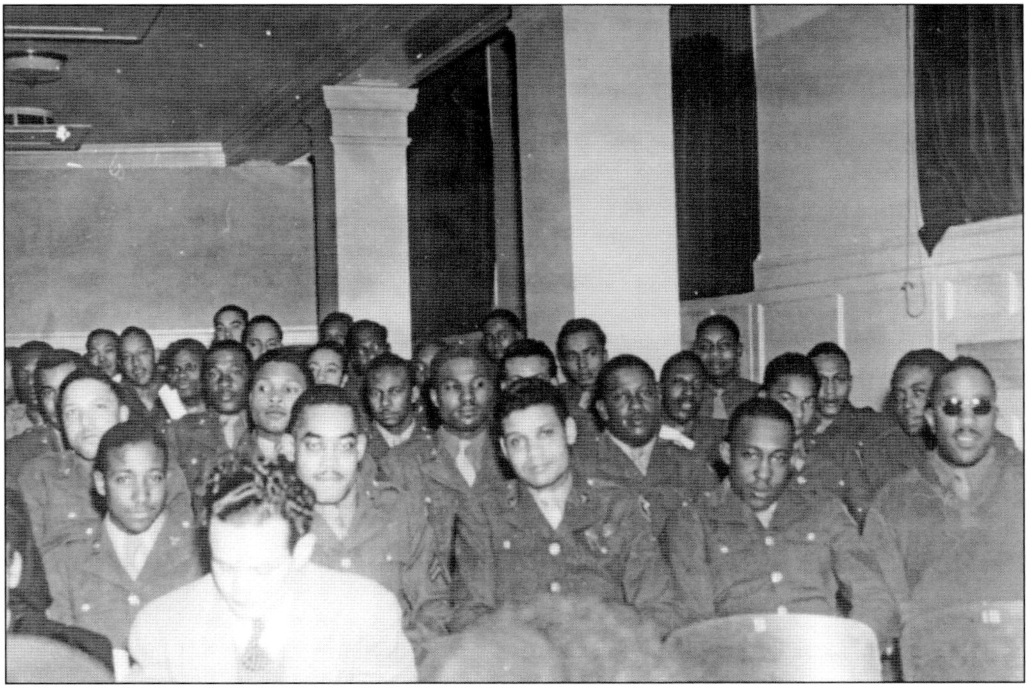

World War II brought much excitement to Portland, and the shipbuilding industry transformed the city overnight. In 1940, the US Maritime Administration approved the production orders of the Liberty ships that were primarily manufactured by local companies. In January 1941, industrialist Henry J. Kaiser developed the huge Oregon Shipbuilding Corporation, and it launched its first Liberty ship, the *Star of Oregon*, on May 19, 1941. At the peak of wartime production in 1943 and 1944, metropolitan Portland counted 140,000 defense workers; 15,000 of those defense workers were African Americans. An influx of African American soldiers was an active part of Portland community life as well. The Williams Avenue YWCA was partially converted into an USO to provide services to the African American soldiers and their families. After the war, many discharged veterans remained in the area. Pictured here are African American soldiers sitting together in an unidentified public auditorium. (Courtesy of the Oregon Historical Society.)

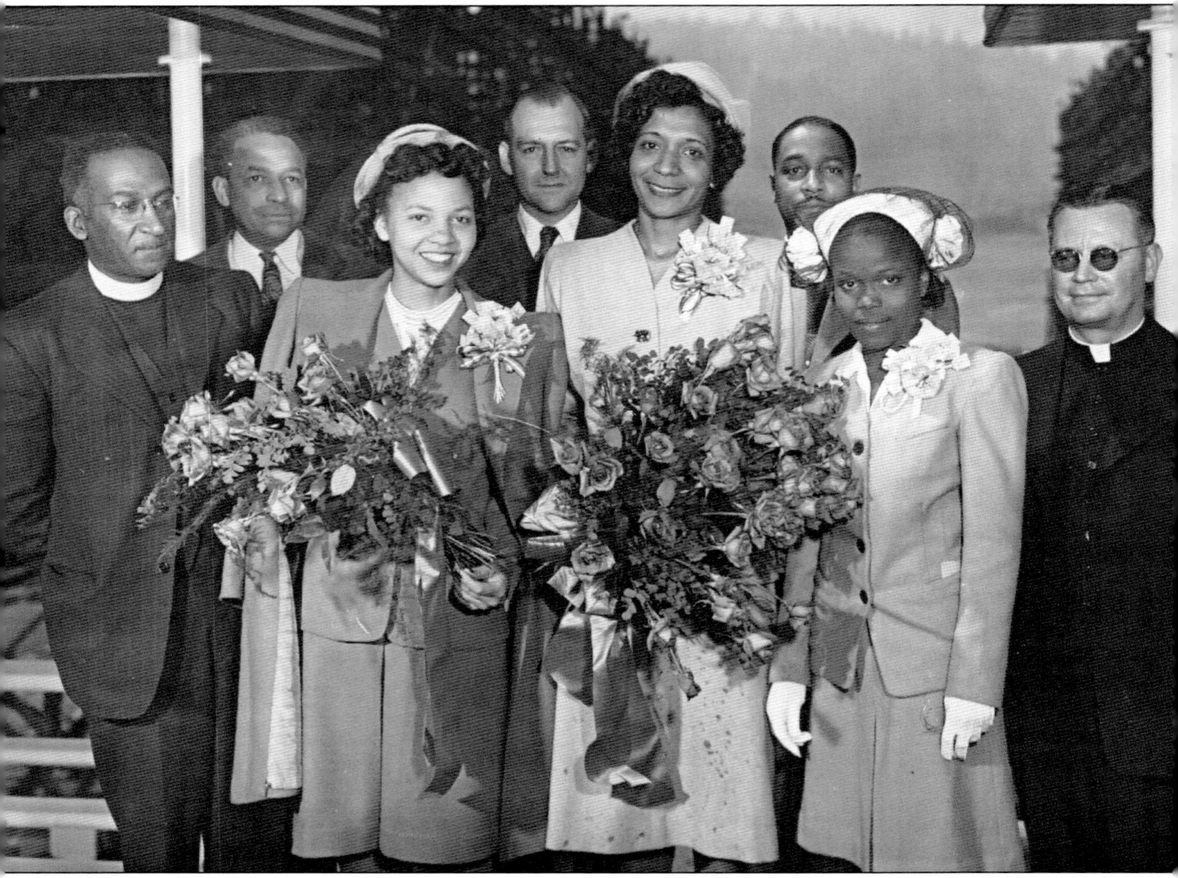

On May 8, 1945, two special VE Day launchings were held to "mark the close cooperation of all races and creeds in American war industry." The Klamath and Modoc Indians joined in one launching, and members of the black community participated in the launching of the *Tuskegee Victory*. The *Tuskegee Victory* was christened by Charlotte Moton, the daughter of the late Robert Moton, who succeeded Booker T. Washington as president of the Tuskegee Institute. An article in the *Oregonian* reports that the event was attended by a group of 20 Tuskegee graduates, most of whom were shipyard employees, and five wounded Negro soldiers from Barnes Hospital who were guests of honor. Guest speaker Fr. Thomas Tobin declared that color prejudice is unwarranted and asserted that 20 labor unions still excluded Negroes from membership while others allowed only limited rights. Pictured here from left to right are (first row) Bennie Gragg, Jefferson High School student; Charlotte Moton, sponsor; Darnice Crockett; and Fr. Thomas Tobin; (second row) Rev. Lee Owen Stone, Dr. DeNorval Unthank, Albert Bauer, and Kenneth Smith. (Courtesy of the Oregon Historical Society.)

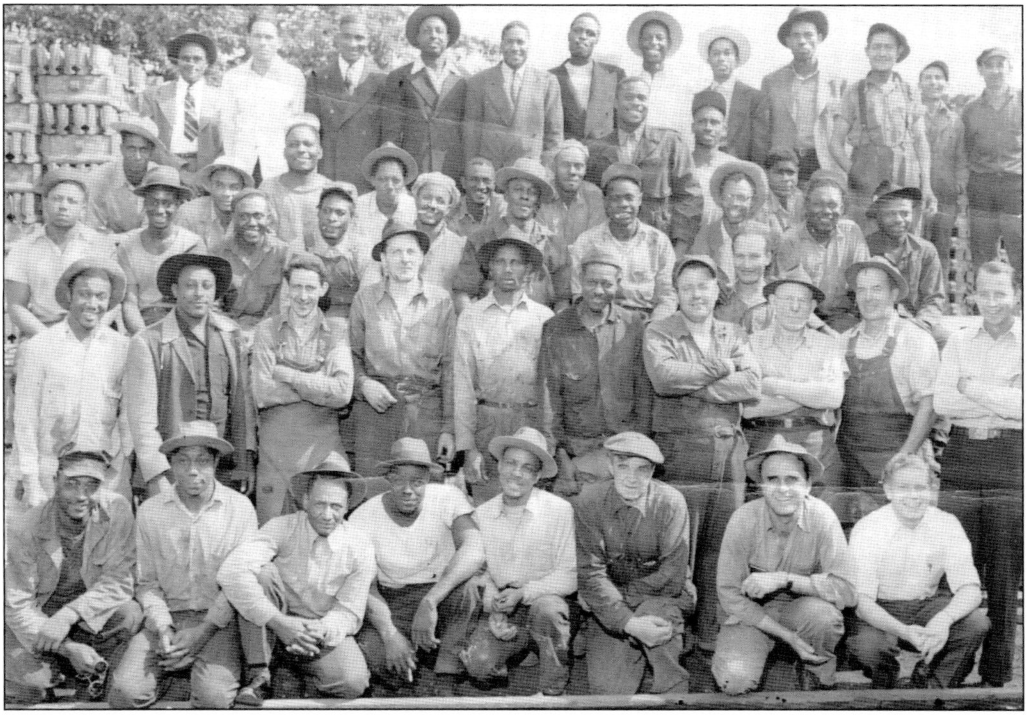

Other employment opportunities (besides shipbuilding) were available during World War II. According to historian Rudy Pearson, several steel-casting, scrap iron, and other industrial companies selected the Portland-Vancouver region, given its access to the Columbia River, for production sites. This 1940s photograph of American Brakeshoe Iron and Steel Foundry employees exemplifies a non-shipbuilding employment opportunity available to African Americans from 1940 to 1945. The foundry was located in Linton, Oregon. Pictured in the back row, far left, are Mitchell Horsley (wearing hat) and Ivy Campbell (white shirt). (Courtesy of City of Portland Archives.)

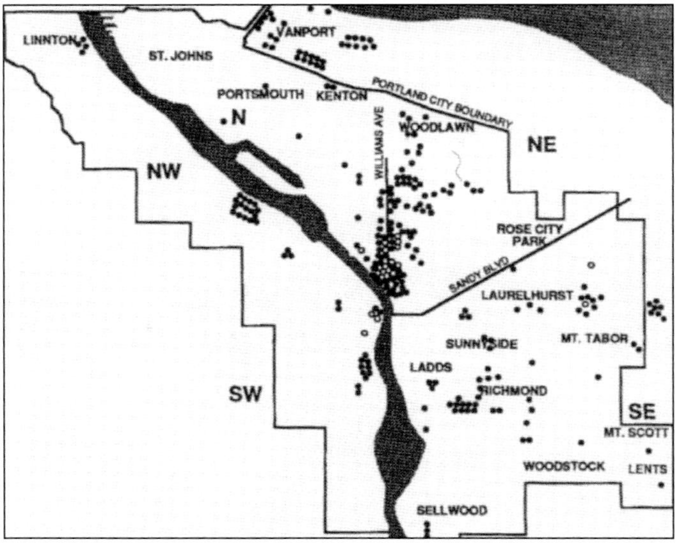

Since the 1930s, as African Americans gradually began to settle on the east side, black community life was centered on and around Williams Avenue. The number of black-owned businesses increased during and after World War II. At right is the "Black Population Distribution Map," published by the Portland City Club in 1945. The solid dots represent dwellings occupied by blacks, and the circle represents black-owned businesses. (Courtesy of the Portland City Club.)

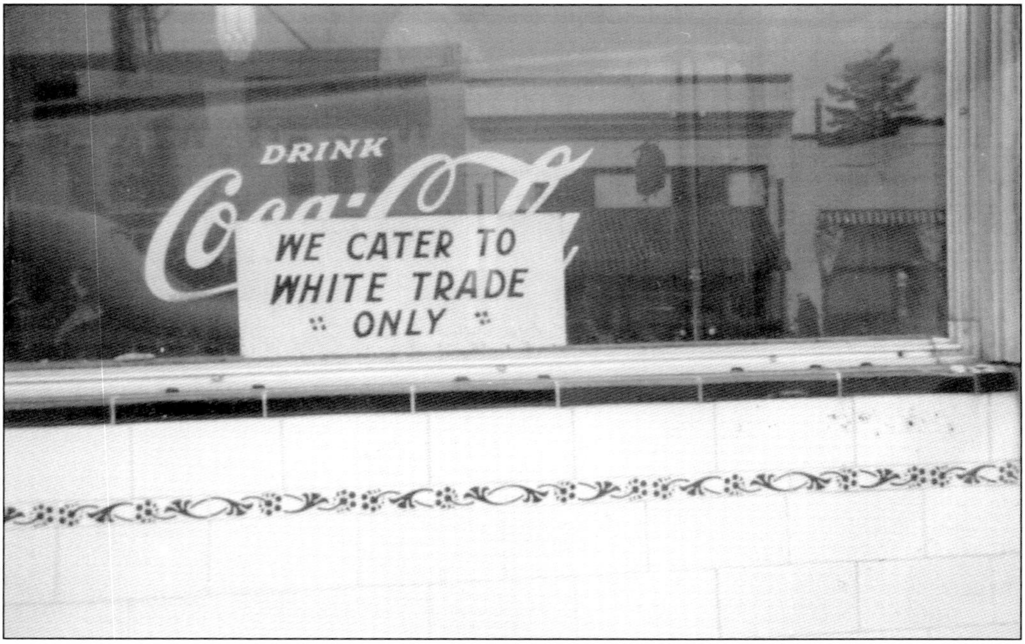

Between 1941 and 1943, the African American population in Portland increased tenfold, from roughly 2,000 to 20,000. Historian Dr. Darrell Millner, author of *The Urban League of Portland: On the Road to Equality*, commented that the rapid increase in population and the different cultural qualities, expectations, and orientation of new immigrants spelled doomed for the old pattern of race relations. Conflict was inevitable, and Jim Crow signs, like the one shown here, greeted newcomers to Portland. (Courtesy of the Oregon Historical Society.)

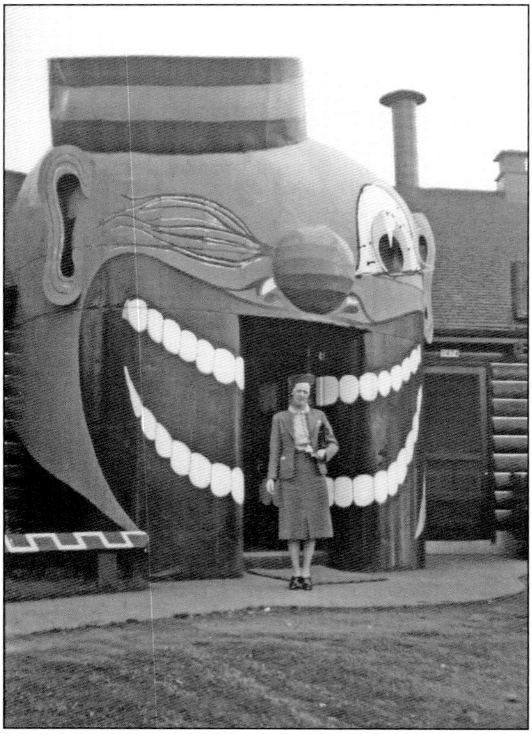

The Coon Chicken Inn restaurant opened in 1931. The name denotes a racial slur, and the trademarks and entrances of the restaurants were designed to look like a big mouth of Sambo caricature. Historian Rudy Pearson commented that the restaurant presented an overt display of prejudice. The restaurant remained a popular eating establishment until the late 1950s. (Courtesy of Alex Blendl, Historical Photos)

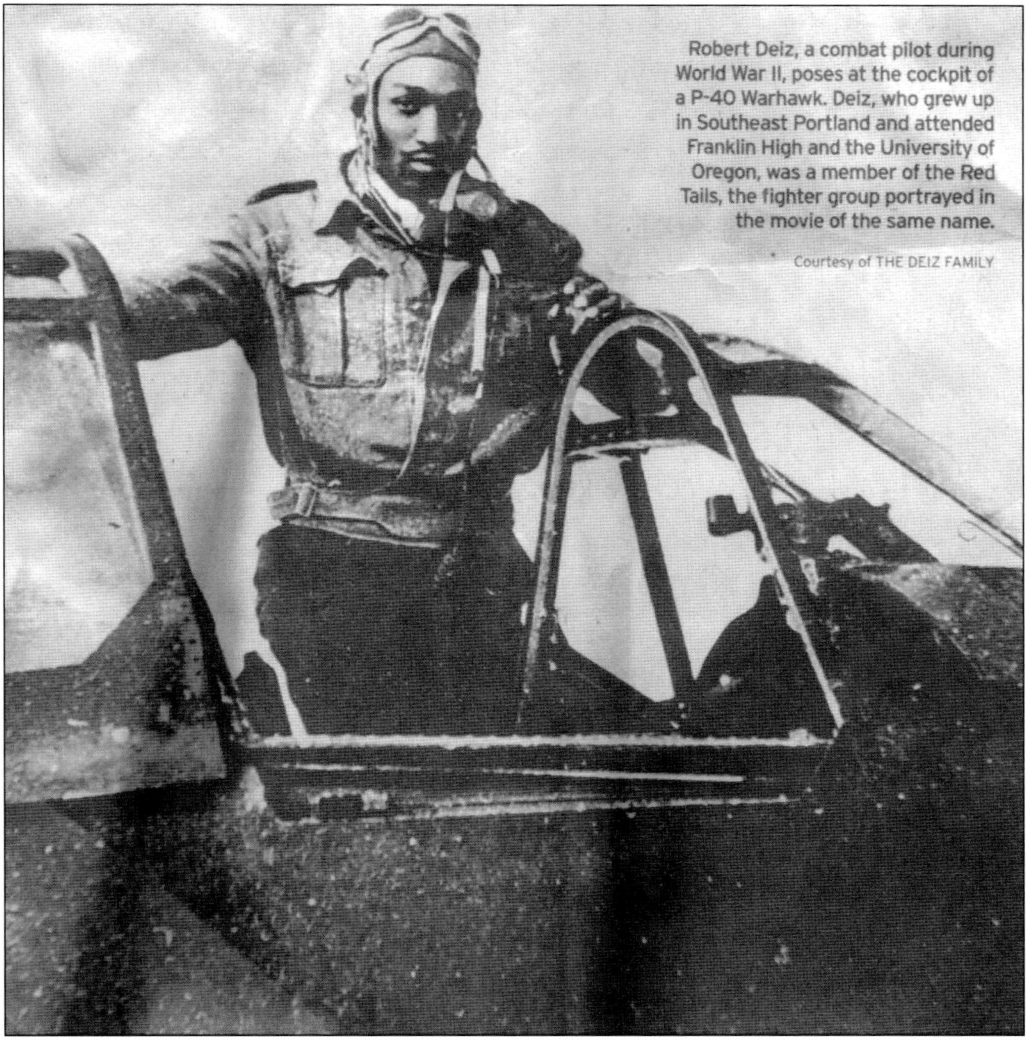

Robert Deiz, a Tuskegee-trained combat pilot during World War II and member of the Red Tails, poses at the cockpit of a P-40 Warhawk. Robert and his brother Carl Deiz were among 12 Oregonians who served as Tuskegee Airmen. Robert was featured in the *Oregonian* when he downed two Nazi fighter planes in two days. In 2004, he was inducted into the Oregon Aviation Hall of Honor. (Courtesy of the Deiz family.)

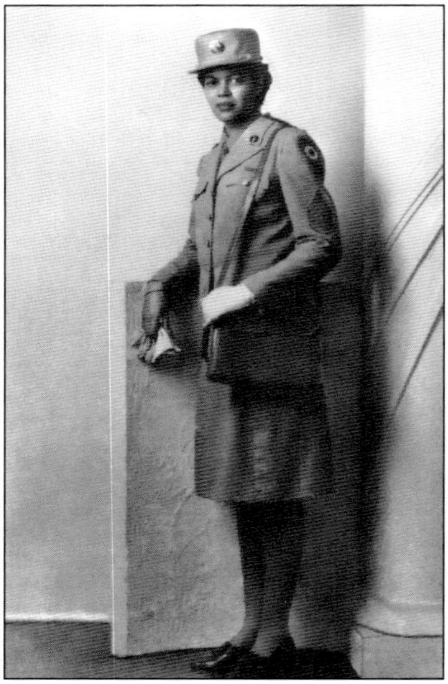

In 1942, Congress approved the creation of the Women's Army Auxiliary Corps (WAAC). Shortly thereafter, Elva May (Poole) Belcher became the first African American woman from Oregon to be sworn into the WAAC. This is a photograph of Elva in her WAAC uniform. She was stationed in Fort Huachuca, Arizona, and was one of 150,000 women who served in the WAAC and, later, the Women Auxiliary Corps (WAC) during World War II. (Courtesy of Elva [Poole] Belcher.)

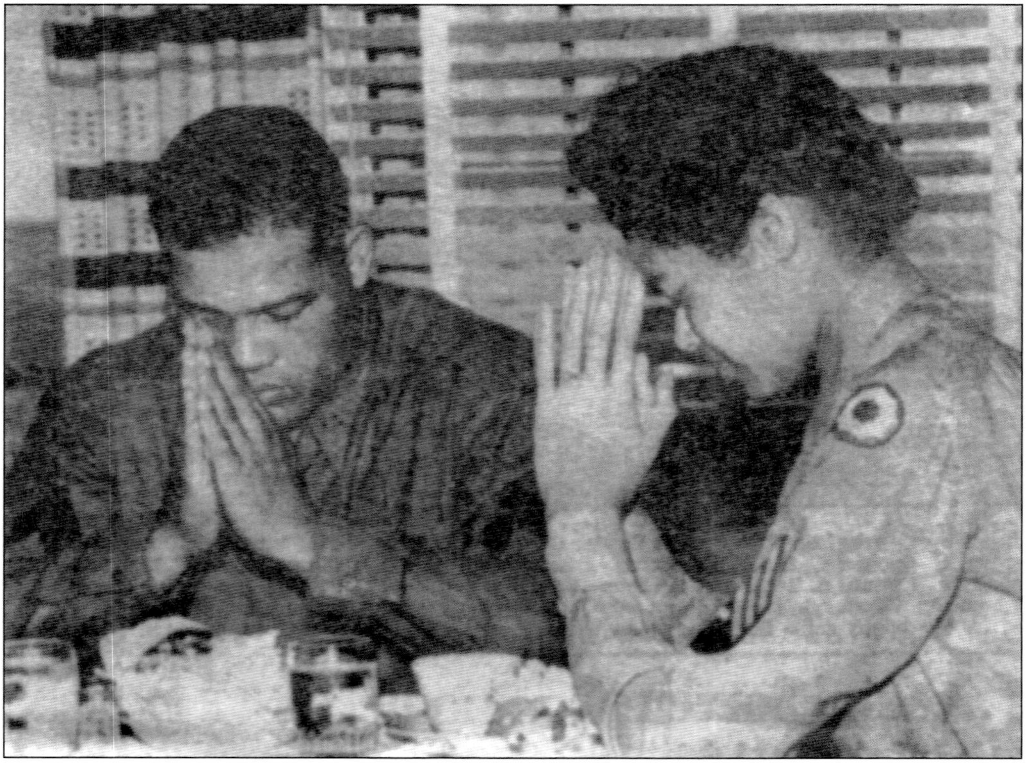

As a soldier, world heavyweight champion Sgt. Joe Louis Barrow traveled more than 21,000 miles and staged 96 boxing exhibitions before two million soldiers. In 1945, such an exhibition occurred in Portland at the auditorium. Elva May Poole escorted the heavyweight champion while visiting Fort Huachuca, Arizona. The caption in the *Apache Sentinel* reads that "Sgt. Joe Louis Barrow is shown with WAC sergeant Elva May Poole, giving thanks for their many blessings." (Courtesy of Elva [Poole] Belcher.)

The Women in the Air Force (WAF), established in 1948 by President Truman, allowed women to serve directly in the military. In this photograph, WAF recruit Mary Abram is being honored by several African American women. Pictured from left to right are (first row) Betty Carden and Mary Abram, Portland's WAF recruit; (second row) Verdell Rutherford and Thelma Minor Unthank. (Courtesy of Oregon State Archives, Urban League Collection.)

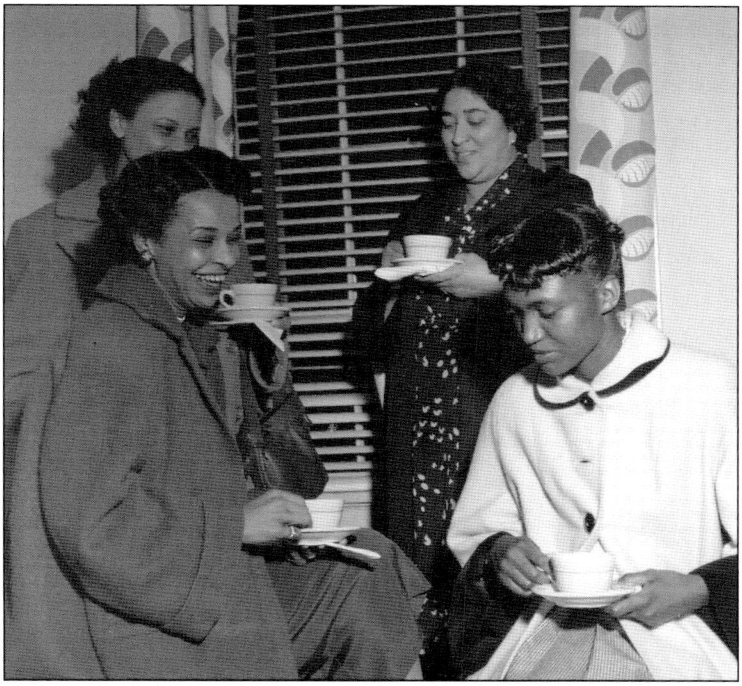

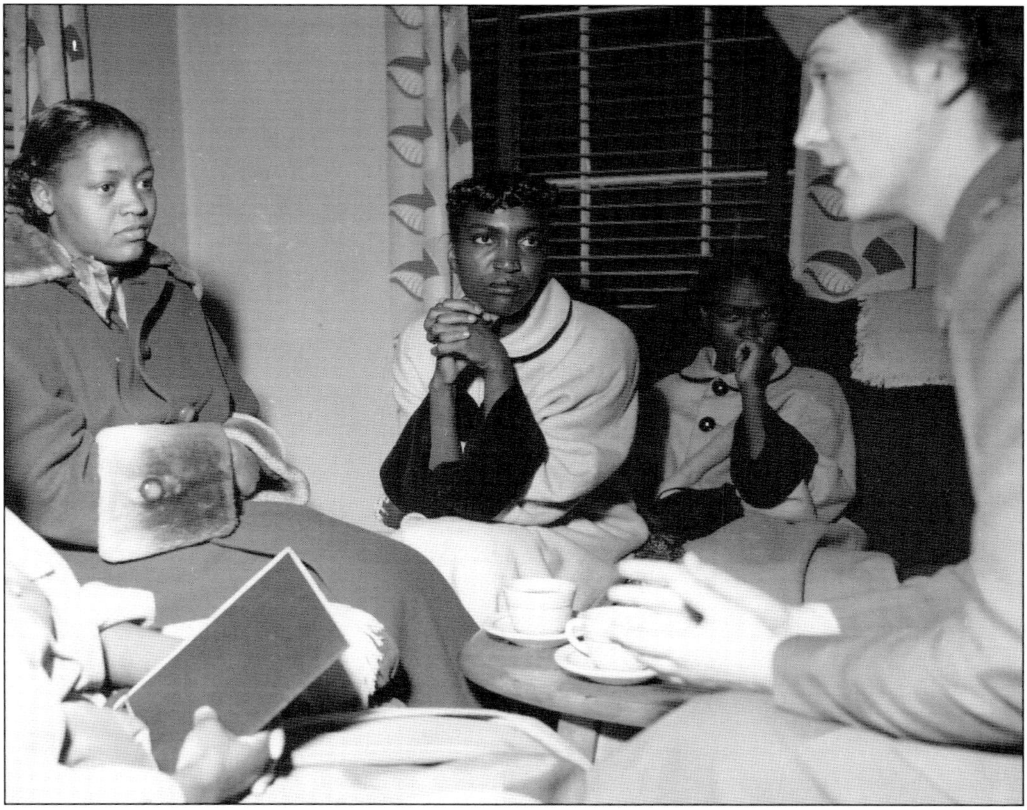

An unidentified WAF recruiter talks to potential recruits. WAF recruit Mary Abram is pictured to the right. (Courtesy of Urban League Collection and OSU Special Collection and Archives.)

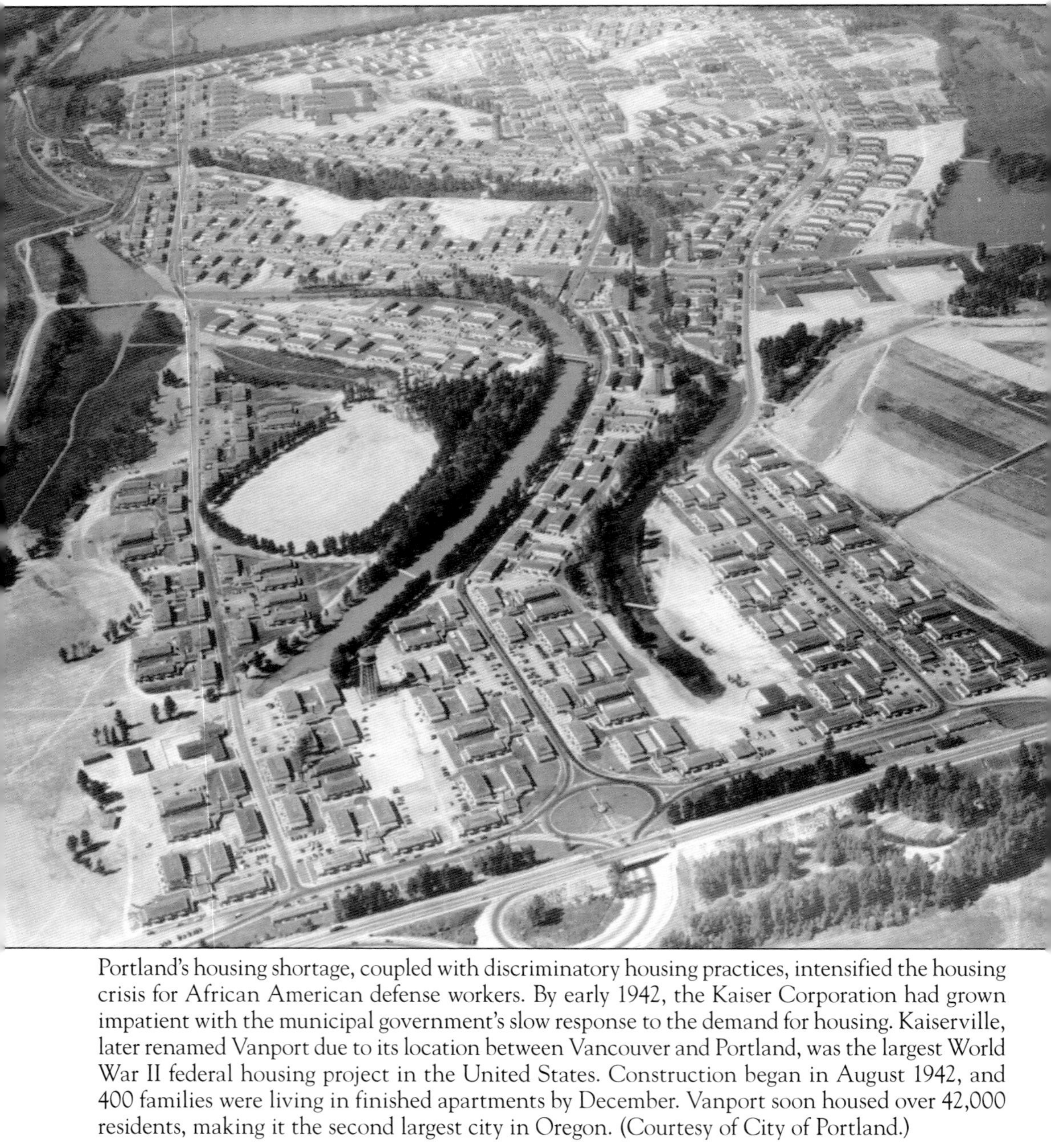

Portland's housing shortage, coupled with discriminatory housing practices, intensified the housing crisis for African American defense workers. By early 1942, the Kaiser Corporation had grown impatient with the municipal government's slow response to the demand for housing. Kaiserville, later renamed Vanport due to its location between Vancouver and Portland, was the largest World War II federal housing project in the United States. Construction began in August 1942, and 400 families were living in finished apartments by December. Vanport soon housed over 42,000 residents, making it the second largest city in Oregon. (Courtesy of City of Portland.)

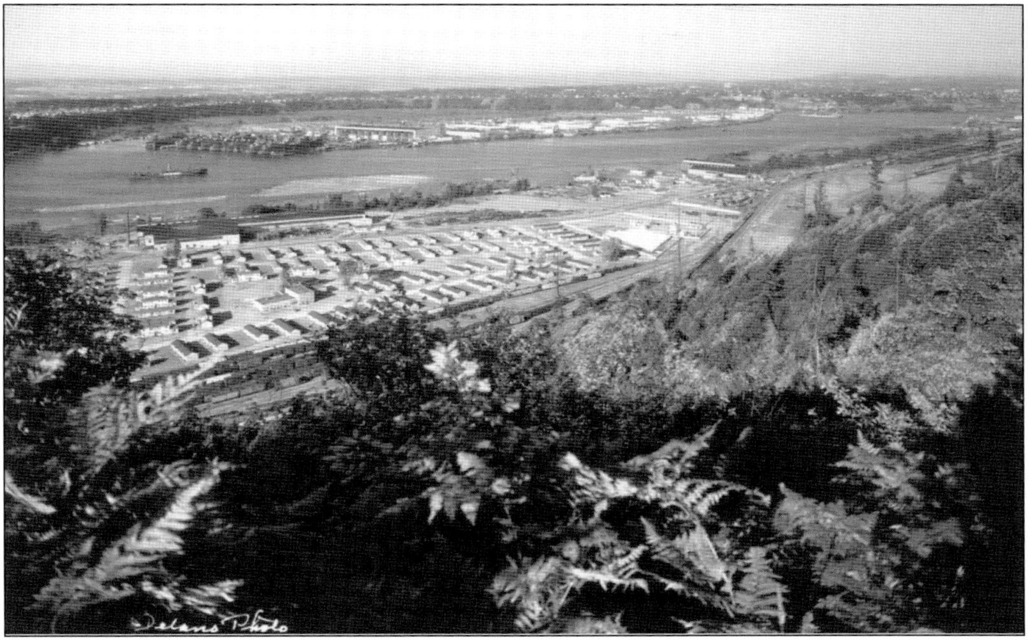

Located at the former site of the 1905 Lewis and Clark Exposition, Guild's Lake Courts provided homes for roughly 10,000 war workers and their families in 2,606 housing units. Approximately 2,000 African American families lived in the far northern end. Shown here is a 1944 aerial view of Guild's Lake Courts. (Courtesy of City of Portland Archives.)

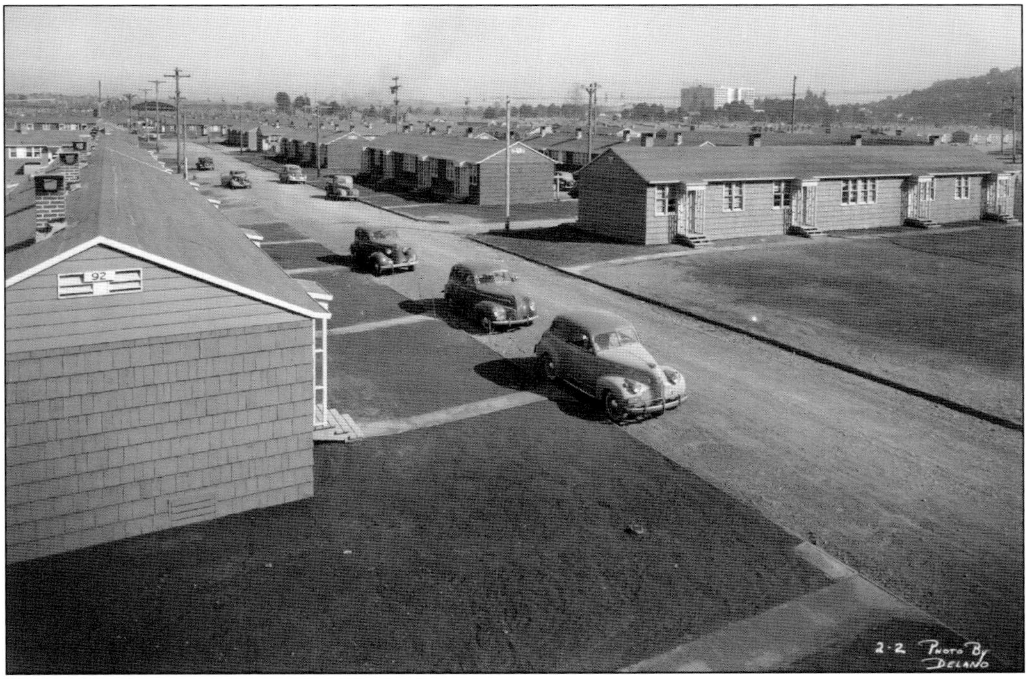

Shown here is a 1942 photograph of the recently built Guild's Lake Courts. According to Dr. Tanya Lyn March, residents were enticed with furnished units in modern, electrified structures, with hard-to-obtain appliances, access to public schools and extensive childcare opportunities, and a short commute to the shipyard. (Courtesy of City of Portland Archives.)

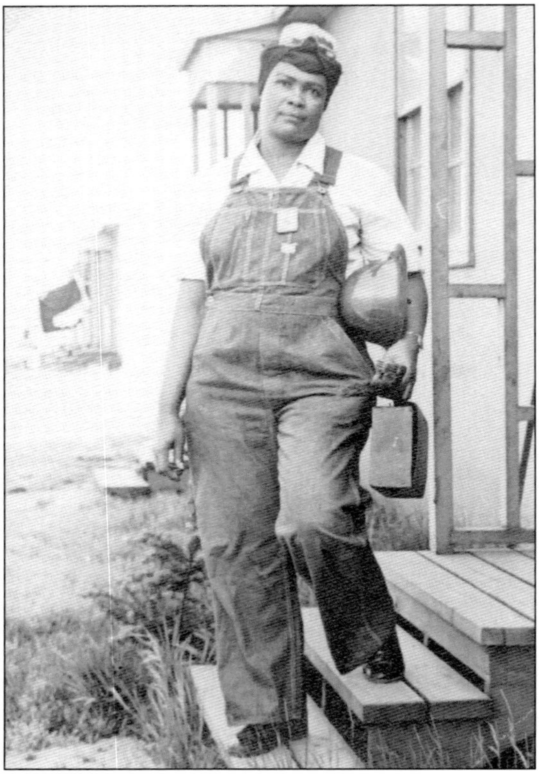

World War II changed women's position in the workplace forever. Due to the shortage of workers, women were recruited to work in the shipyards and other war plants. The typical dress for women defense workers is displayed in this compelling 1943 photograph of Ninie Mae Locke, native of Napchez, Mississippi and Guild Lake Courts. (Courtesy of City of Portland Archives.)

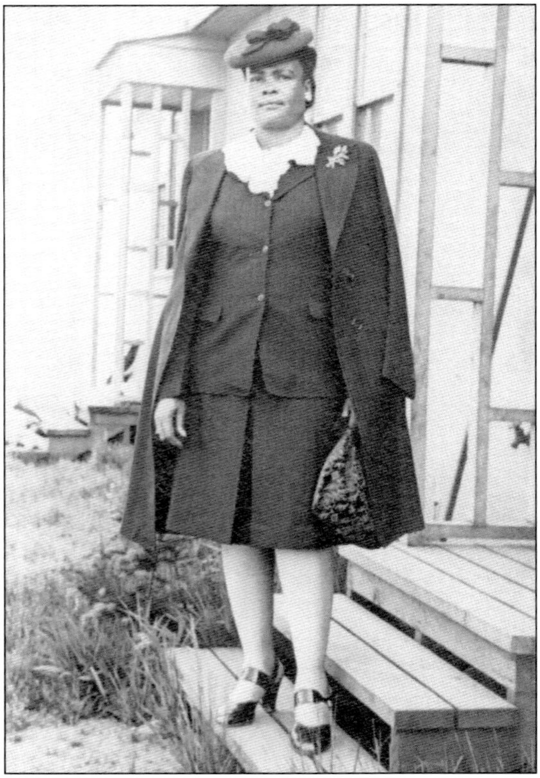

Ninie Mae Locke, native of Napchez, Mississippi and Guild Lake Courts, is shown here in her Sunday best attire. This photograph demonstrates the economic prosperity experienced by all defense workers, particular African Americans. Wartime employment opportunities presented greater economic opportunities for African Americans who migrated from southern states with limited employment opportunities and low wages. (Courtesy of City of Portland Archives.)

In many ways, the federal housing projects were more progressive in race relations. Vanport and Guild's Lake Court children pictured here play at the Guild's Lakes Fruit and Flower Day Care. Gloria Campbell Cash is the young girl bouncing on the board in a black dress. (Courtesy of City of Portland Archives.)

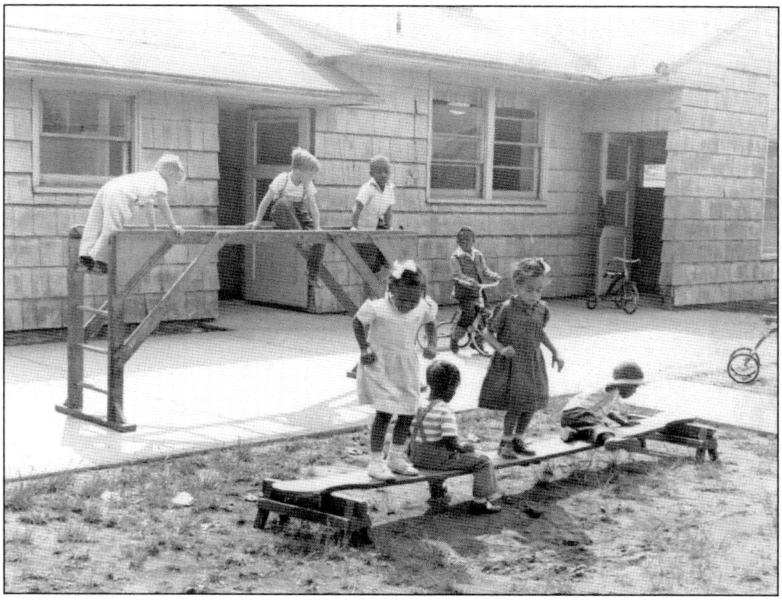

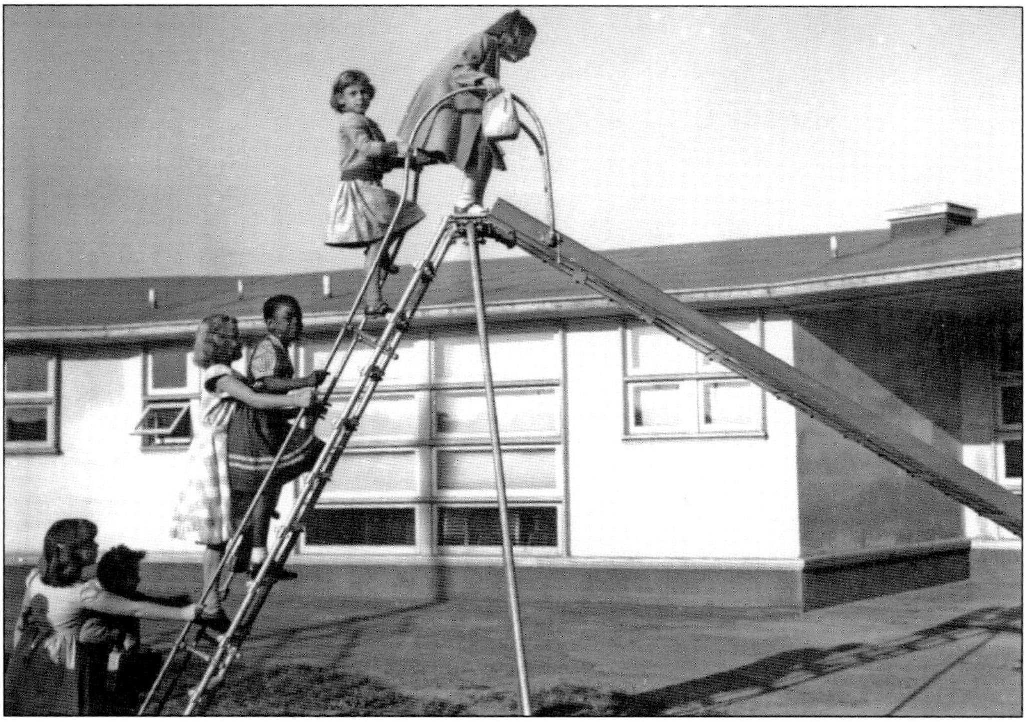

The Oregon Ship School, located near the Parkside Homes development of the Housing Authority of Portland, provided children with integrated classrooms and social experiences. Pictured here are white and black children climbing the slide on the playground. (Courtesy of Urban League Collection and OSU Special Collection and Research Archive Center.)

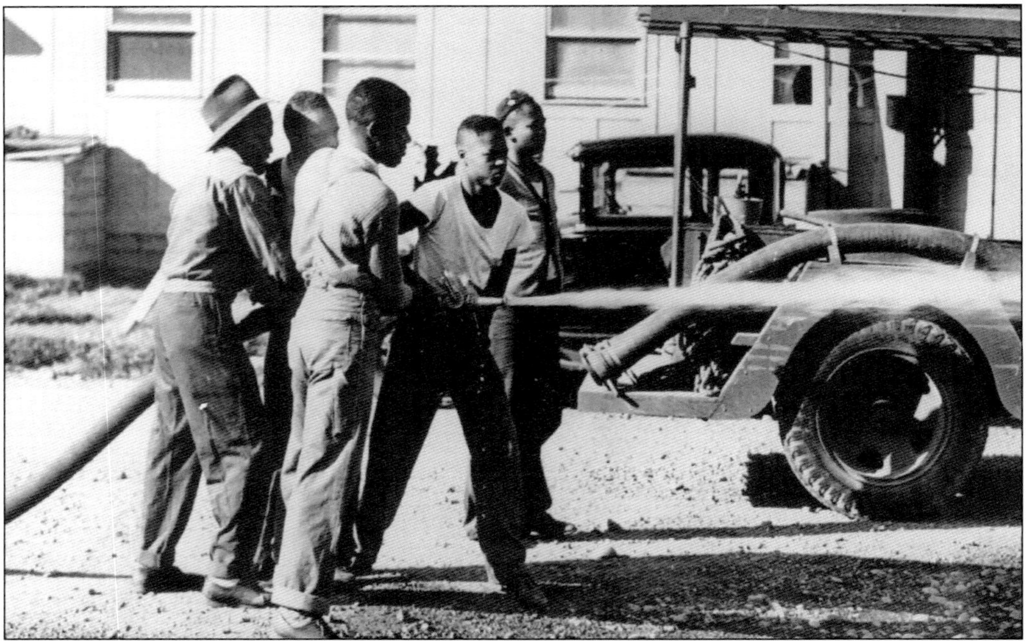

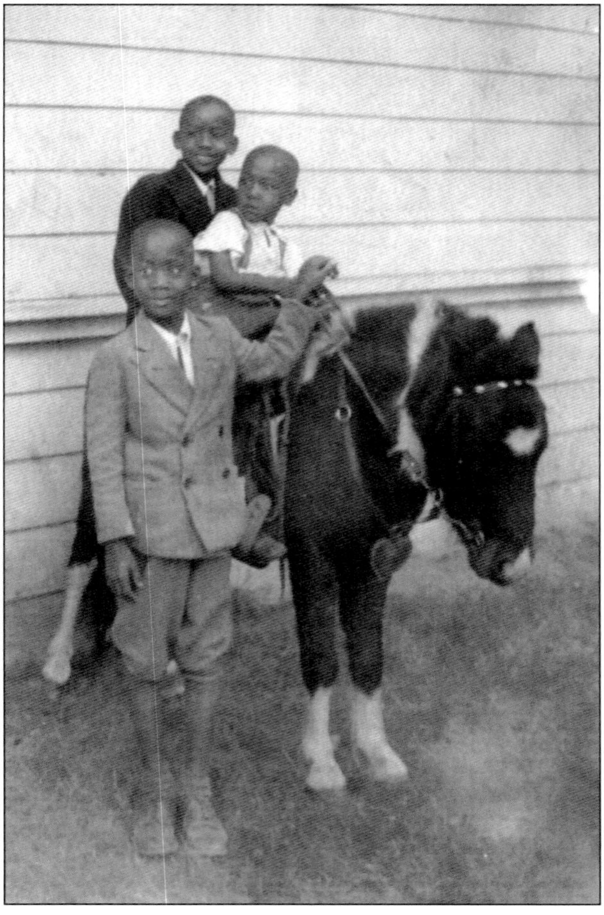

Children residing in Guild's Lake Courts participated in volunteer fire brigades and in the racially integrated Junior Police Patrol. Shown here are African American members of the Junior Fire Squad. (Courtesy of City of Portland Archives.)

Occasionally, Vanport residents were visited by traveling photographers who went door-to-door with a pony, looking for willing subjects. Shown here, the Washington brothers Billy and Joe (also known as Smitty, in front of Billy) sit on top of the pony as Ed (also known as Sonny) stands beside. This photograph is one of the few items belonging to their mother, Virgie Washington, that survived the Vanport Flood. (Courtesy of Ed Washington.)

The Bethelites were among several women's groups that banded together to support the war efforts. (Courtesy of the Rutherford Family Collection and PSU Library.)

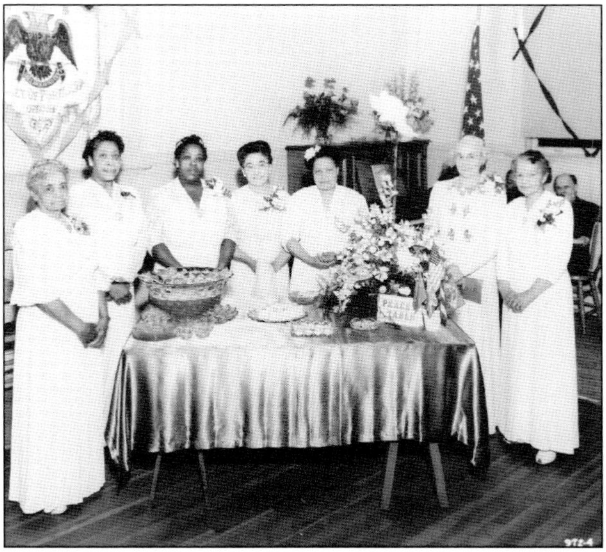

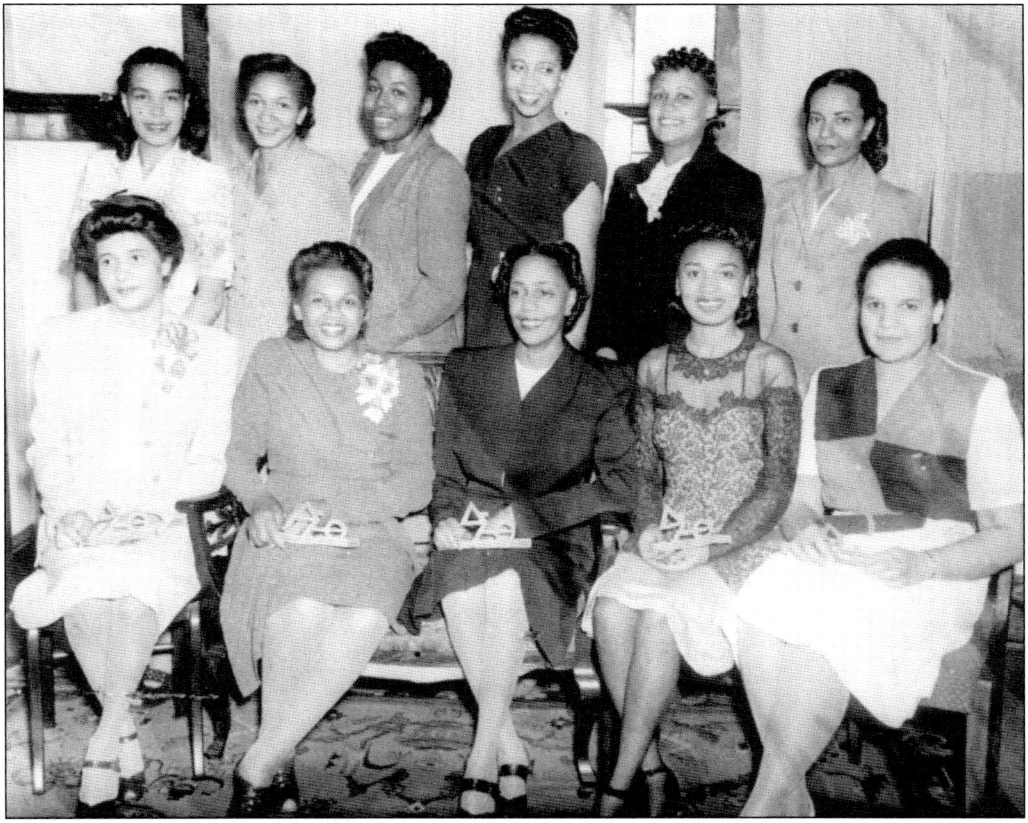

In 1942, Portland natives Lena Hillsman and Ellen Torrence were initiated in Alpha Omicron in Seattle and promoted the ideal of Delta Sigma Theta in Portland. In March 1945, a Portland Alumnae Beta Psi chapter was chartered in Portland, becoming the first and only chapter of the Delta Sigma Theta Sorority, Inc., in Oregon. The charter members volunteered at the Negro USO, providing aid to soldiers and their families. (Courtesy of the Beta Psi and Portland Alumnae Chapters of the Delta Sigma Theta.)

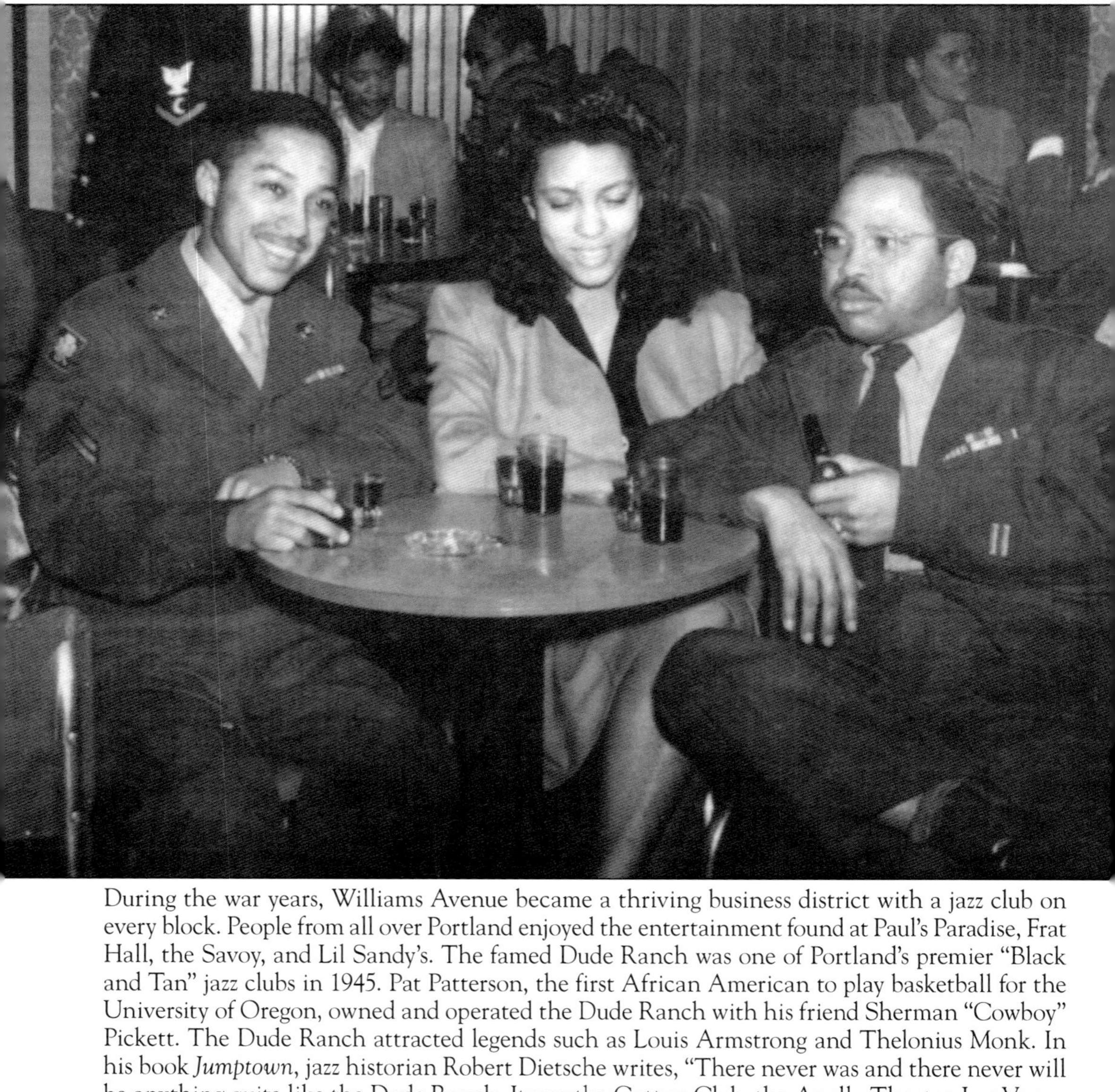

During the war years, Williams Avenue became a thriving business district with a jazz club on every block. People from all over Portland enjoyed the entertainment found at Paul's Paradise, Frat Hall, the Savoy, and Lil Sandy's. The famed Dude Ranch was one of Portland's premier "Black and Tan" jazz clubs in 1945. Pat Patterson, the first African American to play basketball for the University of Oregon, owned and operated the Dude Ranch with his friend Sherman "Cowboy" Pickett. The Dude Ranch attracted legends such as Louis Armstrong and Thelonius Monk. In his book *Jumptown*, jazz historian Robert Dietsche writes, "There never was and there never will be anything quite like the Dude Ranch. It was the Cotton Club, the Apollo Theater, Las Vegas, and the Wild West rolled into one." Enjoying an evening at the Dude Ranch are Pauline Miller (center), her then-fiancé John Bradford (right), and his brother Joe Bradford (left). The brothers were both stationed in the South Pacific and were reunited that evening at the Dude Ranch. (Courtesy of Pauline Miller Bradford.)

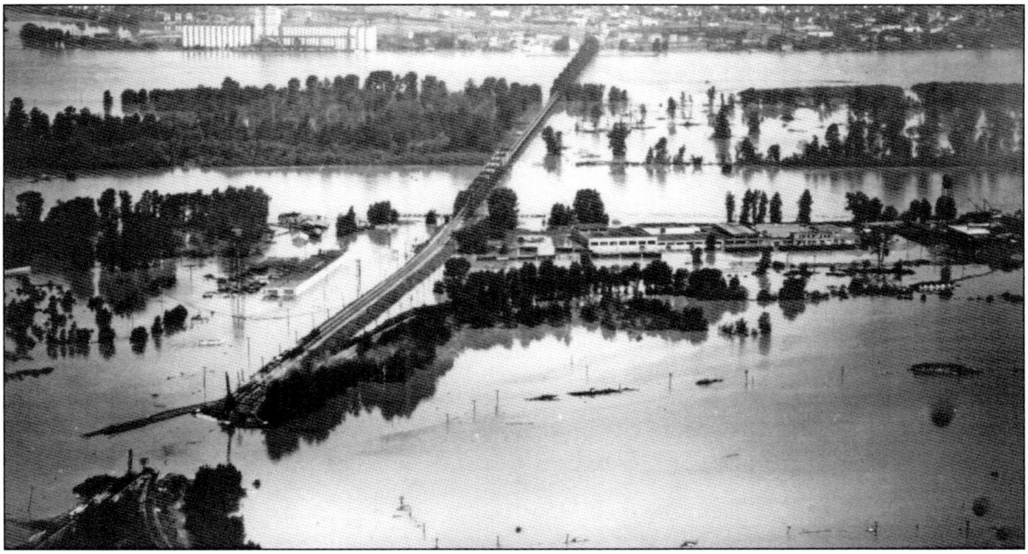

After the war, only 10,000 of the original 20,000 to 25,000 blacks who migrated to Portland during the war remained in the city. A housing shortage, restrictive housing practices, and limited economic resources confined approximately 4,500 blacks to Vanport. On May 30, 1948, a disastrous flood wiped out the entire Vanport housing project in a matter of minutes. In his book *Portland in Three Centuries*, historian Carl Abbott writes that the Columbia River was swollen by weeks of heavy rain, and that the water breached the Northern Pacific Railway embankment and backfilled the low-lying community. Vanport residents had 35 minutes to escape the floodwaters. (Courtesy of the Gerald W. Williams Collection and OSU Special Collections and Archive Research Center.)

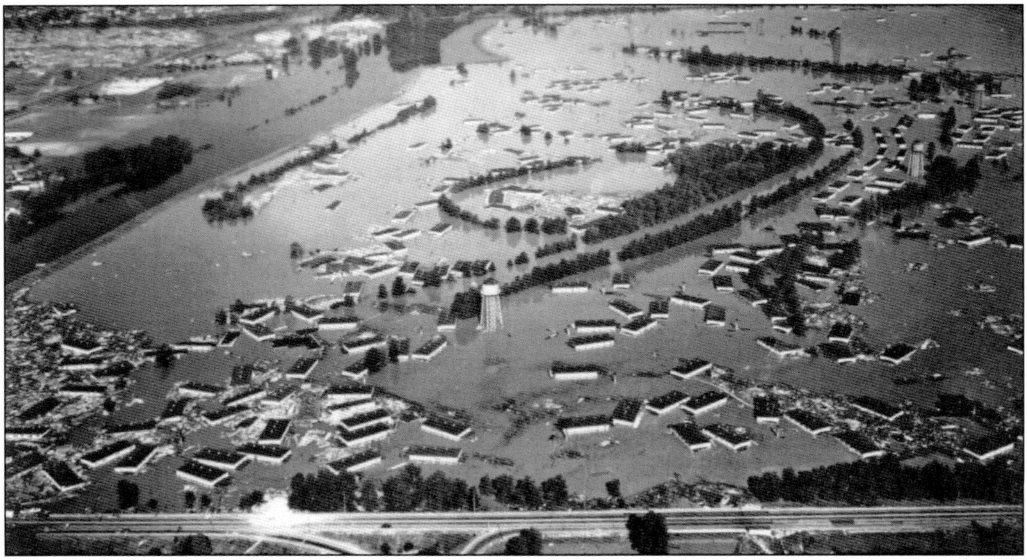

The quickly built Vanport housing units were no match for the waves of floodwaters that spread over Vanport. As the waves began to roll, the houses were wrenched apart. The water reached the highest part of the housing project near Denver Avenue, and all the vehicular traffic was quickly flooded out. The destruction of the housing project is visible in this aerial view of the Vanport Flood. (Courtesy of the Gerald W. Williams Collection and OSU Special Collections and Archive Research Center.)

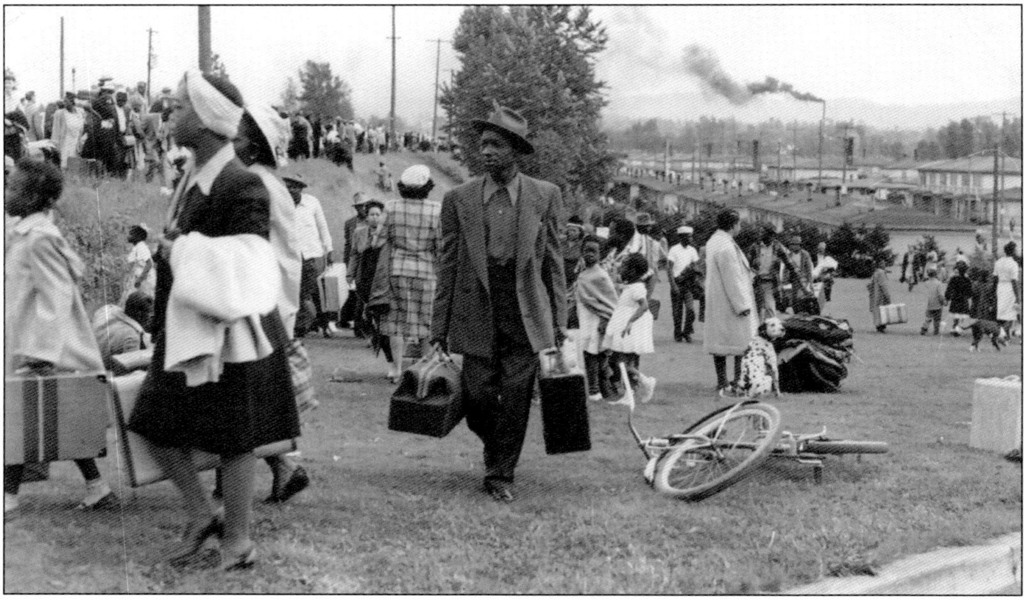

The Vanport Flood was a tragic and frightening time for the Portland metropolitan area. Photographs like this one appeared in the local paper. The *Oregonian* caption for this 1948 image claims, "thousands of men, women and children, some clutching belongings, made their way up the sloping embankment that separates Vanport from Denver Avenue soon after the dike broke." (Courtesy of the *Oregonian*.)

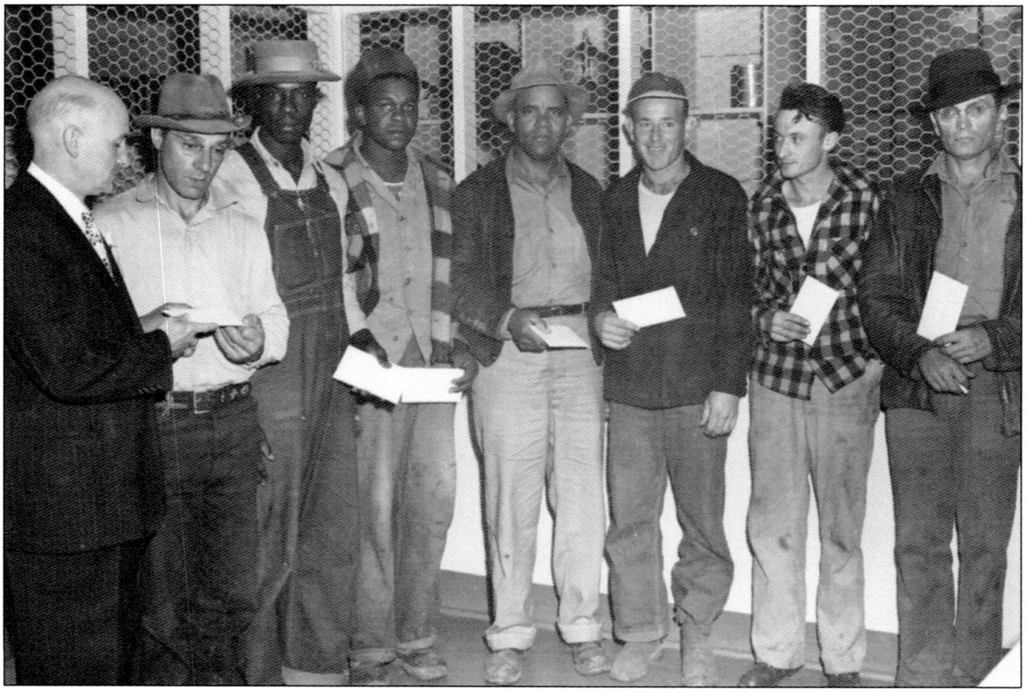

Emergency relief efforts took place immediately. There was a strong surge of community support, and many residents, both black and white, opened their homes. Commissioner William A. Bowes delivered relief checks donated by the employees of the Bureau of Public Works to victims of the Vanport Flood who were employees of the bureau. (Courtesy of City of Portland Archives.)

After the Vanport Flood of 1948, many of the displaced Vanport residents relocated to Guild's Lake Courts. By this time, the majority of Guild's Lake Courts housing units were dismantled, and the former Vanport residents were housed in temporary trailers. Gloria Campbell Cash is shown standing to the far right with her neighbors at Guild's Lake Courts. The trailers can be seen in the background. (Courtesy of City of Portland Archives.)

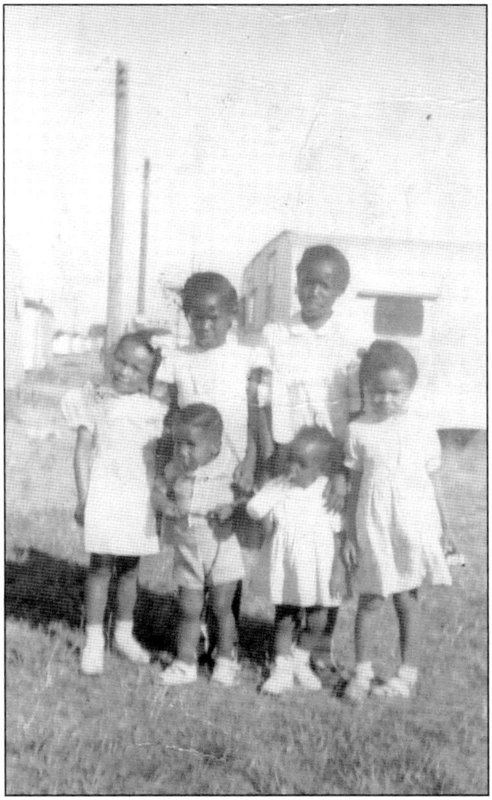

Pictured here are youth volunteer traffic safety patrollers at Guild's Lake Courts, comprising former Vanport residents. (Courtesy of Ed Washington.)

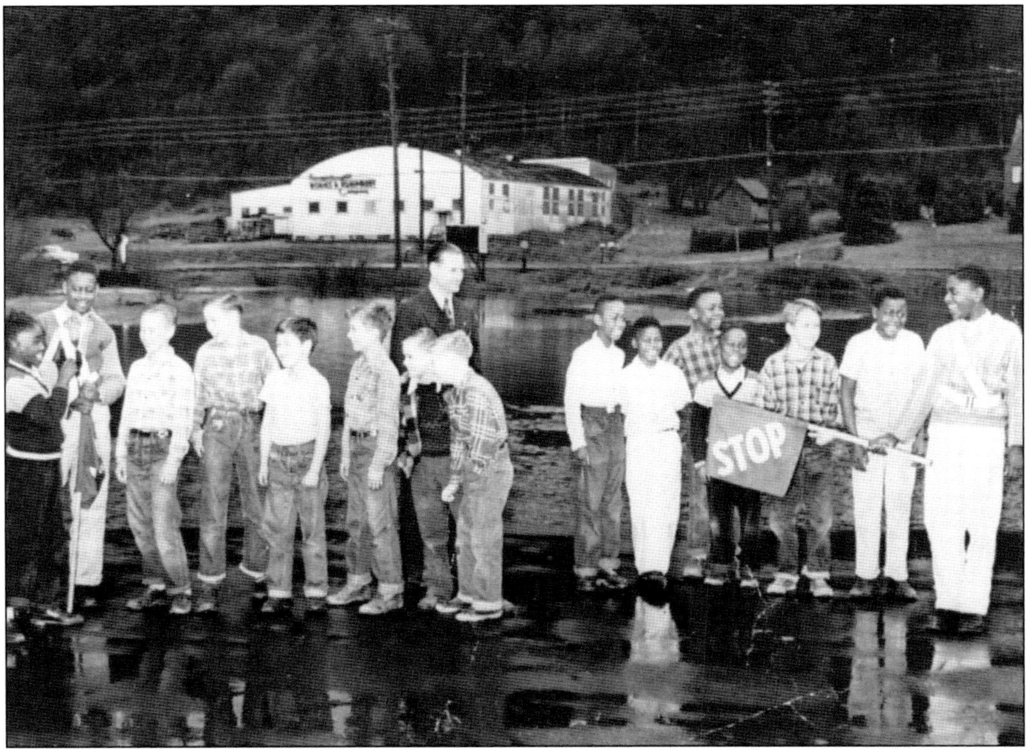

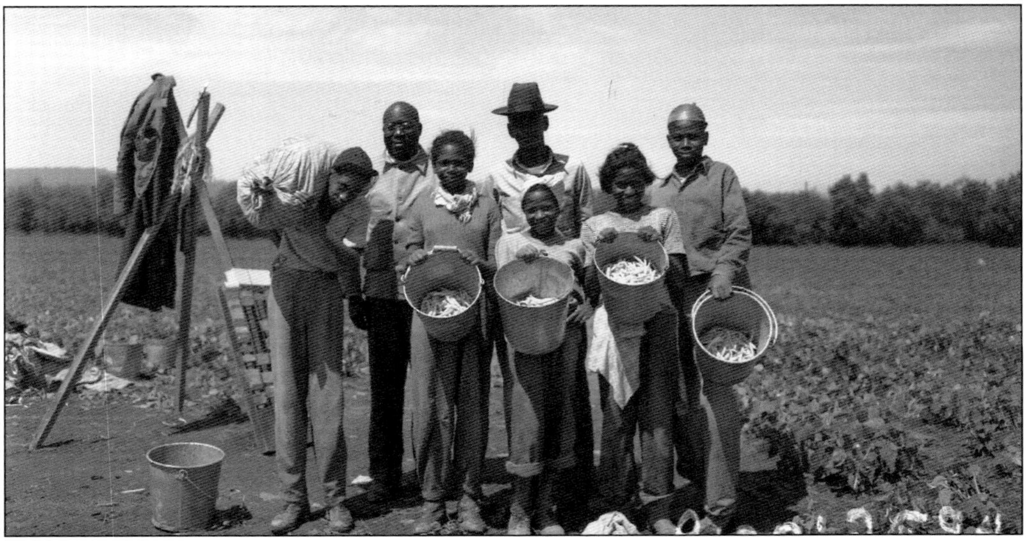

After the war, former shipyard workers sought farmwork as a source of income. Seen here is an African American family working in a bean field near Scappoose, Oregon, led by Rev. M.C. Cheek of Guild's Lake Community Church. (Courtesy of Urban League Collection and OSU Special Collection and Research Archive Center.)

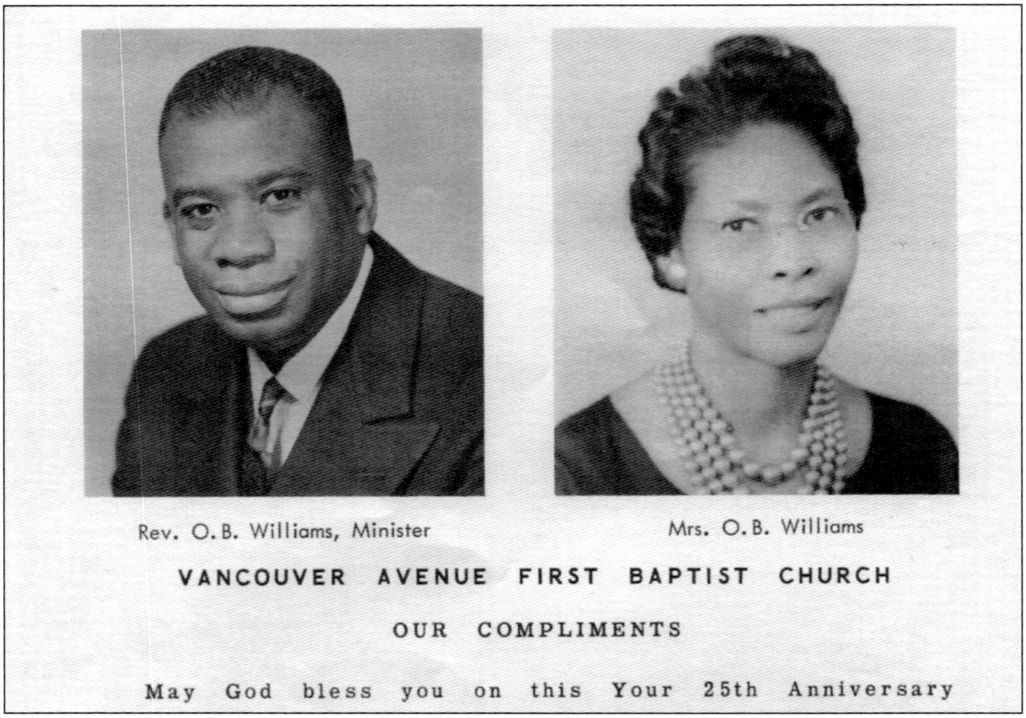

Small groups of shipyard workers organized prayer bands in military housing developments that evolved into churches that met regularly in the housing project's recreational center. Rev. Oliver Booker Williams and his wife, Willia, began their church journey in the Burton Homes federal housing project, located in Vancouver, Washington. On April 15, 1945, the young Rev. O.B. Williams was installed as pastor of the First Baptist Church of Burton Homes. (Courtesy of Mount Olivet Baptist Church.)

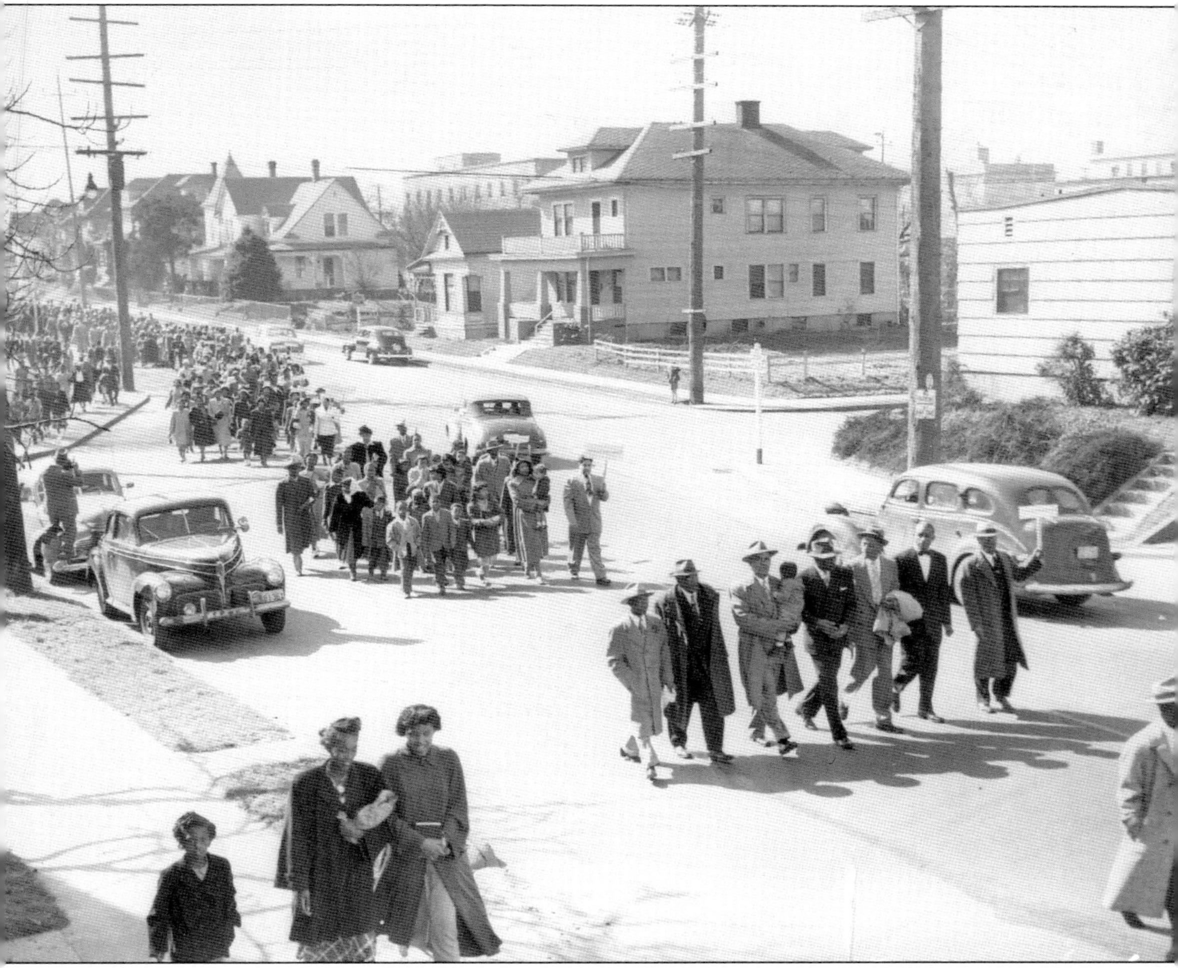

Upon the closure of Burton Homes, Pastor O.B. Williams moved to the Bagley Downs housing project and found a temporary place of worship. Upon the closure of Bagley Downs in 1946, many of the former defense workers moved from Washington and into Oregon. Pastor Williams moved to Vanport, and the congregation began to worship at the Masonic temple in Portland. The congregation soon outgrew the Masonic temple and purchased a condemned rooming house on Vancouver Avenue; hence, the church was named to Vancouver Avenue First Baptist Church. On the morning of May 18, 1947, members of the congregation marched to the newly renovated church. Four years later, in 1951, the congregation purchased the former Central Methodist Church at Vancouver Avenue and Fargo Street, and it remains there today. (Courtesy of the Oregon Historical Society.)

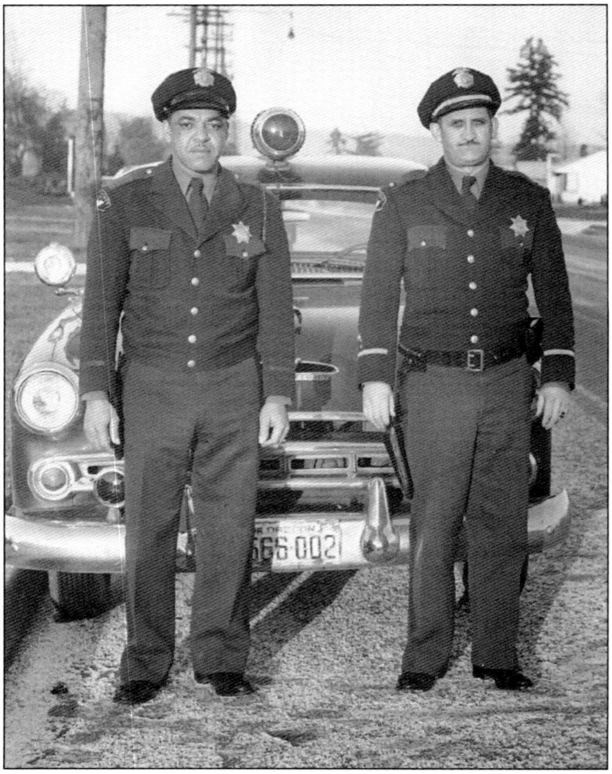

Vanport hired two black sheriffs, Matt Dishman and Bill Travis; both were then hired as Multnomah County sheriffs. In honor of Dishman's community service, members of the Lion's Club renamed the Knott Street Center the Matt Dishman Center. Pictured here to the left is Bill Travis. (Courtesy of the Oregon Historical Society.)

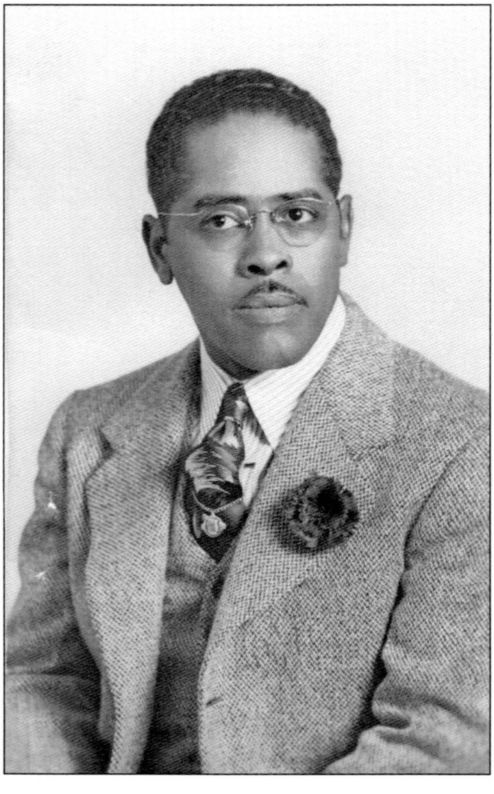

Robert G. Ford moved to Portland in 1943 to work in the Vancouver, Washington, shipyard. In 1945, he became one of the first two African American teachers in the Portland Public School System. Leota Stone, wife of St. Philip father Lee Owen Stone, was hired a few months later to become Portland's second African American teacher. In 1952, Robert Ford became the first African American to receive an appointment in a Portland high school. He taught English and social studies at Roosevelt High School. In 1971, he was chosen as Teacher of the Year by the Portland Association of Teachers. (Courtesy of Urban League Collection and OSU Special Collection and Research Archive Center.)

Five

Democracy's Unfinished Business

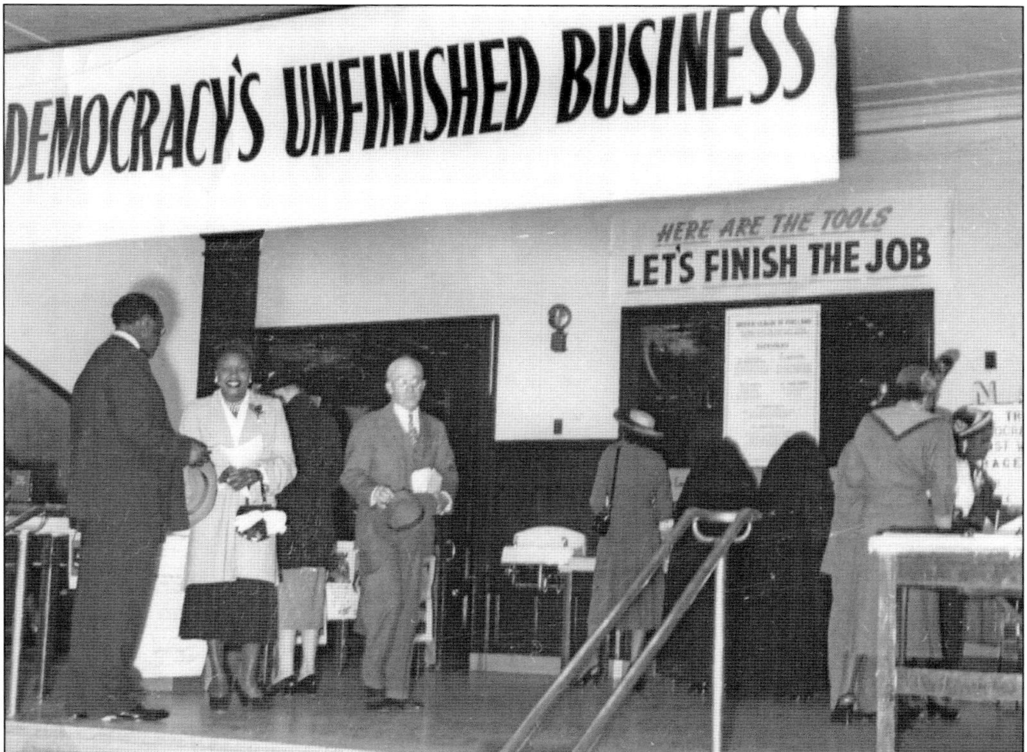

The Urban League's "Democracy's Unfinished Business" banner epitomizes the black community's focus and priorities during the postwar era. In 1945, the Oregon Senate rejected another civil rights bill by a 24-6 vote. The passage of the Fair Employment Practice Law in 1949 encouraged a renewed attack on other discriminatory practices. The newly created Urban League, NAACP, and other community organizations began to shift their resources and attention to passage of a public accommodation law. (Courtesy of Urban League Collection and OSU Special Collection and Research Archive Center.)

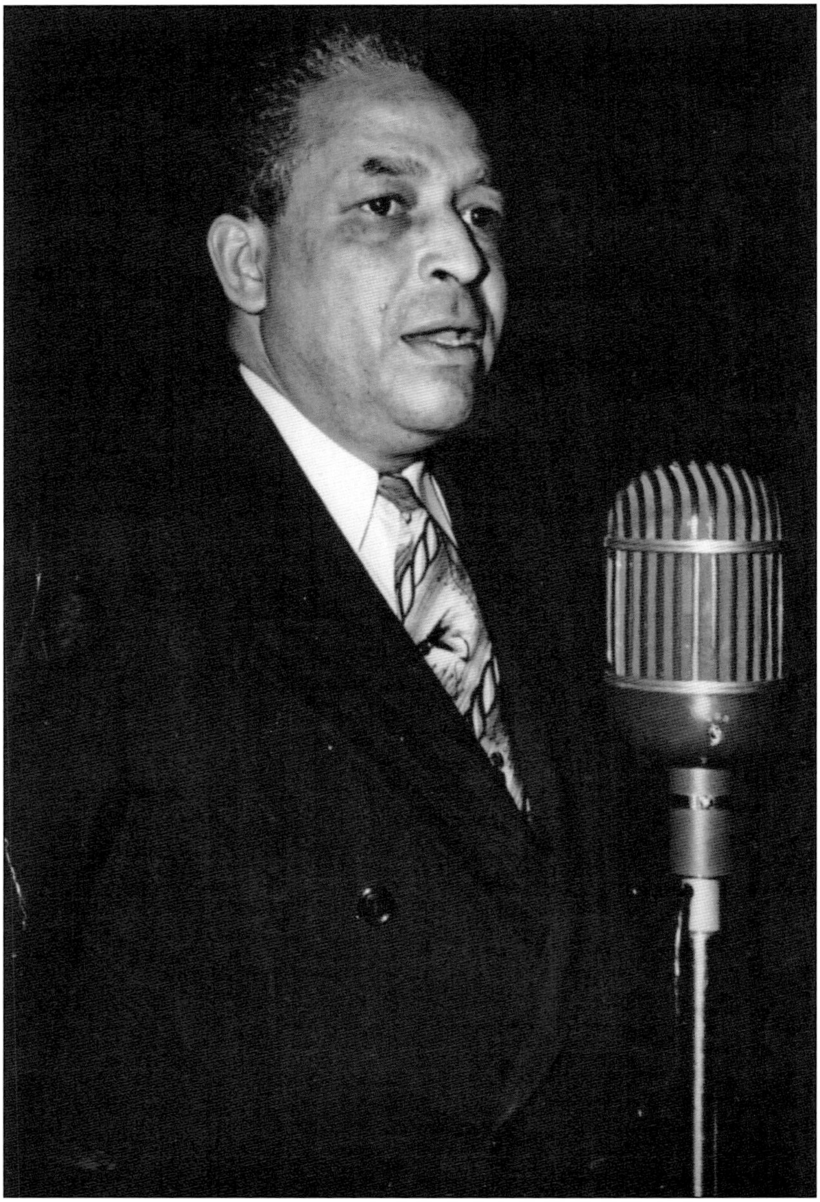

Dr. DeNorval Unthank was a dedicated doctor and civil rights activist. He was born in 1899 in Allentown, Pennsylvania. He received his medical degree in 1926 from Howard University in Washington, DC. He moved to Portland in 1929 and replaced Dr. James Merriman, the Union Pacific's previous medical doctor. Throughout the 1930s, he was the only black doctor in Portland and faced various forms of discrimination since his arrival in Portland. Dr. Unthank and his wife, Thelma, had to move four times before they were able to settle peacefully. He provided care to so many Vanport residents that the Red Cross used his medical records as a way to account for families and individuals during the Vanport Flood. Often called "the father of the Urban League," Dr. Unthank played a leading role in convincing the National Urban League to open a Portland affiliate. Between 1946 and 1964, Dr. Unthank served as president of the Urban League of Portland three times. (Courtesy of Urban League Collection and OSU Special Collection and Research Archive Center.)

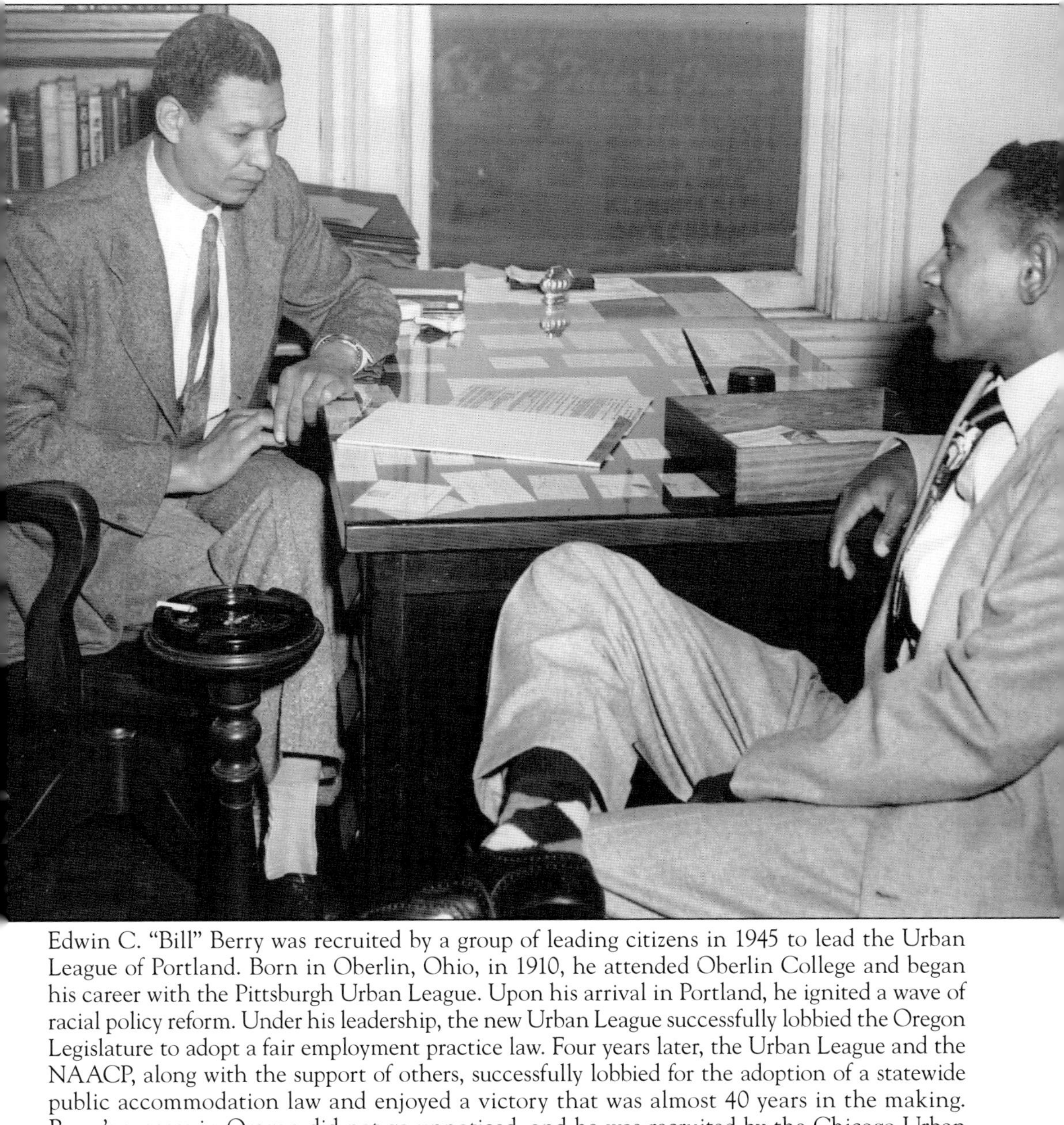

Edwin C. "Bill" Berry was recruited by a group of leading citizens in 1945 to lead the Urban League of Portland. Born in Oberlin, Ohio, in 1910, he attended Oberlin College and began his career with the Pittsburgh Urban League. Upon his arrival in Portland, he ignited a wave of racial policy reform. Under his leadership, the new Urban League successfully lobbied the Oregon Legislature to adopt a fair employment practice law. Four years later, the Urban League and the NAACP, along with the support of others, successfully lobbied for the adoption of a statewide public accommodation law and enjoyed a victory that was almost 40 years in the making. Berry's success in Oregon did not go unnoticed, and he was recruited by the Chicago Urban League in 1955 to serve as its director. In 1983, Berry led the transition team for Mayor Harold Washington, the first African American mayor of Chicago. In this photograph, director Berry counsels a young student. (Courtesy of Urban League of Portland and OSU Special Collections and Archive Research Center.)

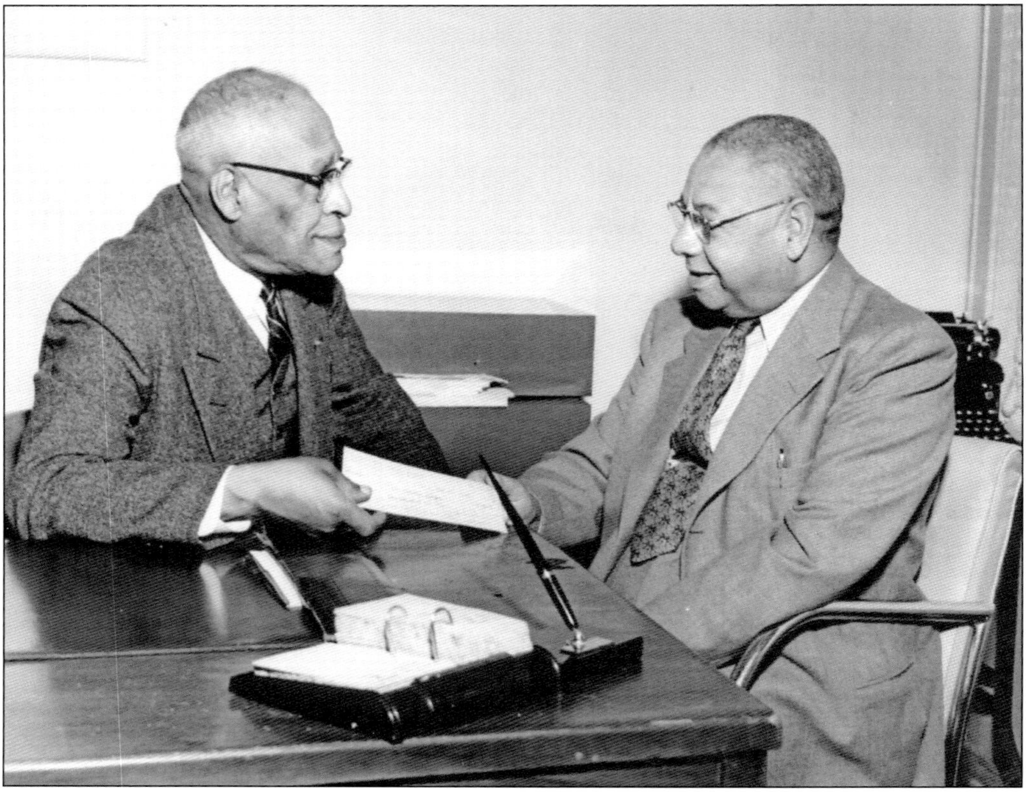

Portland white elite preferred to deal with black underworld figures like Tom Johnson, who allegedly controlled much of the vice in Albina. New black leadership and new city leadership, particularly that led by socially conservative mayor Dorothy McCullough, changed the way the city conducted business. In this picture, Tom Johnson (left) presents a check to a Mr. Baker, an Urban League representative. (Courtesy of Urban League of Portland and OSU Special Collection and Archive Research Center.)

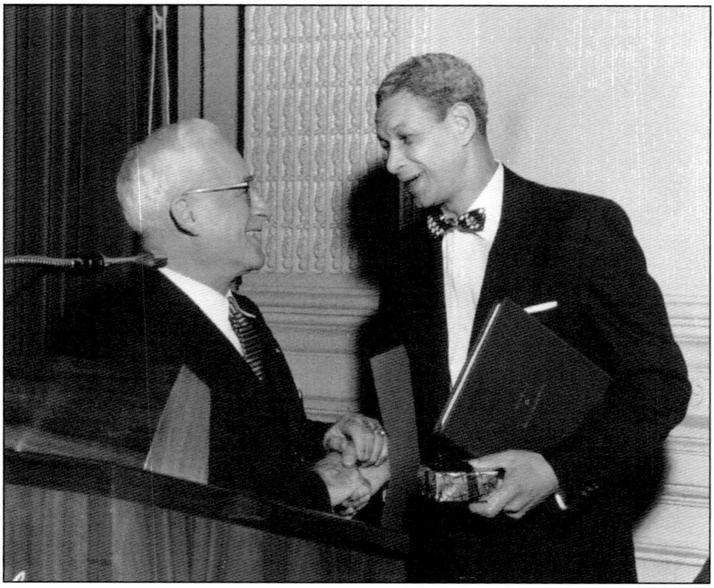

Berry's charismatic and strategic leadership paved the way for racial policy reform unseen in previous generations. Upon his first visit to Portland, he held meetings with the established leadership in both the black and white communities. Berry is pictured in 1955 with Francis J. "Frank" Ivancie at a Portland City Club meeting at Benson High School. (Courtesy of Urban League of Portland and OSU Special Collection and Archive Research Center.)

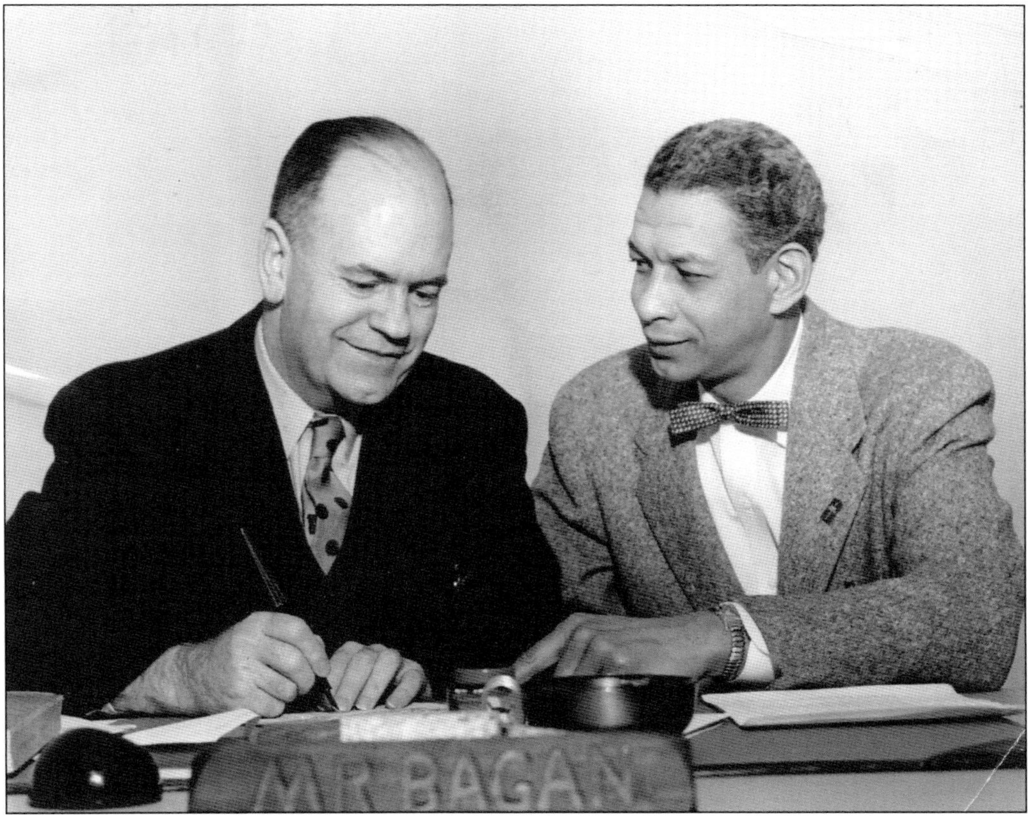

The loss of wartime production jobs and the Vanport Flood's displacement of 4,500 African Americans forced Portland to deal with segregated housing and employment practices of the past. According to historian Dr. Darrell Millner, the first focus of the Urban League was employment, and director Berry worked closely with state officials to open the job market for Portland's black community. Shown here are James Bagan, the manager of the Portland office of Oregon Employment Service, and Berry conferring on employment opportunities for non-whites in Portland. (Courtesy of Urban League of Portland and OSU Special Collection and Archive Research Center.)

Over the years, the Urban League was able to open up employment opportunities for minorities. This was primarily due to Berry's strategic and charismatic leadership style, his resourceful interracial board of directors, and the dedication of the Urban League staff. This group photograph includes, from left to right, James Bagan, E. Shelton Hill, Edwin C. Berry, R.P. Gantenbein, and unidentified. (Courtesy of Urban League of Portland and OSU Special Collection and Archive Research Center.)

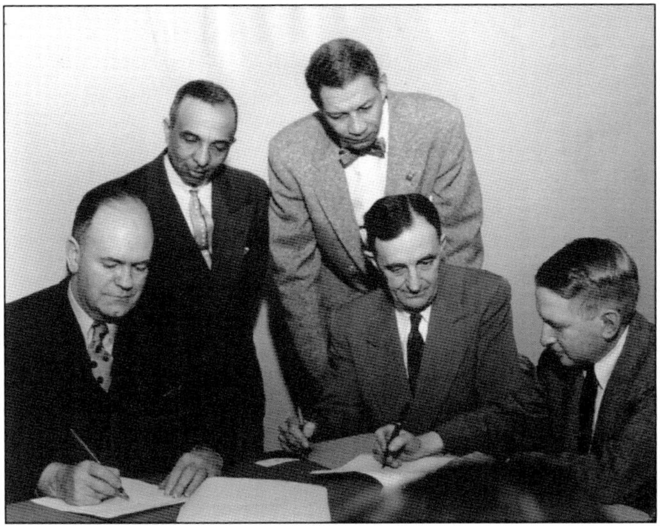

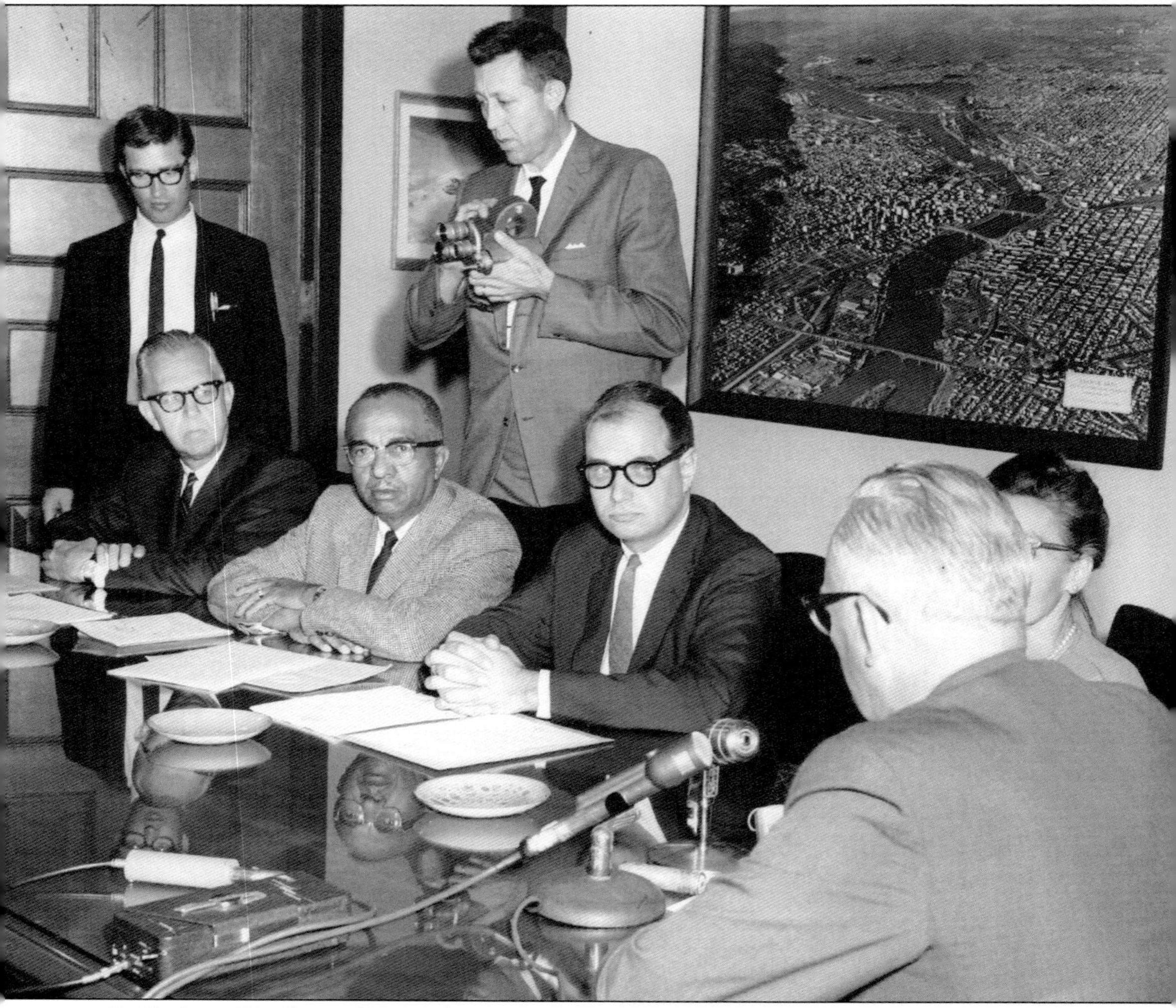

E. Shelton "Shelly" Hill served as president of the Urban League from 1959 to 1973. He was born on a Native American reservation in Oklahoma and graduated from Western University in Kansas. He arrived in Portland in 1941 as a railroad employee after he found it difficult to land a job with a degree in chemistry in the Midwest. He has been described as "the Harriet Tubman of the Northwest," bringing more than 300 blacks to Portland to work for the railroad. During the war, he served as special service officer at the Portland air base. In 1947, after the war, he joined the Urban League staff as the job development specialist. One by one, Hill took on businesses and industries that had traditionally closed their doors on African Americans. During his leadership, Portland saw its first blacks hired as teachers, school principals, bus drivers, and bank officers. His wife, Helloise, taught at Vanport and was hired as Portland's first black school principal. Hill later received the Whitney Young Jr. Medallion, a national award for people who have been active in the Urban League for 20 years or more. The picture above shows Mayor Terry Shrunk, with his back to the camera, discussing Portland school issues with E. Shelton Hill (seated second from left), Maxine Selling (seated to the right of Terry Shrunk), and others. (Courtesy of Urban League of Portland and OSU Special Collection and Archive Research Center.)

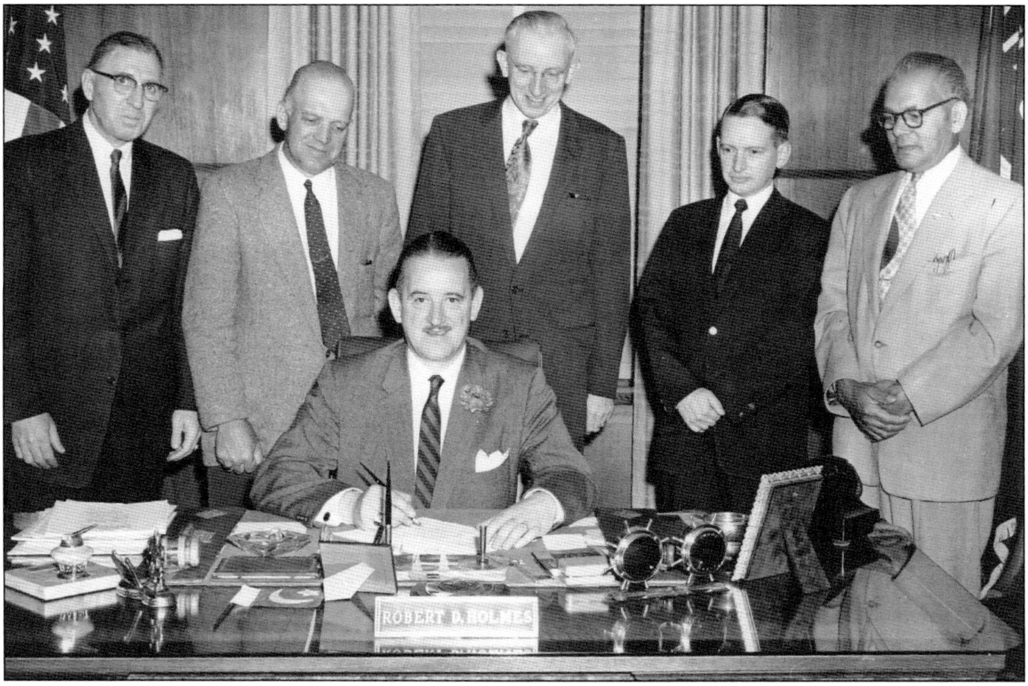

In this picture, Gov. Robert D. Holmes signs House Bills 646 and 647, which expanded Oregon civil rights statutes. Standing behind the governor from left to right are Milton Goldsmith, chairman of the Federal Employment Practice Advisory Committee; labor commissioner Norman O. Nilsen; Dr. John Rademaker, professor at Willamette University; R.P. Gantenbein, chairman of Oregon Committee for Equal Rights; and Phil Reynolds, who helped pass civil rights legislation and was installed as president of the Portland Branch of the NAACP in 1957. Reynolds started working for the railway in 1914 and retired from the Union Pacific after 35 years as a redcap at the Portland Union Station. (Courtesy of Urban League of Portland and OSU Special Collection and Archive Research Center.)

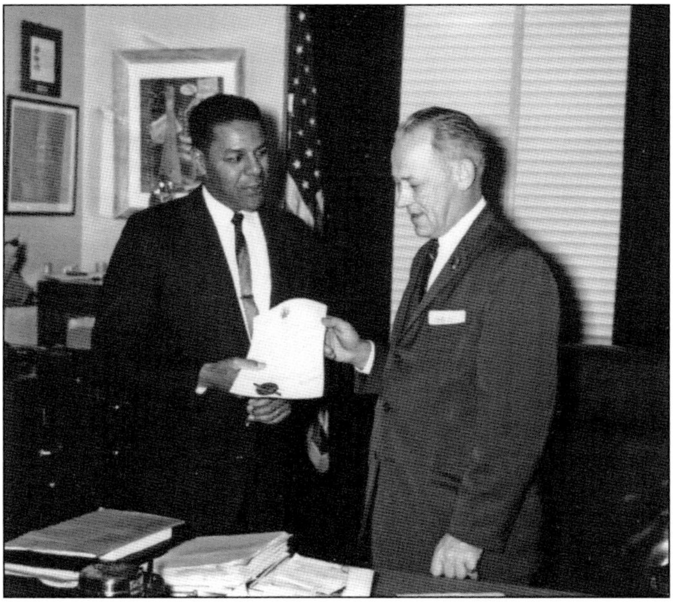

Dr. Walter C. Reynolds (left), pictured with Mayor Terry Shrunk, joined the US Army and served in the Philippines in World War II. In 1949, Dr. Reynolds was the first African American graduate of the University of Oregon Medical School. Dr. Reynolds was mentored by Portland physician Dr. DeNorval Unthank and served as president of the Urban League from 1959 to 1961. He served as president of the medical staff at Emanuel Hospital. (Courtesy of Urban League of Portland and OSU Special Collection and Archive Research Center.)

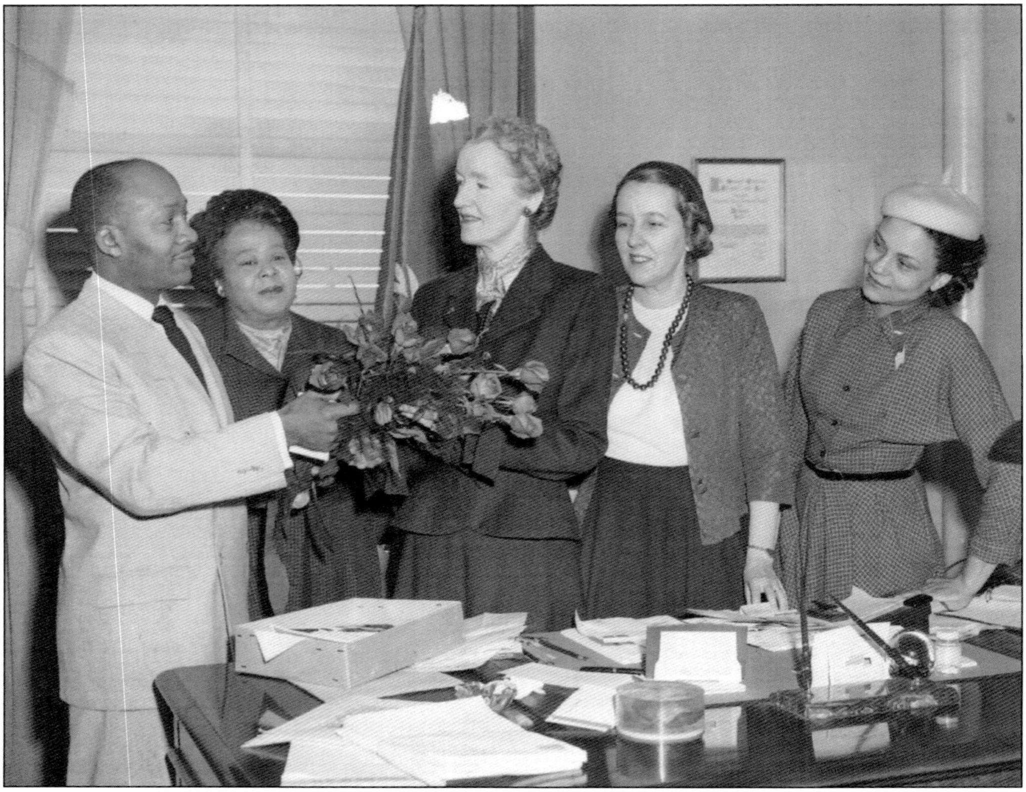

Dorothy McCullough Lee, described as a socially conservative reformer, was elected the mayor of Portland in 1949. In 1950, under her administration, the City of Portland worked with a multiracial committee of prominent individuals and organizations to prepare a public accommodation law that was adopted by the city council. Opponents initiated a referendum to place the issue before the voters, who repealed the new law before it ever went into effect. In this picture, a NAACP committee honors Mayor Lee for her leadership. (Courtesy of the Oregon Historical Society.)

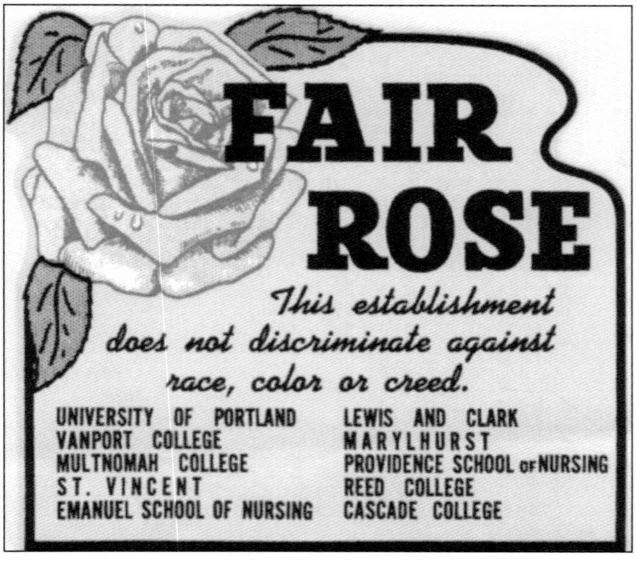

The Fair Rose decal was designed to encourage the Portland City Council to pass the public accommodation law. Students from local colleges listed on the decal provided the design. Those who promised not to discriminate placed the decal in their store. In an oral interview, a former Reed College student commented that "the kids went downtown, went door to door, store to store, particularly restaurants, to get them to put up Fair Rose signs. Businesses that refused the sign were boycotted." (Courtesy of City of Portland Archives.)

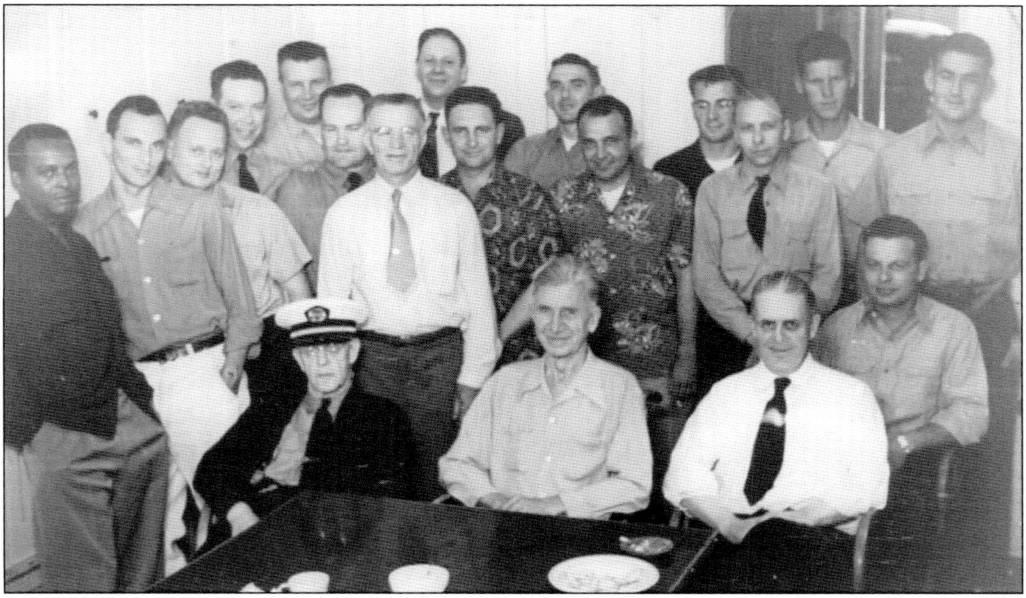

Pictured here is the retirement party for Robert Simpson at Portland Fire Station No. 8 in 1952. Standing to the far left is William Carr, the first African American appointed to the Portland Fire Department in 1952. (Courtesy of City of Portland Archives.)

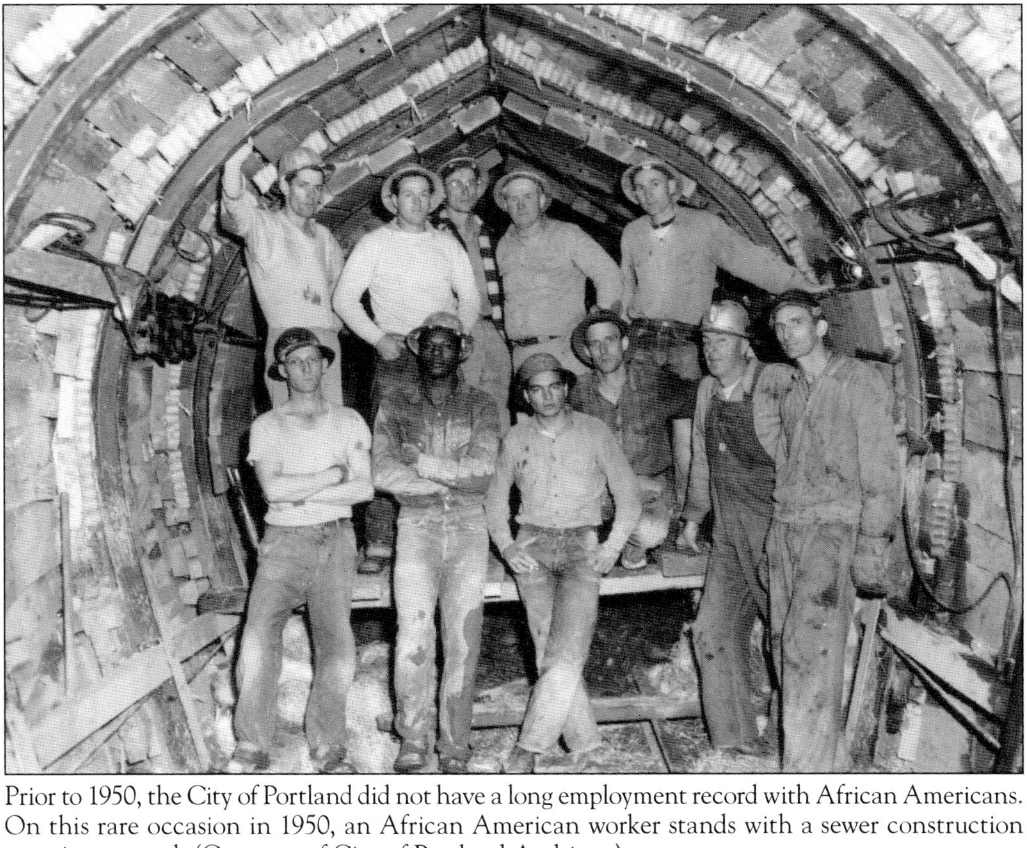

Prior to 1950, the City of Portland did not have a long employment record with African Americans. On this rare occasion in 1950, an African American worker stands with a sewer construction crew in a tunnel. (Courtesy of City of Portland Archives.)

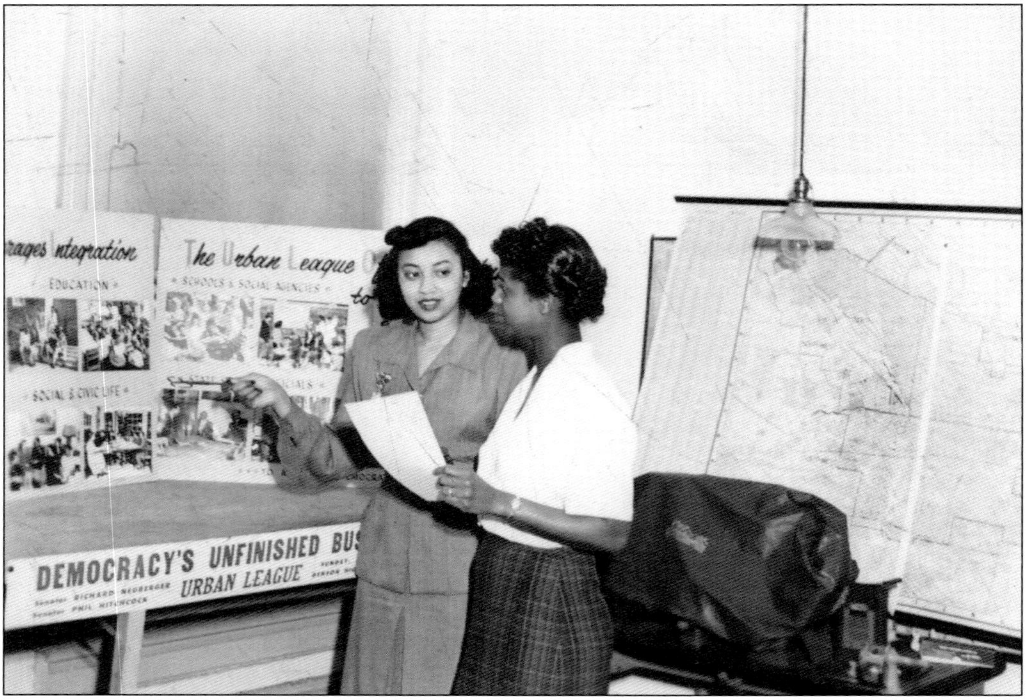

Pictured here is Myrtle White Carr (right) with Gertrude Rae. Carr, a longtime Urban League employee, received recognition for 20 years of service in 1965. Her husband, William, was the first African American to work for the Portland Fire Bureau. (Courtesy of Urban League of Portland and OSU Special Collection and Archive Research Center.)

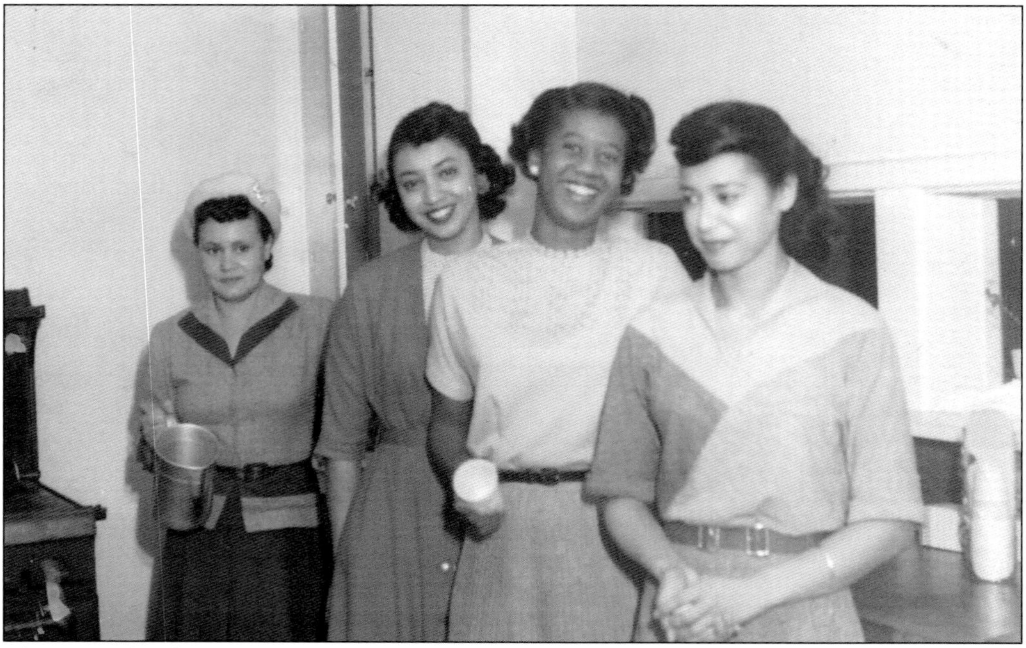

The original Urban League staff members are pictured here. From left to right are Dorthy Berry, Gertrude Rae, Myrtle Carr, and Delores Casanosas. (Courtesy of Urban League of Portland and OSU Special Collection and Archive Research Center.)

The Portland Branch of the NAACP was long involved in the final effort to pass the much-celebrated public accommodation law of 1953. Pictured here are civil rights activists and four past presidents of the Portland Branch of the NAACP; from left to right, they are Otto Rutherford, Marie Smith, Lorna Marple, and Mayfield Webb. Marie Smith was one of the founders of the Oregon Association of Colored Women's Clubs, the first female president of the Portland NAACP, and the first woman to receive a Metropolitan Human Relations Commission (MHRC) Russell A. Peyton Award. (Courtesy of Urban League of Portland and OSU Special Collection and Archive Research Center.)

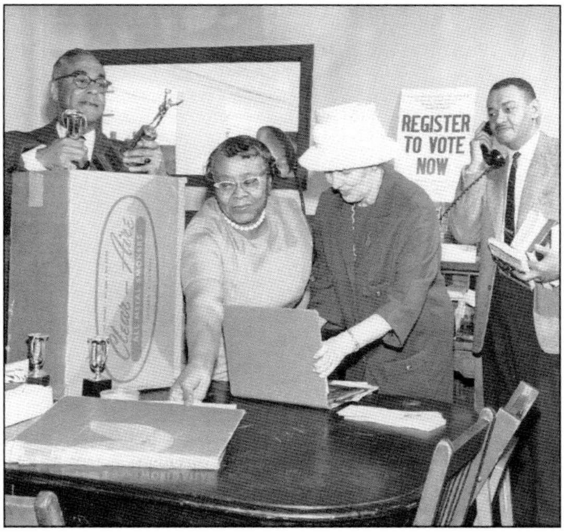

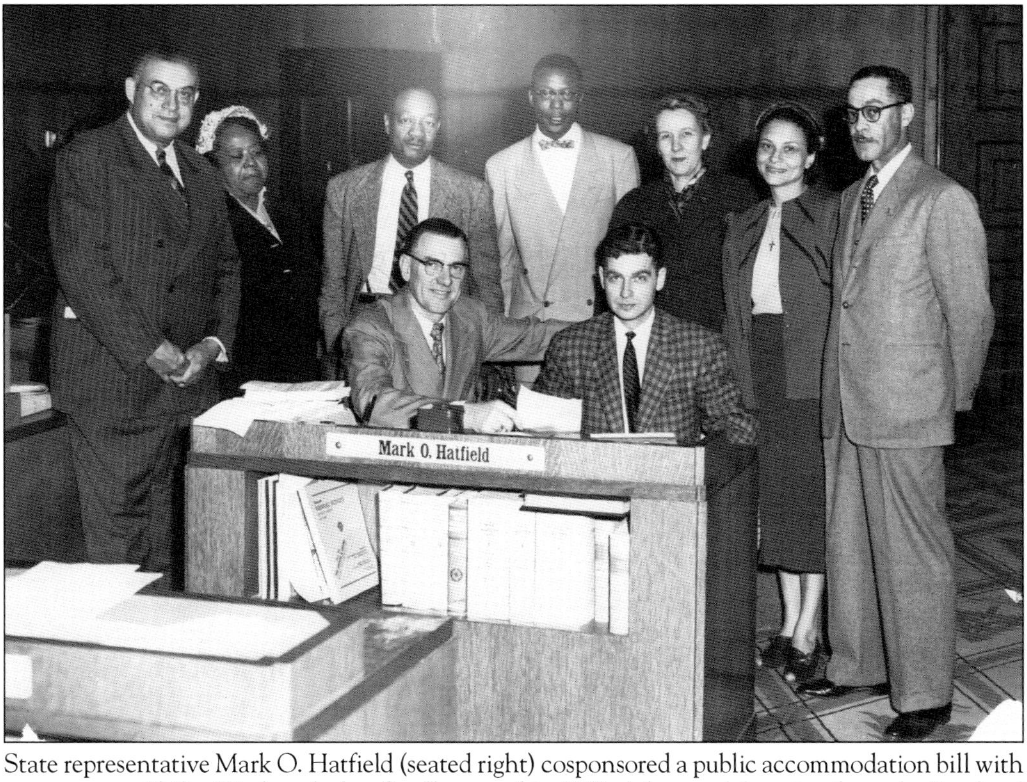

State representative Mark O. Hatfield (seated right) cosponsored a public accommodation bill with state senator Philip Hitchcock that finally passed in 1953. A happy delegation from the Portland NAACP Branch included, from left to right, Edgar Williams, Marie Smith, Ulysses Plummer, Rev. J. Harold Jones, Lorna Marple, Verdell Burdine Rutherford, and Otto Rutherford. Since 1893, black people lobbied the legislature to repeal exclusion laws and the ban on intermarriage and to pass a public accommodation law. On April 13, 1953, the Oregon Legislature approved a state civil rights bill. Under the leadership of Otto Rutherford, the Portland Branch of the NAACP devoted much of its energy to passage of the bill. Edgar Williams had been battling for a civil rights bill ever since he came to Oregon in 1918. Such a bill had been introduced in 17 legislative sessions beginning 1919. (Courtesy of the Oregon Historical Society.)

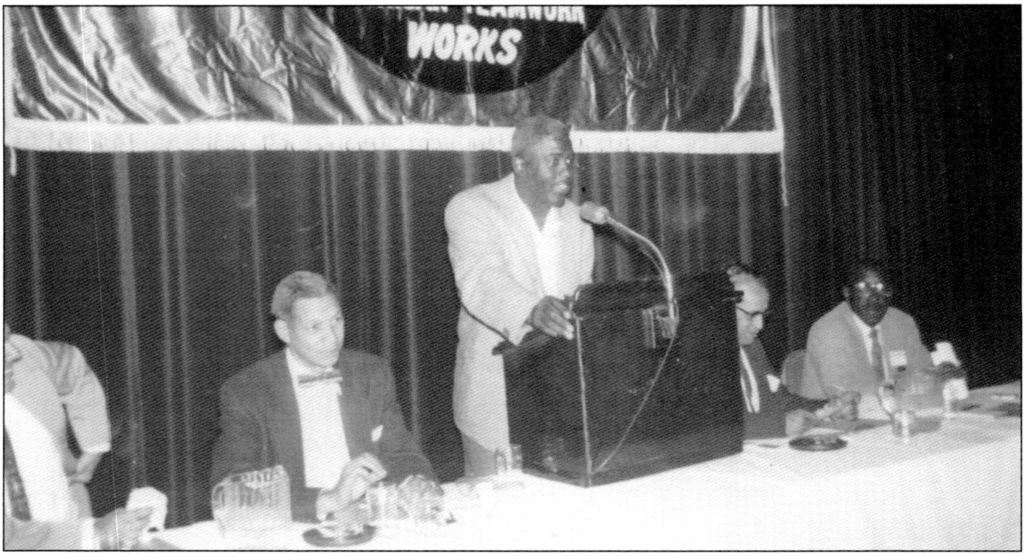

In April 1965, Jackie Robinson, the first African American major league baseball player, was a keynote speaker at the 20th-anniversary meeting of the Urban League of Portland. At this time, Robinson, a chairman of the Freedom National Bank in New York, was very active in the national civil rights movement. According to the *Oregonian*, Robinson was scheduled to speak at Benson High School, but he made an informal stop at Jefferson High School. (Courtesy of Urban League of Portland and OSU Special Collection and Archive Research Center.)

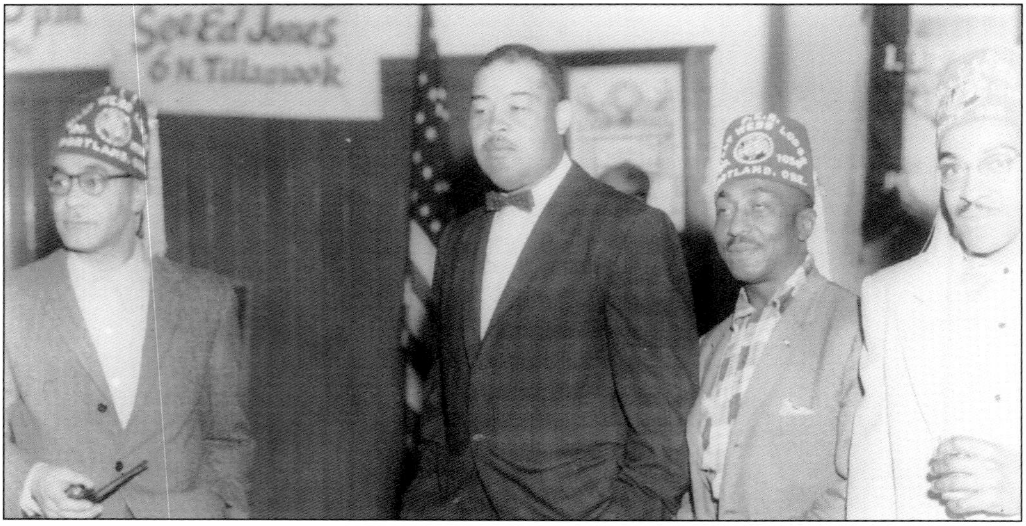

Since 1883, fraternal lodges have provided social, political, and charitable functions within Portland's black community. The Masonic and Odd Fellow lodges were organized in Portland in 1883. The Black Elks Lodge and the Rose City Lodge (with its women's auxiliary) were organized in 1906. Pictured here is former heavyweight champion Joe Louis with Otto Rutherford, president of the Portland NAACP, and members of the Billy Webb Elks Lodge No. 1050 of the Improved Benevolent and Protective Order of the Elks (IBPOE). In 1958, the *Oregonian* reported that Louis was an honored guest at the Bethel AME "Build Bethel" banquet at Columbia Athletic Club. A new church was constructed at Northeast Eighth Avenue and Jarrett and Simpson Streets when the historic Bethel church was razed to make room for Memorial Coliseum. (Courtesy of the Oregon Historical Society.)

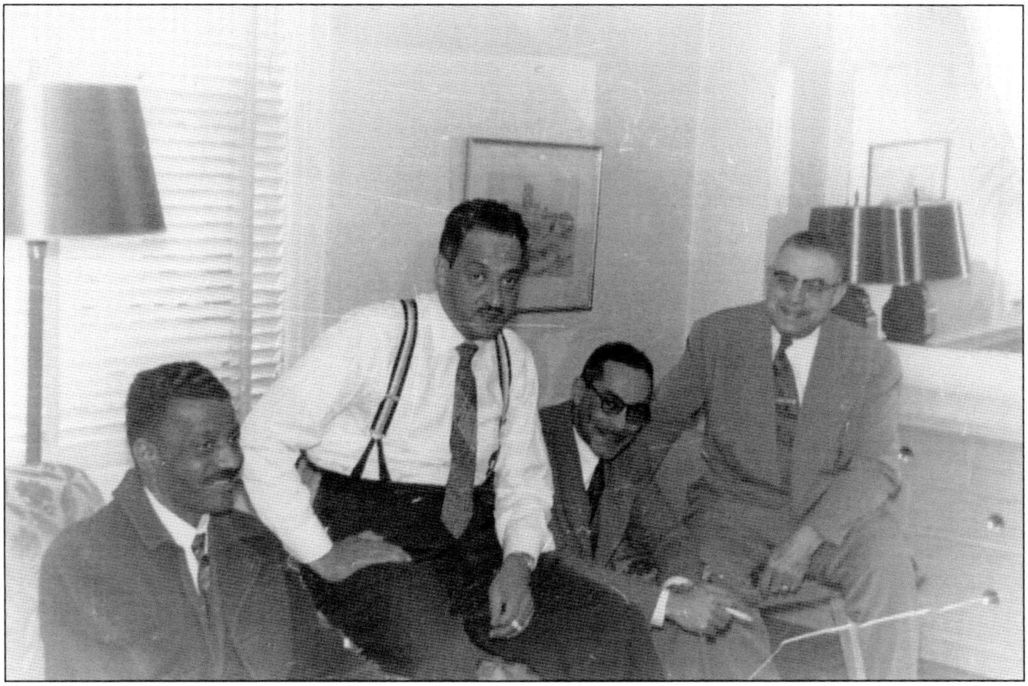

In 1954, Thurgood Marshall, the chief legal counsel of the NAACP, was the principal speaker at a Fight for Freedom rally held at First Presbyterian Church and sponsored by the Portland Branch of the NAACP. His visit to Portland was the same year as his famous case *Brown v. Board of Education of Topeka*. Marshall was confirmed as the 96th justice of the Supreme Court in 1967 and its first African American. (Courtesy of the Rutherford Family Collection and PSU Library.)

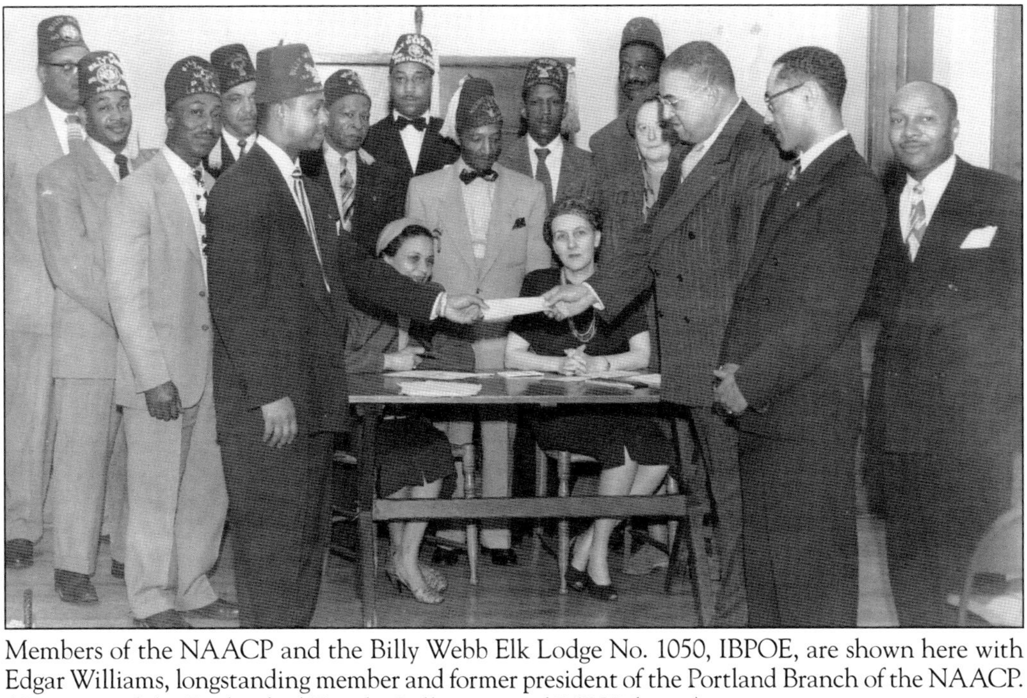

Members of the NAACP and the Billy Webb Elk Lodge No. 1050, IBPOE, are shown here with Edgar Williams, longstanding member and former president of the Portland Branch of the NAACP. (Courtesy of the Rutherford Family Collection and PSU Library.)

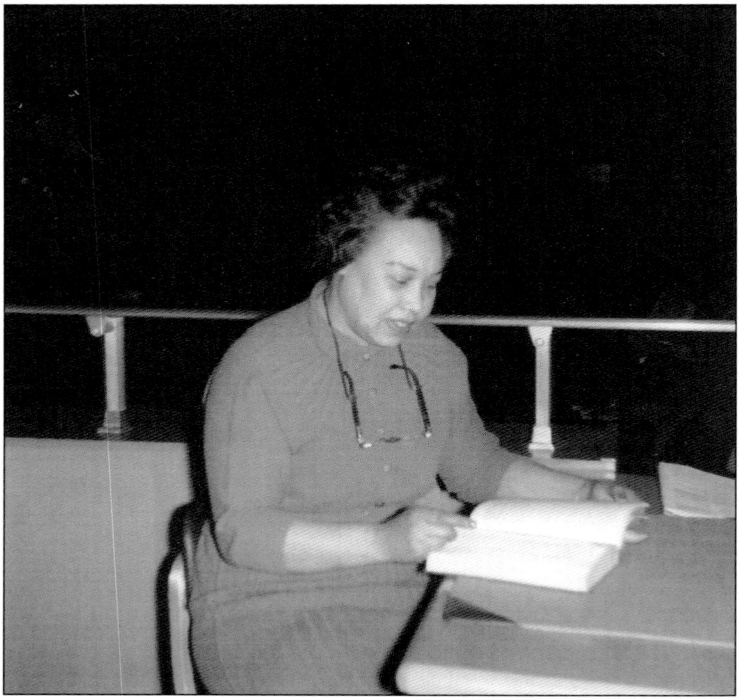

Ida Flowers McClendon was a librarian with the Library Association of Portland. Her husband, Bill, was the publisher of the *People's Observer*, a newspaper established in 1938. Later, Bill established another black newspaper and was also the founding director of Reed College's black studies department. Ida was the managing editor of the *People's Observer*. (Courtesy of Urban League of Portland and OSU Special Collection and Archive Research Center.)

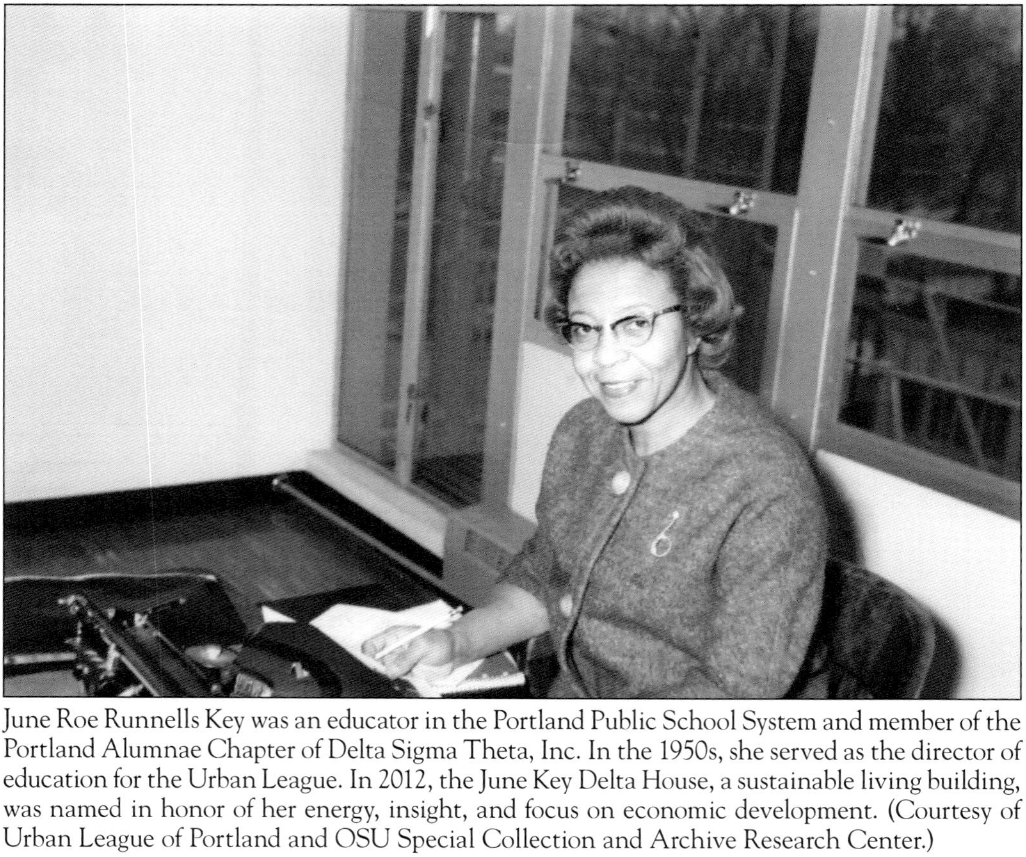

June Roe Runnells Key was an educator in the Portland Public School System and member of the Portland Alumnae Chapter of Delta Sigma Theta, Inc. In the 1950s, she served as the director of education for the Urban League. In 2012, the June Key Delta House, a sustainable living building, was named in honor of her energy, insight, and focus on economic development. (Courtesy of Urban League of Portland and OSU Special Collection and Archive Research Center.)

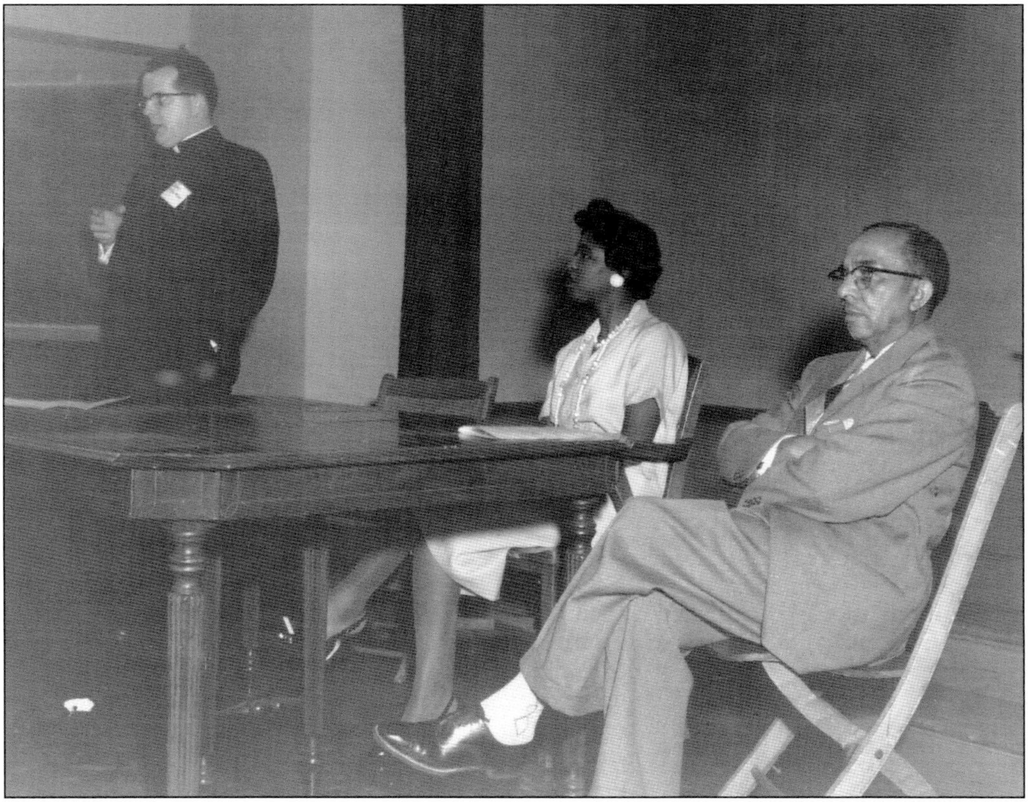

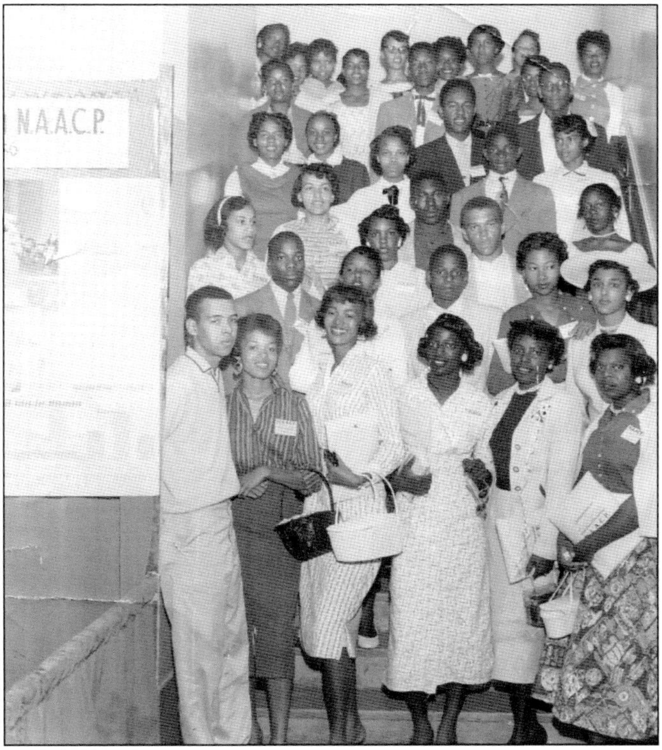

The Beta Psi Chapter of Delta Sigma Theta, Inc., and the Urban League sponsored the Job Opportunity Clinic at St. Philip the Deacon Episcopal Church. Seated at the table are E. Shelton Hill and Urban League of Portland member Sadie Grimmett as Fr. David H. Fosselman of the University of Portland speaks at the clinic. Sadie Grimmett was the Delta president, and E. Shelton Hill was the Urban League director of industrial relations. (Courtesy of Urban League of Portland and OSU Special Collection and Archive Research Center.)

The NAACP organized activities for young people. Picture here is the NAACP Youth Corps. (Courtesy of the Rutherford Family Collection and PSU Library.)

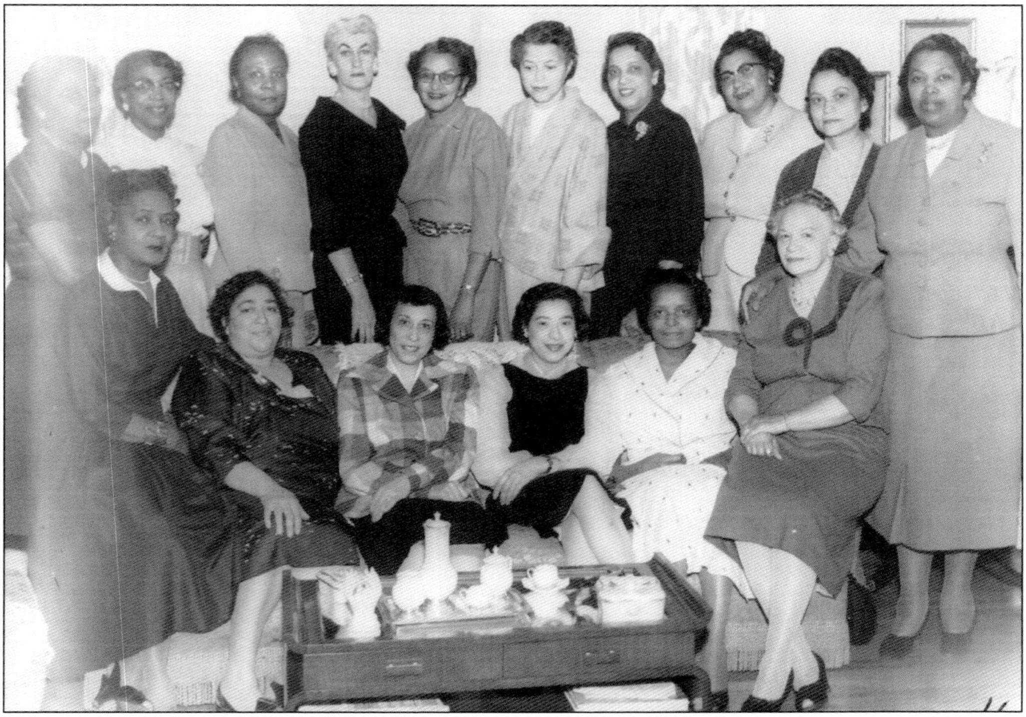

Shown here are members of the Cultured Club, an affiliated club of the Oregon Association of Colored Women's Clubs (OACW). Originally organized as the Colored Women's Council in 1899, the group merged with nine other groups in 1914 to form the Oregon Federation of Colored Women's Clubs. The OACW, through the works of their affiliated clubs, worked closely with NAACP and Urban League to promote the improvement of Portland's African American community's quality of life. (Both, courtesy of the Rutherford Family Collection and PSU Library.)

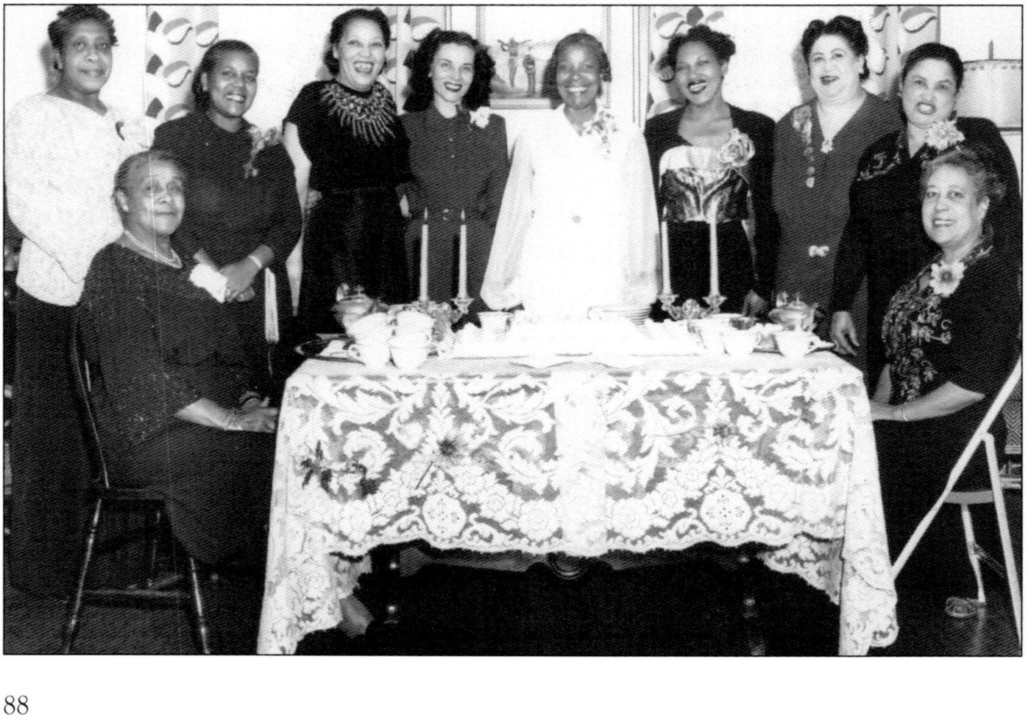

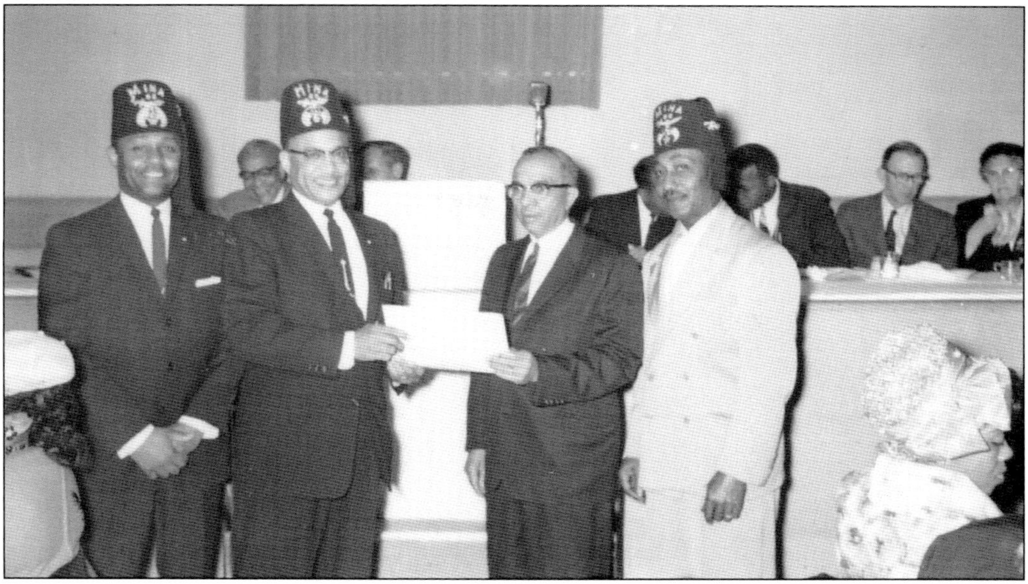

E. Shelton Hill, director of the Urban League, receives an award from members of the Mina Temple No. 68. (Courtesy of the Rutherford Family Collection and PSU Library.)

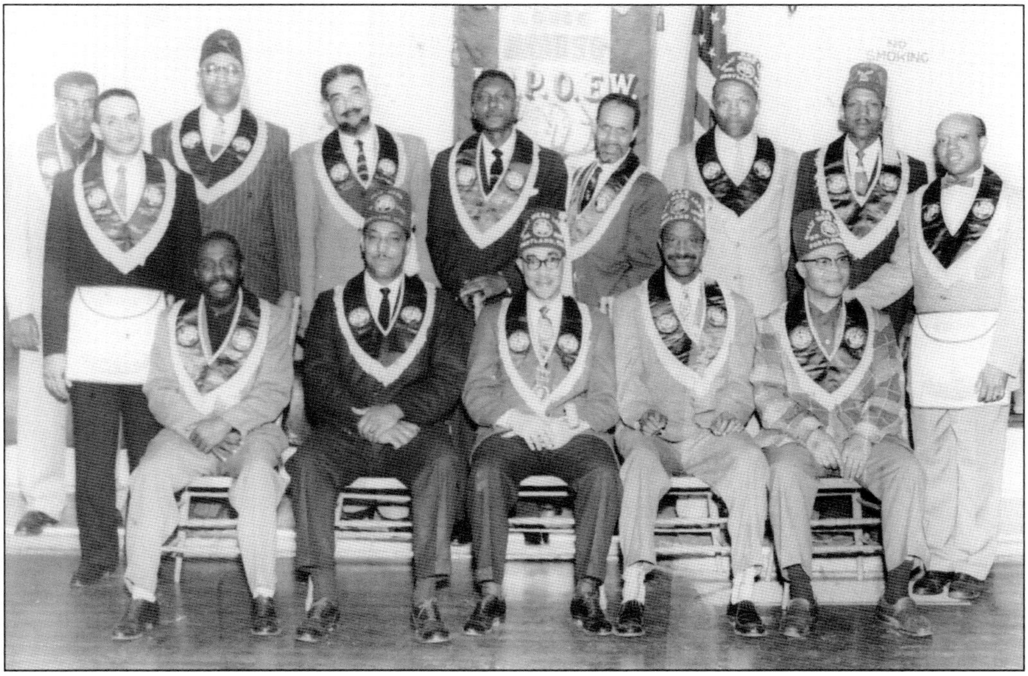

The Billy Webb Elks Lodge was a member of the IBPOE, an African American branch of the Benevolent and Protective Order of the Elks (BPOE). It was first organized in Cincinnati in 1898 by a Pullman Porter, and the first Portland IBPOE lodge dates from 1906. The lodge was named for a prominent musician who led an African American Elks band that played in Portland and on steamships on the West Coast in the 1920s. In 1958, Fraternal Hall, then at 1412 North Williams Avenue, was bulldozed, leaving many black organizations without a place to meet. So the following year, the Elks purchased the Williams Avenue branch of the YWCA. (Courtesy of the Rutherford Family Collection and PSU Library.)

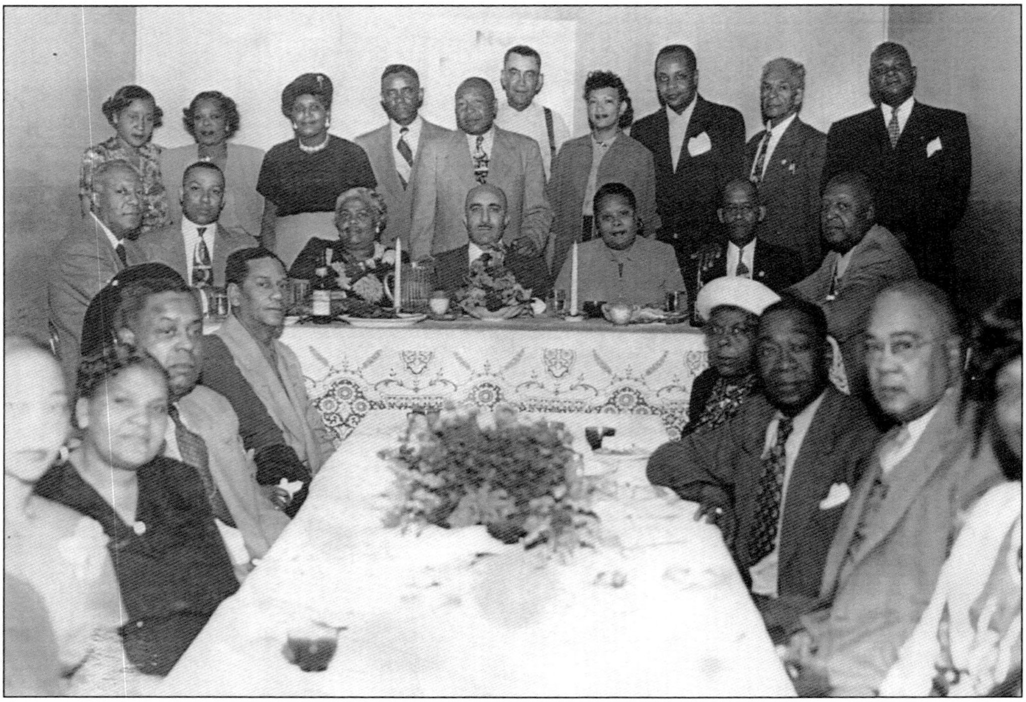

At this banquet in 1954, A. Philip Randolph was the honored guest at the Williams Avenue YWCA, formerly called the Colored YWCA. (Courtesy of Avel Gordly.)

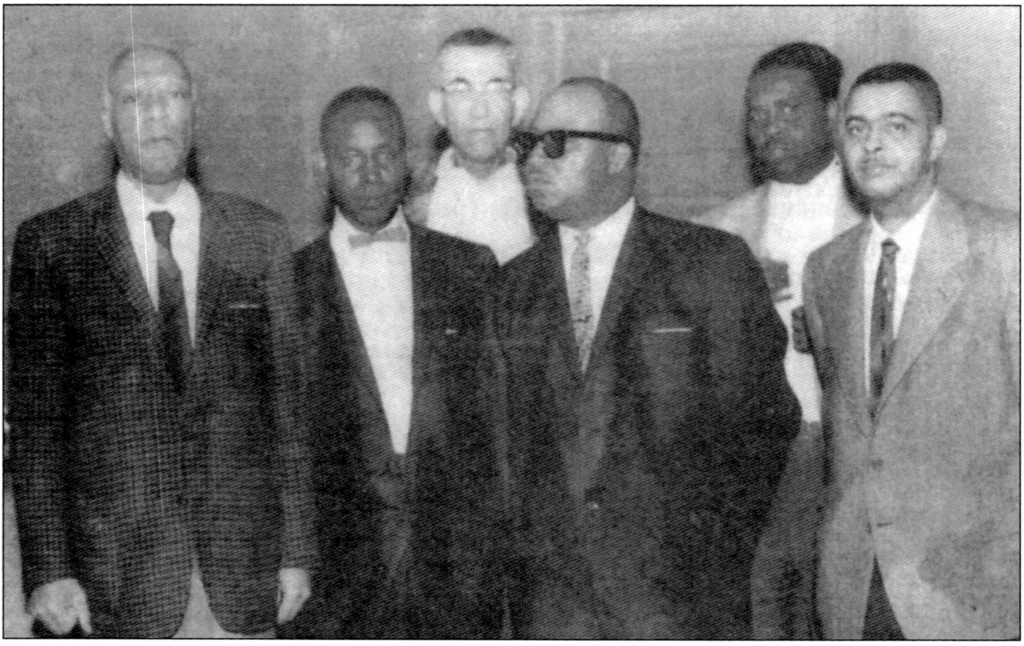

Pictured here in 1962, A. Philip Randolph poses with members of the Portland Chapter of the Brotherhood of Sleeping Car Porters. Included in the picture are Randolph, vice president of the AFL-CIO and president of International Brotherhood of Sleeping Car Porters, and union members C. Johns, Fay Gordly, and McKinley Williams. As an auxiliary policeman, Fay Gordly provided security for Randolph during his visit to Portland. (Courtesy of Avel Gordly.)

Six

The Fruits of Their Labor

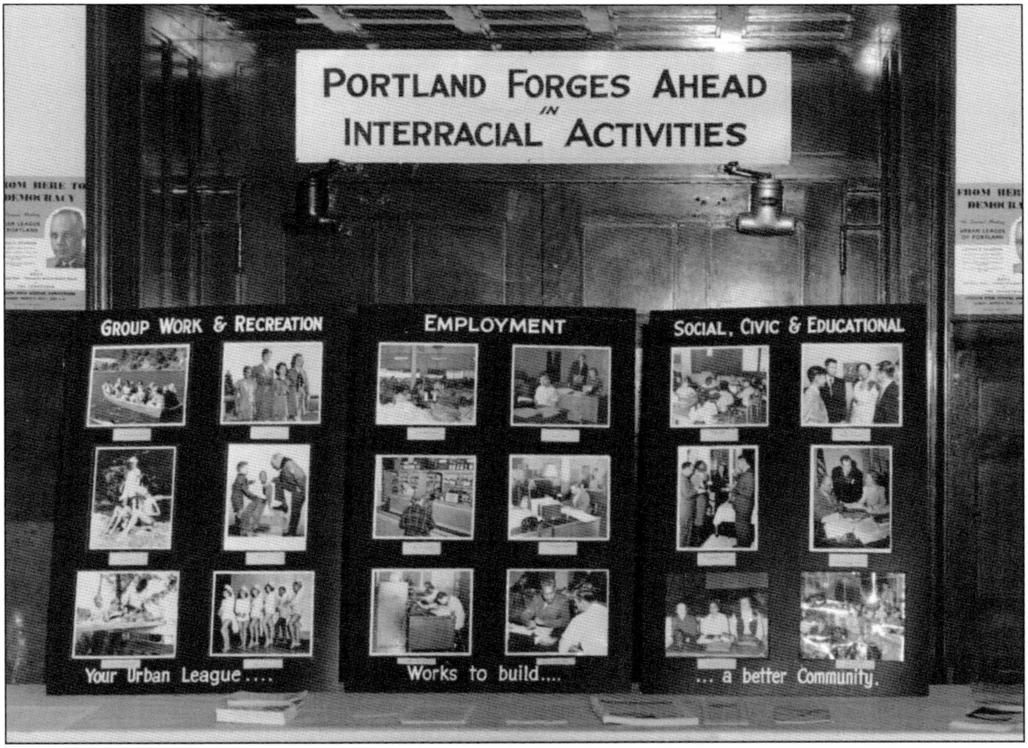

The passage of Oregon's civil rights laws against racial discrimination was pivotal to breaking barriers in employment, education, housing, and public accommodation. During the 1950s and 1960s, Portland's African American community experienced many firsts that were celebrated and chronicled by the *Oregonian*; the Urban League's newspaper, called the *Progress*; and other local black newspapers. In 1954, the first legal action under Oregon's civil rights law involved a refusal of services at a café in the Athena Hotel. The NAACP, with the help of attorney Don S. Willner, negotiated a $200 out-of-court settlement for Godfrey Ibom and his companion. (Courtesy of the Rutherford Family Collection and PSU Library.)

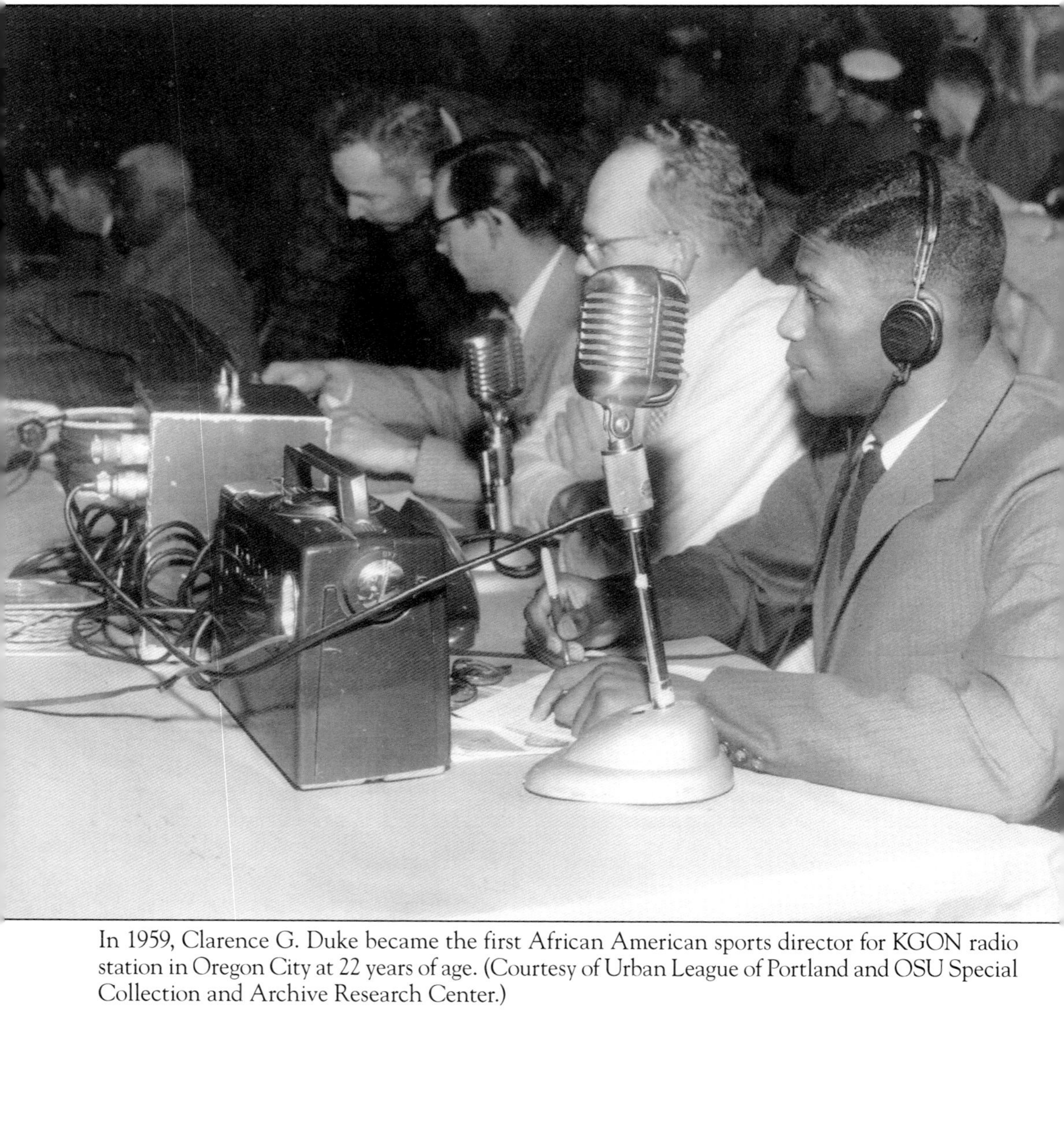

In 1959, Clarence G. Duke became the first African American sports director for KGON radio station in Oregon City at 22 years of age. (Courtesy of Urban League of Portland and OSU Special Collection and Archive Research Center.)

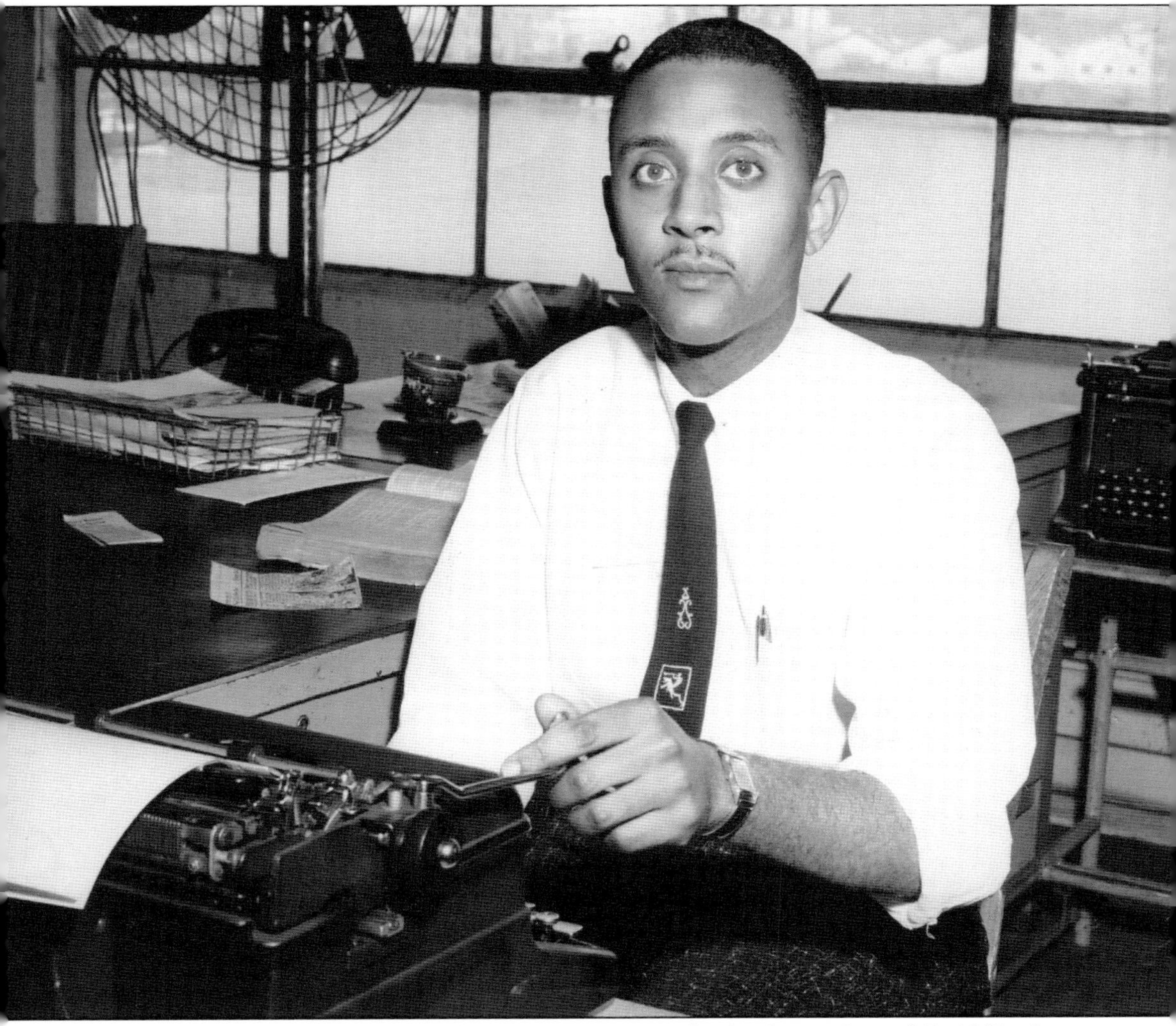

In 1957, Dick Bogle was the first general assignment reporter for the *Oregon Journal*. In 1968, after an eight-year stint as a Portland police officer, Bogle took a job with KATU-TV as Oregon's first African American television journalist. In 1984, two years after Bogle left television to work as an aide to City Commissioner Mildred Schwab, the visibility he had gained as a reporter and later as anchor helped him win a city council seat. He was the second African American elected to the Portland City Council. (Courtesy of Urban League of Portland and OSU Special Collection and Archive Research Center.)

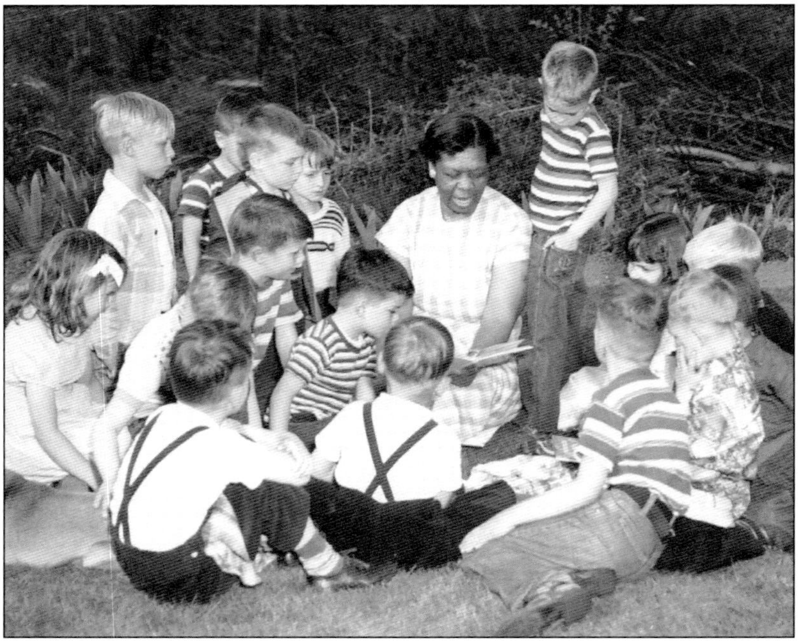

Jeannie Gray reads to a group of children. She was one the first African Americans to teach school in West Linn. (Courtesy of Urban League of Portland and OSU Special Collection and Archive Research Center.)

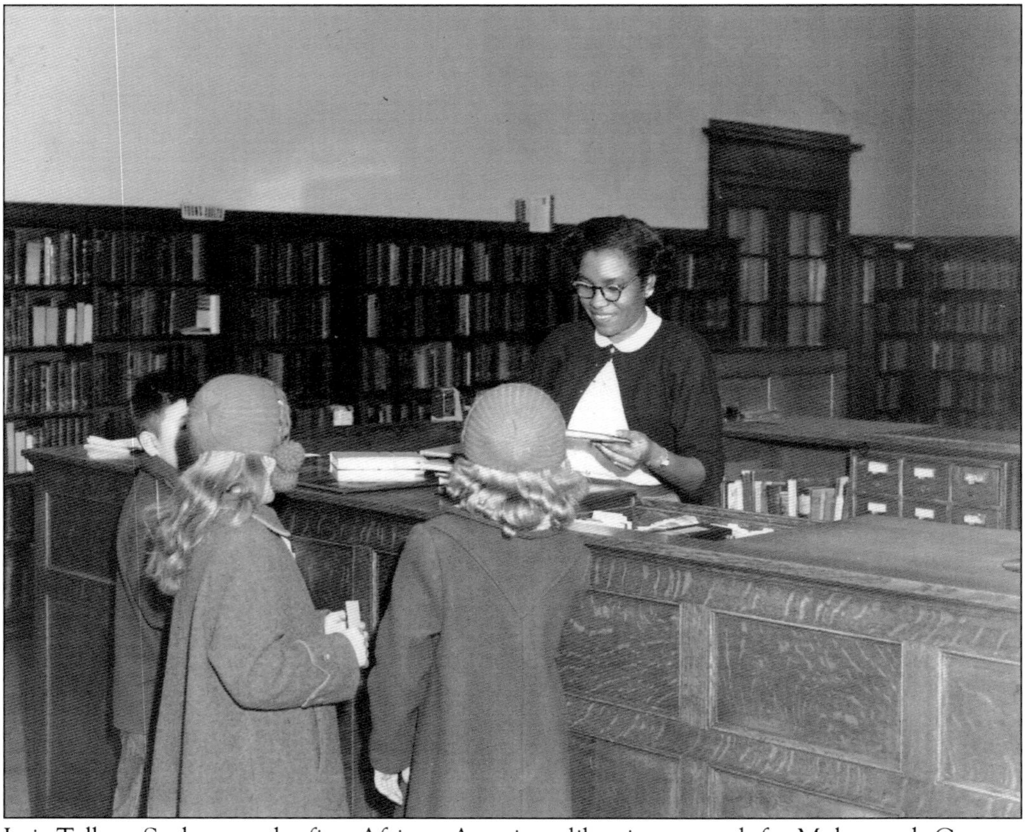

Lois Tolbert Sayles was the first African American librarian to work for Multnomah County, Oregon. She later became the head of the library at Roosevelt High School. (Courtesy of Urban League of Portland and OSU Special Collection and Archive Research Center.)

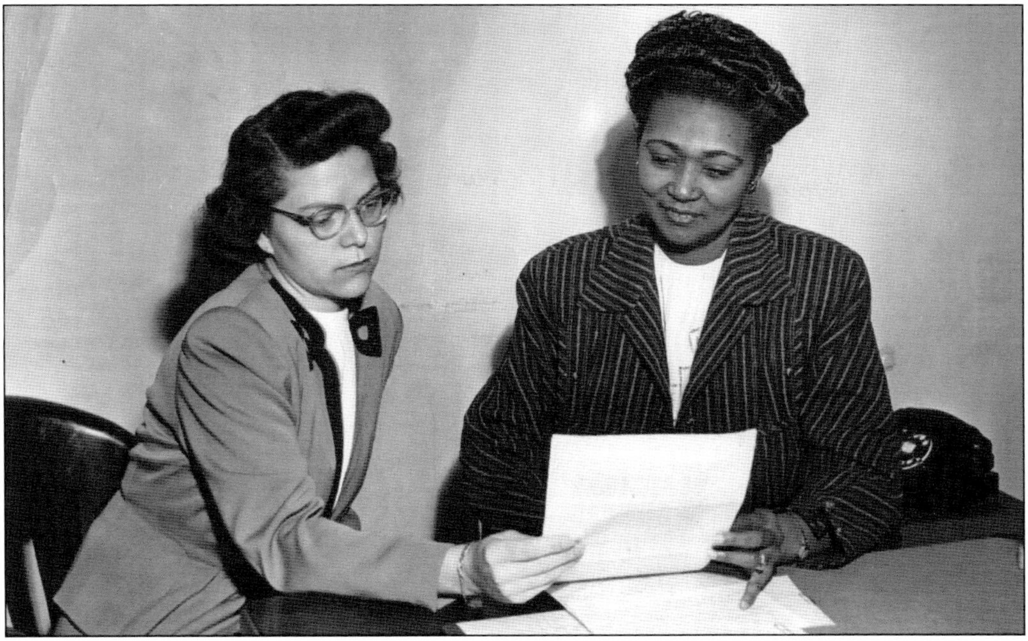

Marjorie Humber Jackson (right) was the first associate director of the Portland YWCA. (Courtesy of Urban League of Portland and OSU Special Collection and Archive Research Center.)

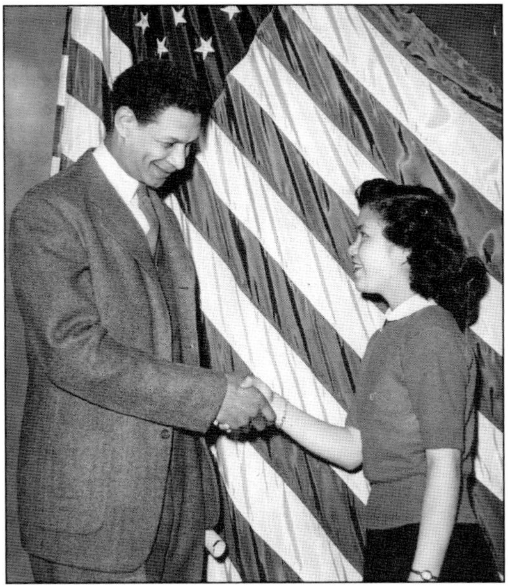

Advancement in social reform was not only enjoyed by the African American community. Shown here is Edwin C. Berry, executive director of the Urban League, congratulating Ruth Fong on her selection as a princess of the Portland Rose Festival. Fong was the first non-white princess to be selected. (Courtesy of Urban League of Portland and OSU Special Collection and Archive Research Center.)

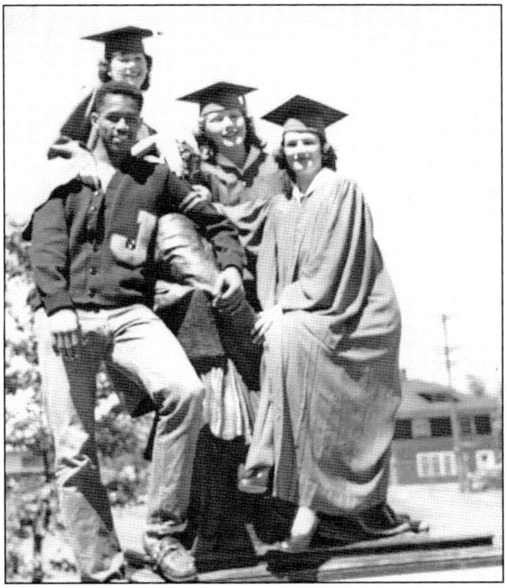

During the 1950–1951 school year, Caley Cook Jr. became the first African American student body president of an integrated school in the West. Cook is shown here with other Jefferson High School students. A gifted athlete, he was a member of the Jefferson High School and, later, Lewis & Clark College track teams. (Courtesy of Urban League of Portland and OSU Special Collection and Archive Research Center.)

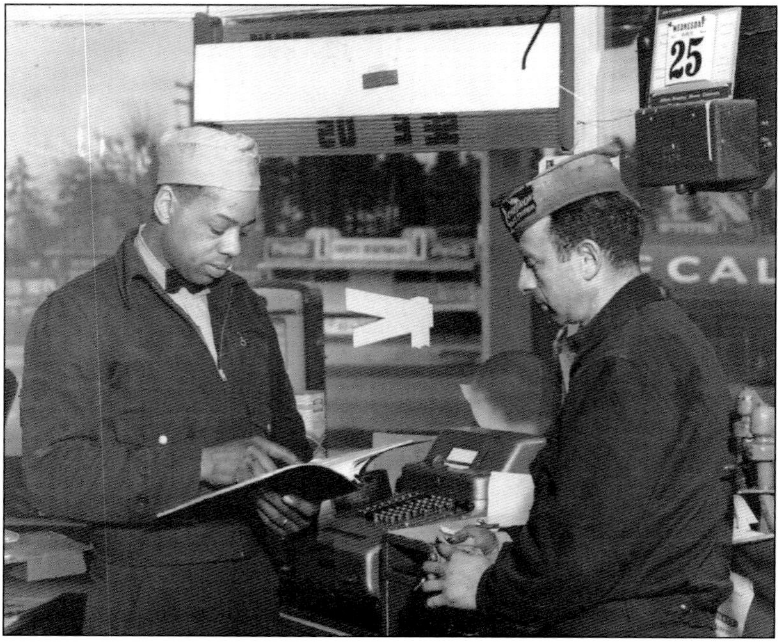

At the close of World War II, a critical mass of small businesses was established in the Albina community. Picture here is Stanley Jordan, the owner-manager of Bozeman Chevron Station, located at 7431 North Vancouver Avenue. (Courtesy of Urban League of Portland and OSU Special Collection and Archive Research Center.)

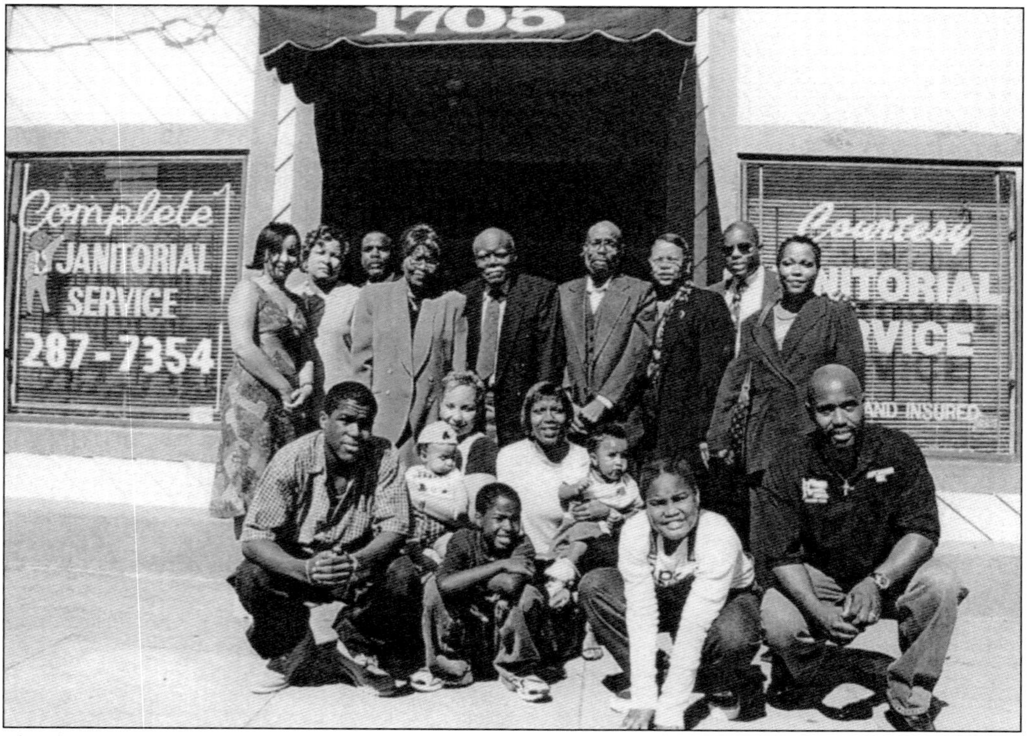

Floyd N. Booker Sr. came to Portland after being discharged from the US Army in 1943. He found employment at the Kaiser Shipyard and worked for the Union Pacific Railroad for 18 years, eventually becoming union shop steward. He later established the Courtesy Janitorial Services, a family-owned business since 1956. The business, located on Alberta Street, continues to operate today as one of the oldest African American businesses in Portland and possibly Oregon. (Courtesy of Marnella Bingham-Mosley.)

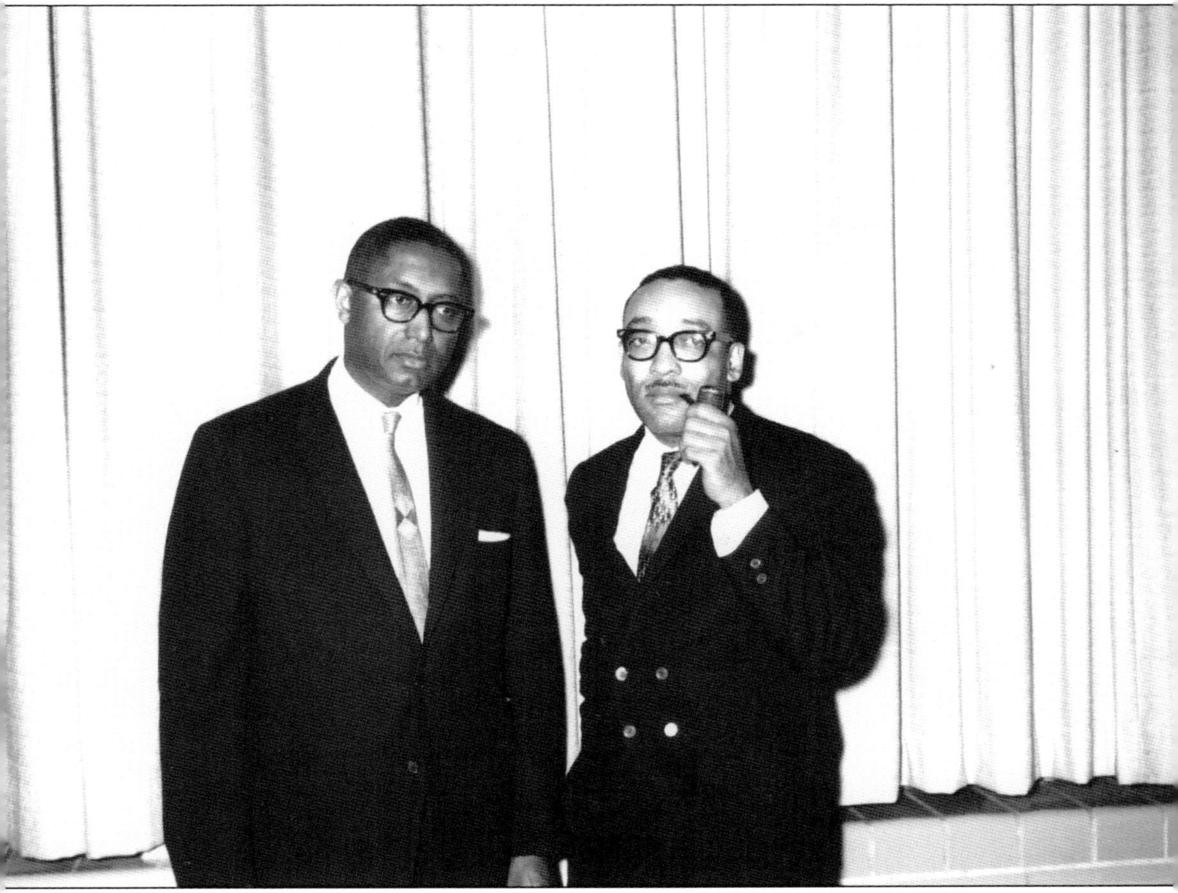

Pictured here are Cleodis Don Vann, mortician and Urban League president (right), and Louis Lomax, keynote speaker at the 1964 Urban League of Portland annual meeting. C. Don Vann and his wife, Roberta, moved to Portland in 1954 and established Oregon's first African American funeral home in 1955. He also served on the Albina War on Poverty Committee. Roberta became Oregon's only African American woman with an Oregon funeral director's license. (Courtesy of Urban League of Portland and OSU Special Collection and Archive Research Center.)

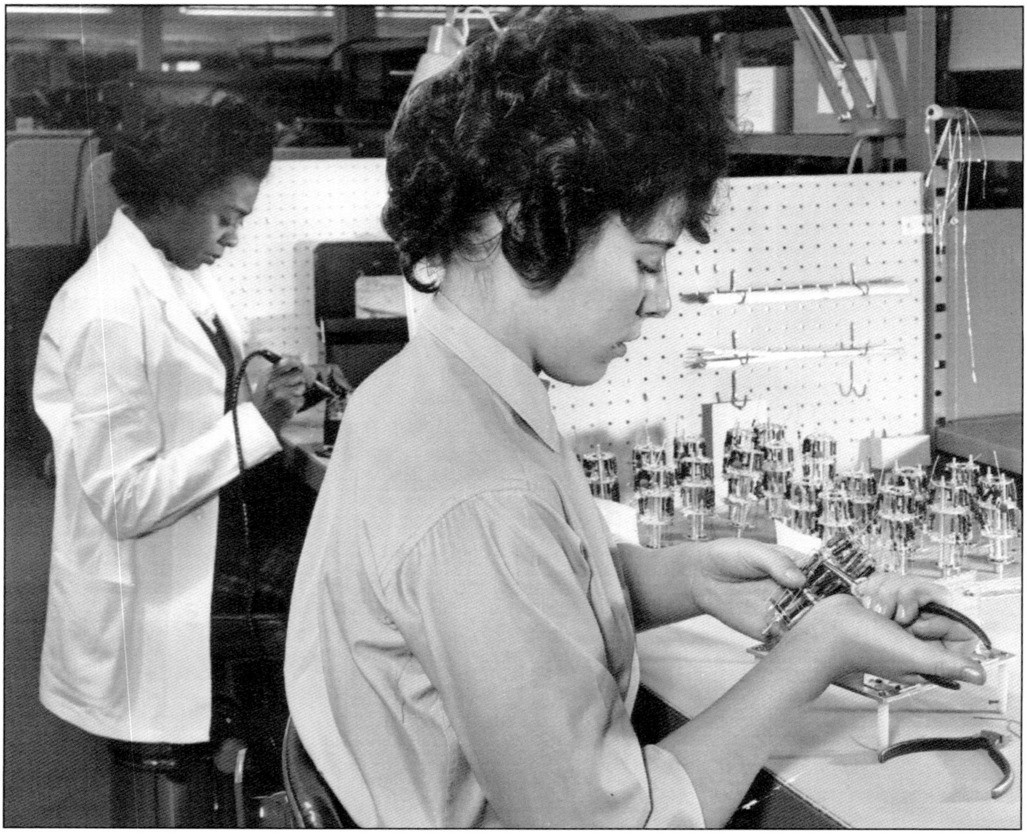

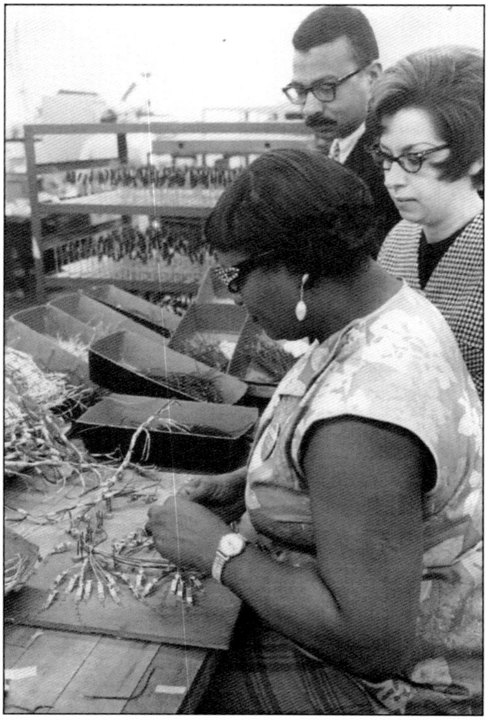

In 1962, through the help of the Urban League, Dian Craig Jackson became the first African American hired at Tektronix. Established in 1946, for many years, Tektronix was the only major electronics manufacturer in Oregon. (Courtesy of Urban League of Portland and OSU Special Collection and Archive Research Center.)

In this image, Tektronix workers perform assembly work at the Albina facility. (Courtesy of Urban League of Portland and OSU Special Collection and Archive Research Center.)

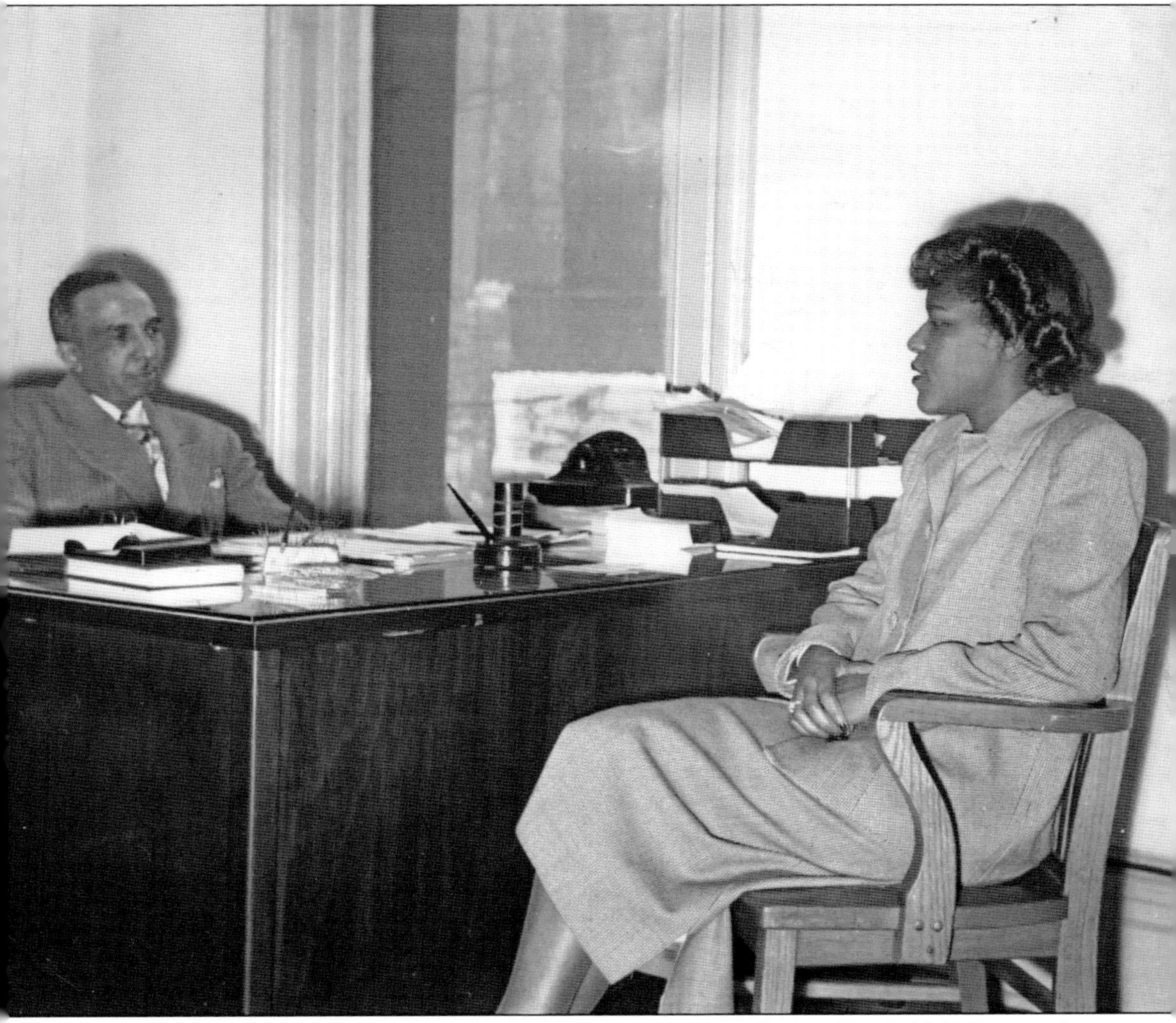

Pictured here are E. Shelly Hill and Joy (Brock) Pruitt, a new graduate of Linfield College and former staff of the Urban League of Portland. Joy later became a school teacher along with her sisters Beverly and Rose Marie, who became the first black Oregon-born and Oregon-educated school teachers in the Portland Public School System. When their mother, Letitia, arrived in Oregon in 1925 as a school teacher from St. Louis, the Portland Public School System would not hire her because she was African American. In 1967, the Brock family was named the National Urban League Family of the year. (Courtesy of Urban League of Portland and OSU Special Collection and Archive Research Center.)

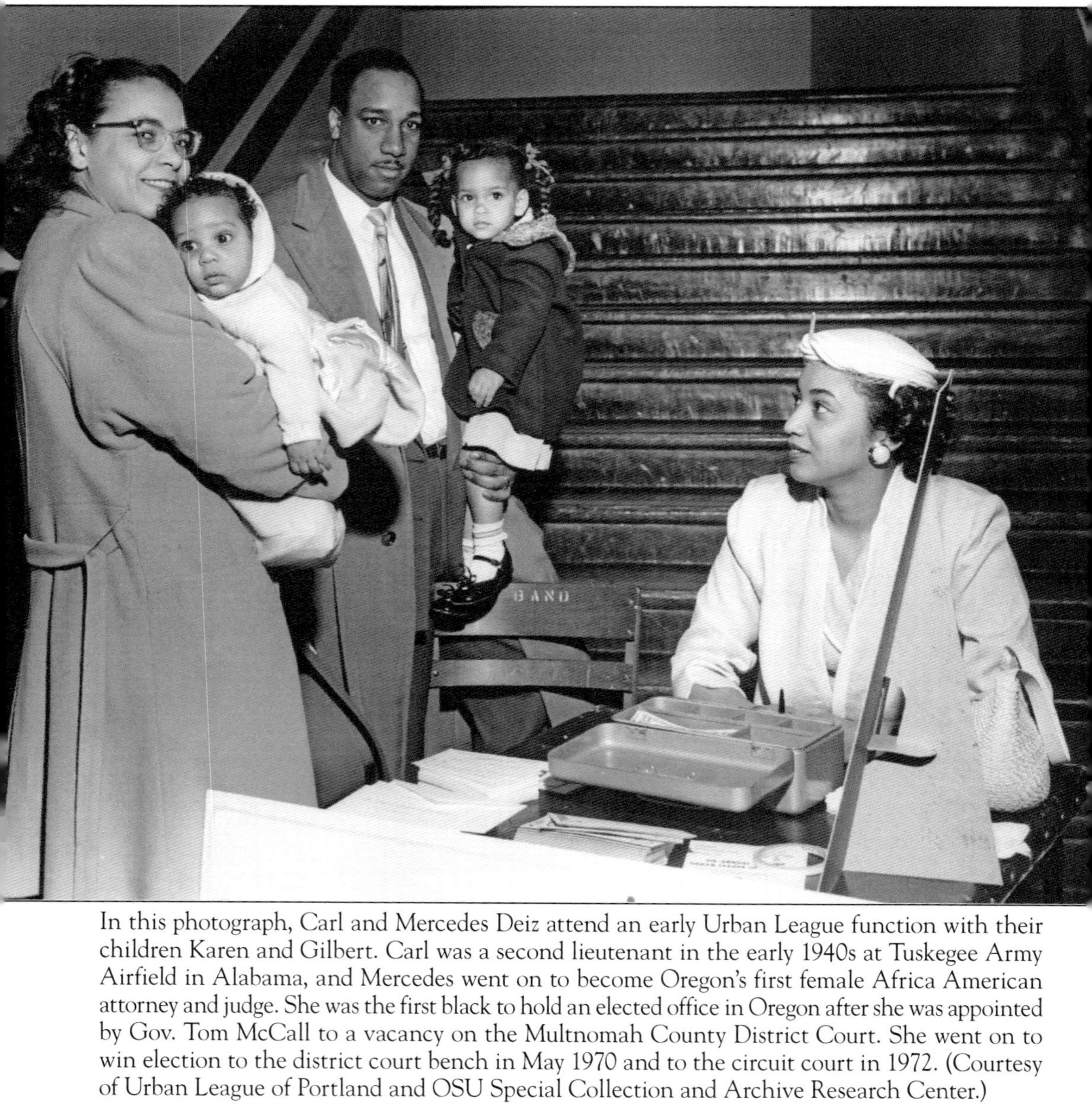

In this photograph, Carl and Mercedes Deiz attend an early Urban League function with their children Karen and Gilbert. Carl was a second lieutenant in the early 1940s at Tuskegee Army Airfield in Alabama, and Mercedes went on to become Oregon's first female Africa American attorney and judge. She was the first black to hold an elected office in Oregon after she was appointed by Gov. Tom McCall to a vacancy on the Multnomah County District Court. She went on to win election to the district court bench in May 1970 and to the circuit court in 1972. (Courtesy of Urban League of Portland and OSU Special Collection and Archive Research Center.)

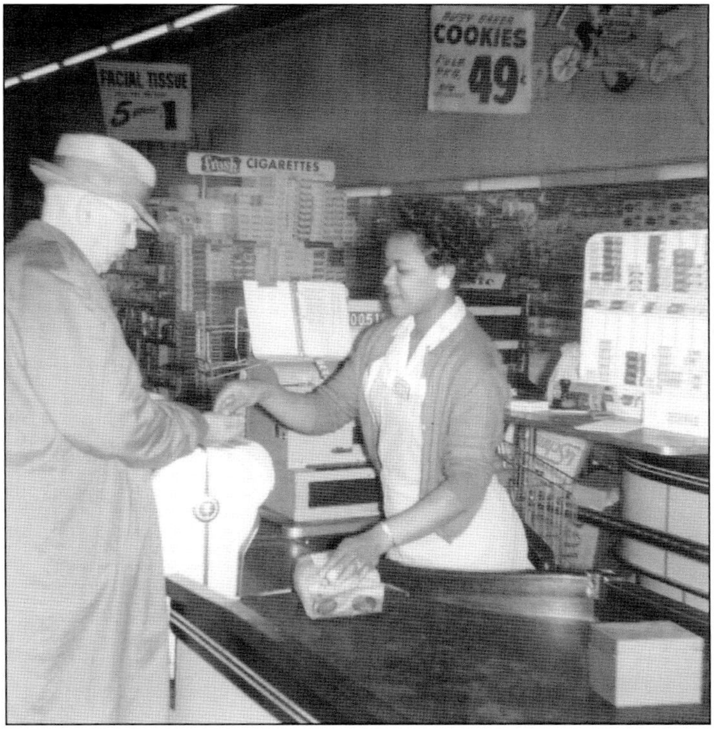

Pictured here is Arizona Warren, one of the first African American sales clerks at Safeway. (Courtesy of Urban League of Portland and OSU Special Collection and Archive Research Center.)

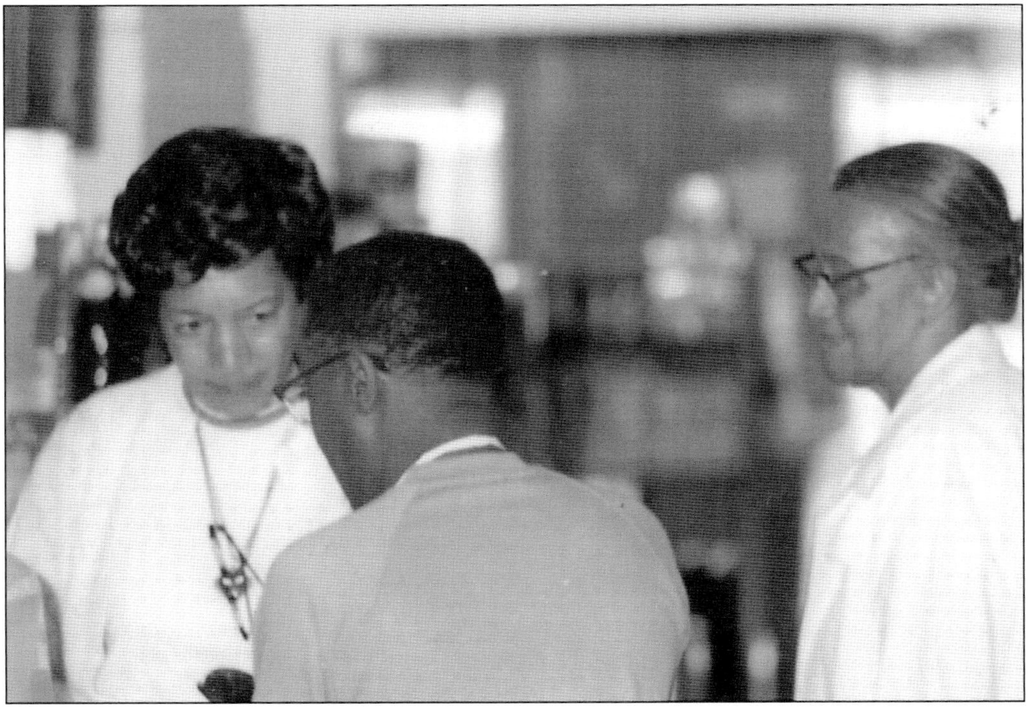

Neighborhood Bill's, one of the first African American grocery stores in Oregon, and was famous for its sausage. Owners Bill, Theresa, and Belle Benton opened the store in 1947 and operated at 2115 North Williams Avenue until 1983. Shown here from left to right are grocery clerk Beatrice Gordly and owners Bill Benton and Theresa Benton. (Courtesy of Avel Gordly.)

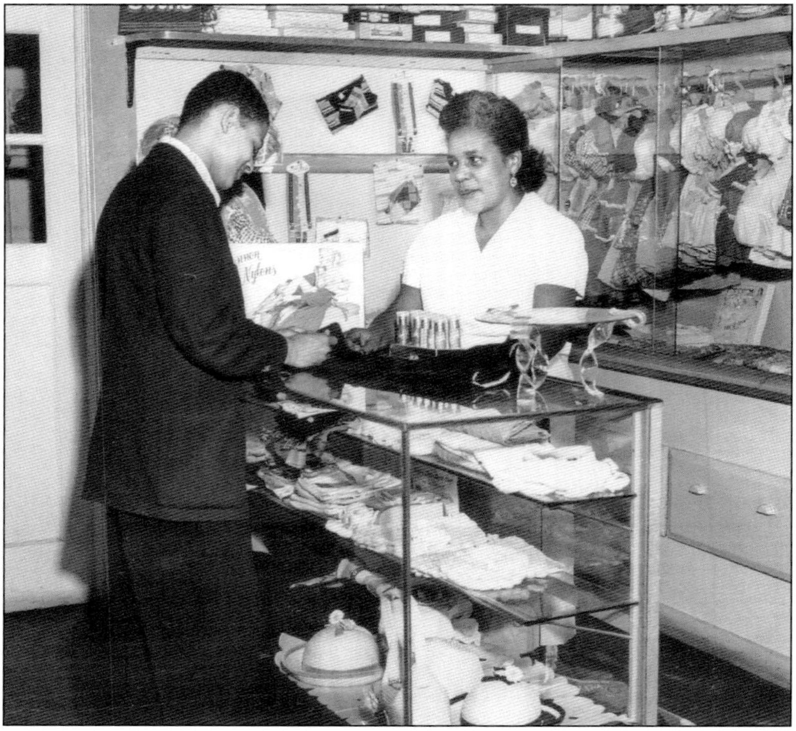

Charlene's Tot Shop was located along Williams Avenue. Etoile Cox stands behind the counter. (Courtesy of Oregon Historical Society.)

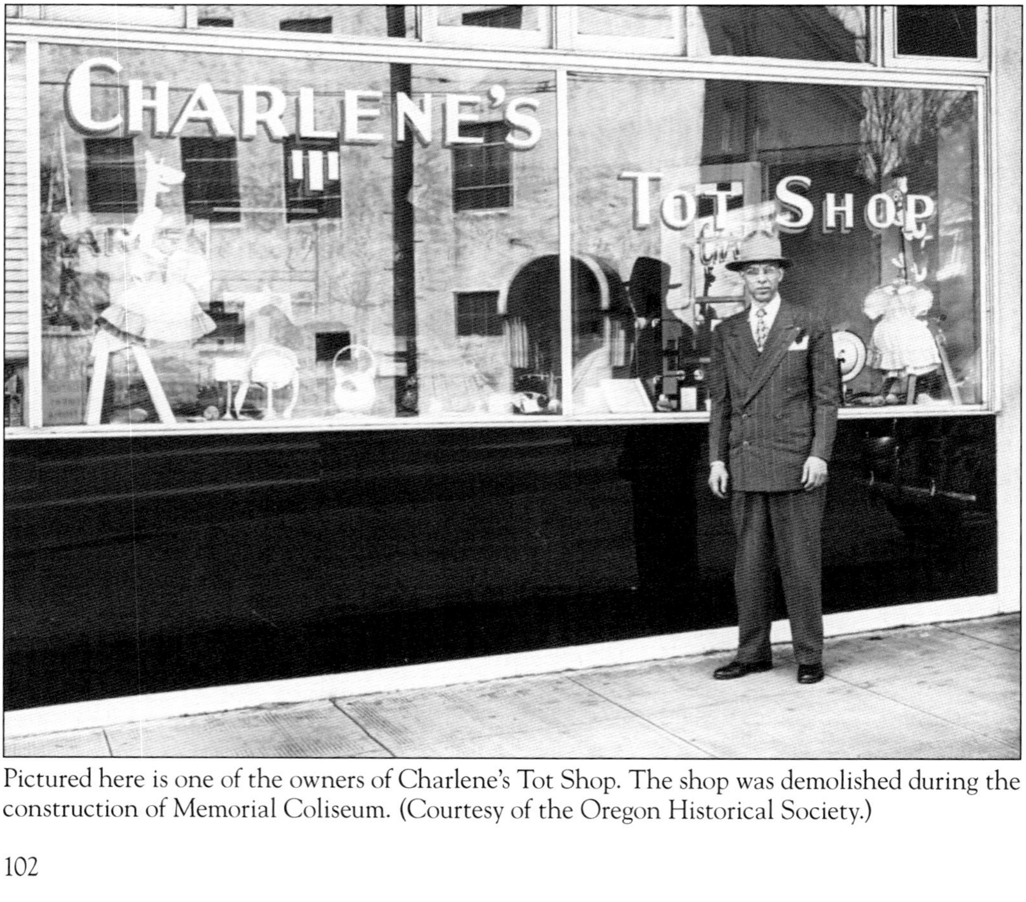

Pictured here is one of the owners of Charlene's Tot Shop. The shop was demolished during the construction of Memorial Coliseum. (Courtesy of the Oregon Historical Society.)

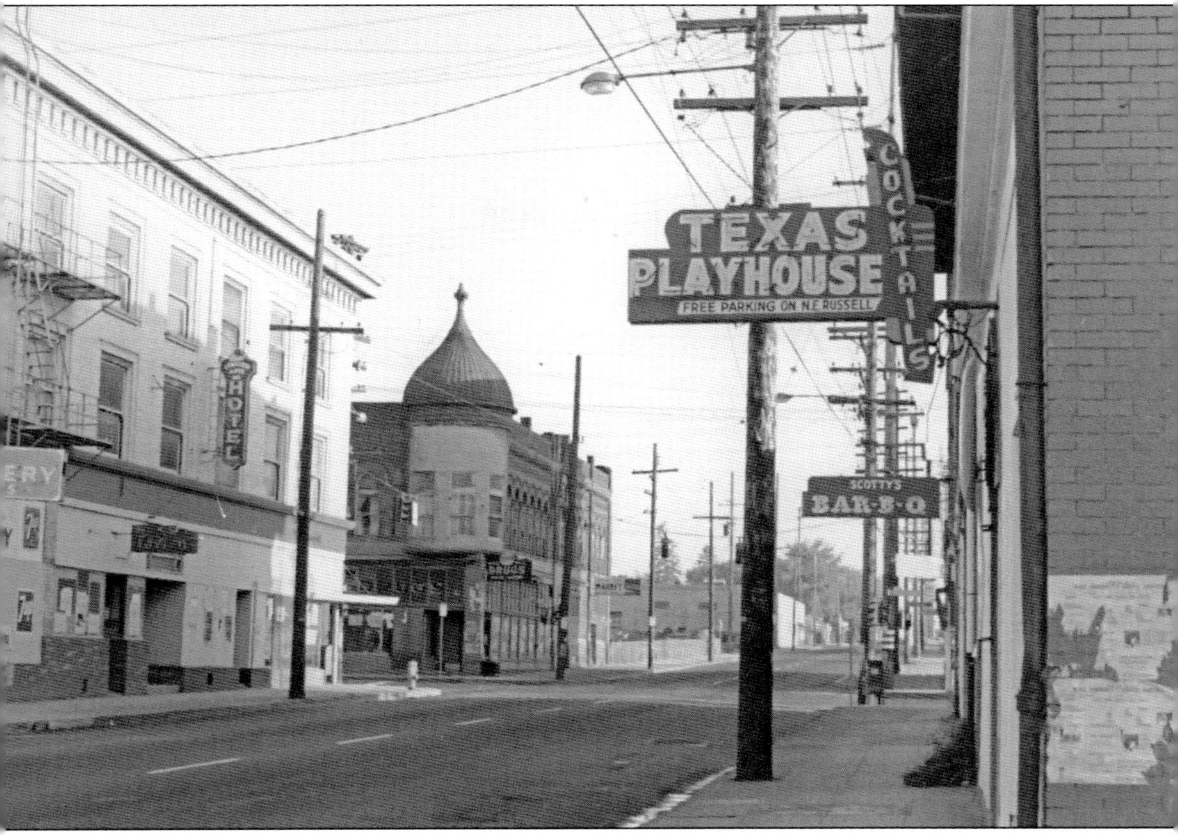

This is a view of Williams Avenue. During World War II, Williams Avenue emerged as a thriving African American business district and continued to serve that community until several federally funded redevelopment projects displaced the business district's customer base; this eventually cleared the southern end of the business district. In the foreground is the onion-domed cupola of the Hill Block Building, once the heart of the business district. This building was razed during the Emanuel Hospital (now Legacy Emanuel Medical Center) urban renewal project. The cupola can be seen today at the Eliot neighborhood's Dawson Park. (Courtesy of Urban League of Portland and OSU Special Collection and Archive Research Center.)

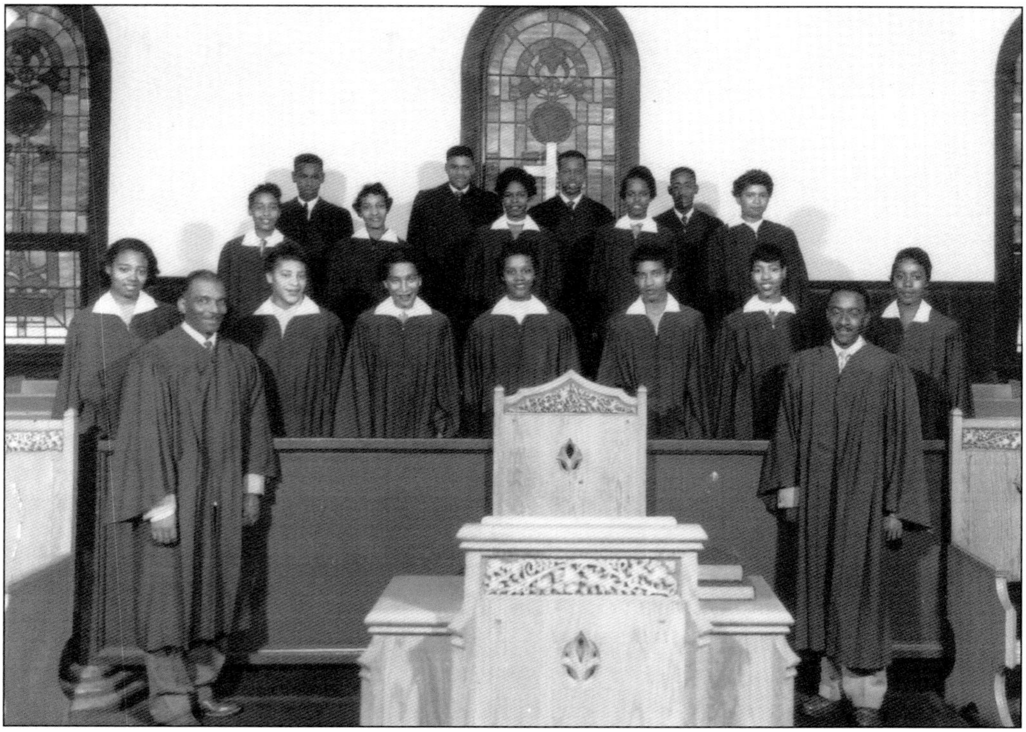

Religious organizations continue to be influential within the African American community as outlets for young people to express their musical talents. Pictured here is the young adult choir of Mount Olivet Baptist Church in the late 1950s. (Courtesy of Ed Washington.)

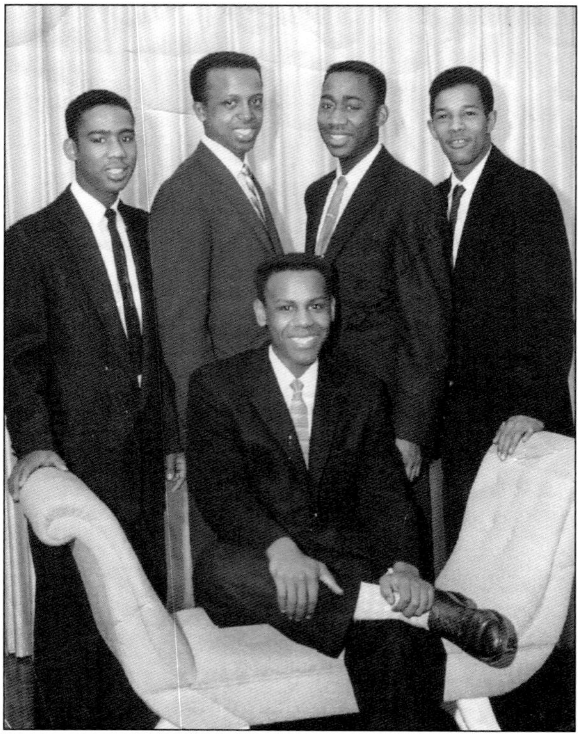

In the 1950s and 1960s, singing groups and bands became increasing popular. In 1957, this singing group was made of friends who lived in the same neighborhood. The group sang in and outside of the church. In church, they were known as the Tempo Tones, and outside of the church, they were called the T Tones. From left to right are Lemuel Robinson, Billy Washington, Manfred Robinson, Eddie Washington, and Onelius Jackson. (Courtesy of Ed Washington.)

The Les Femmes was established in 1951 to teach the youth of the community correct social behavior. According to an article in the *Oregonian*, a debutante must be a high school student from 16 to 19 years of age with a grade point average of at least a C. Good conduct is required, and the prospective debutante must not have attended any public dances or social functions on an adult level. This photograph showcases a debutante court of 1957. (Courtesy of Ed Washington.)

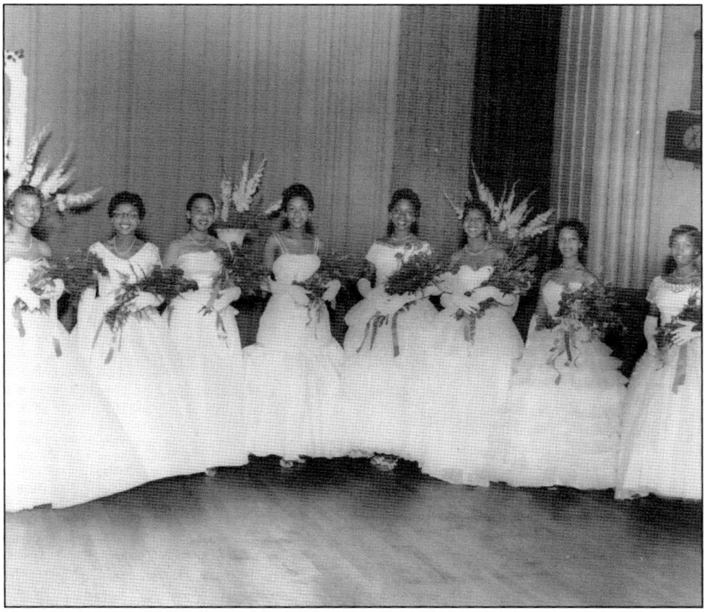

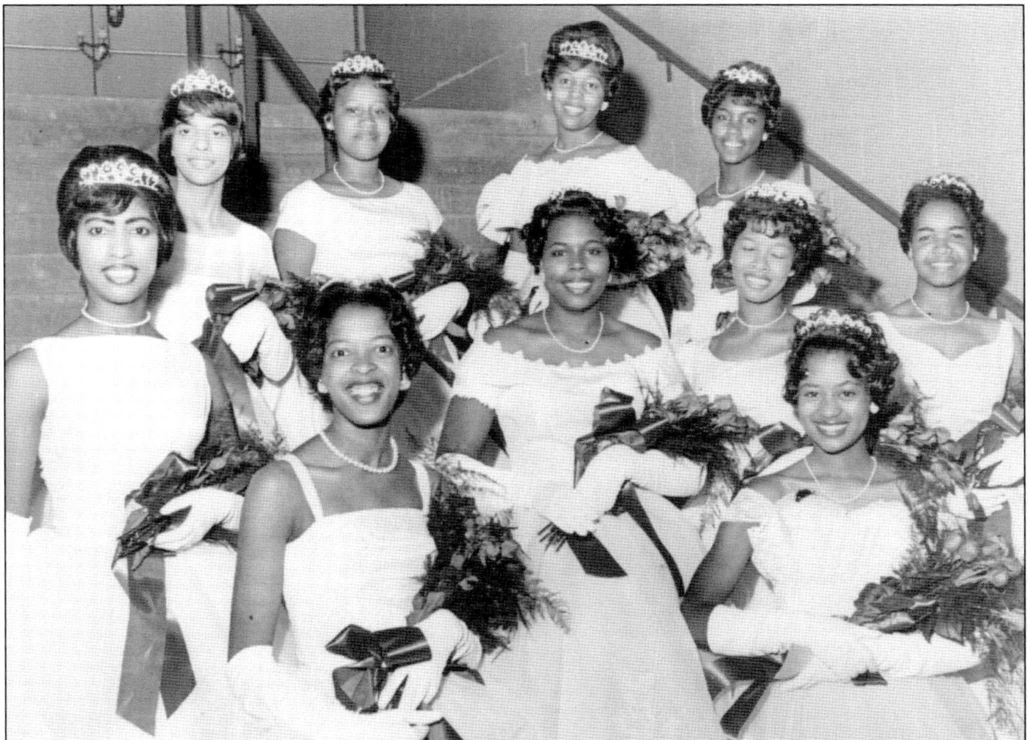

Presented at the 10th annual Les Femmes Debutante Ball are, from left to right, (first row) Delcie Wood and Rosemary Harris; (second row) Evelyn Johnson, Katherine McNeil, Lurlene Johnson, and May Jo Haggerty; (third row) Lilian Irvin, Garnett Robinson, Margo Jones, and Ruby Overton. The formal dance was held in the Georgia-Pacific Room of Memorial Coliseum. (Courtesy of the *Oregonian*.)

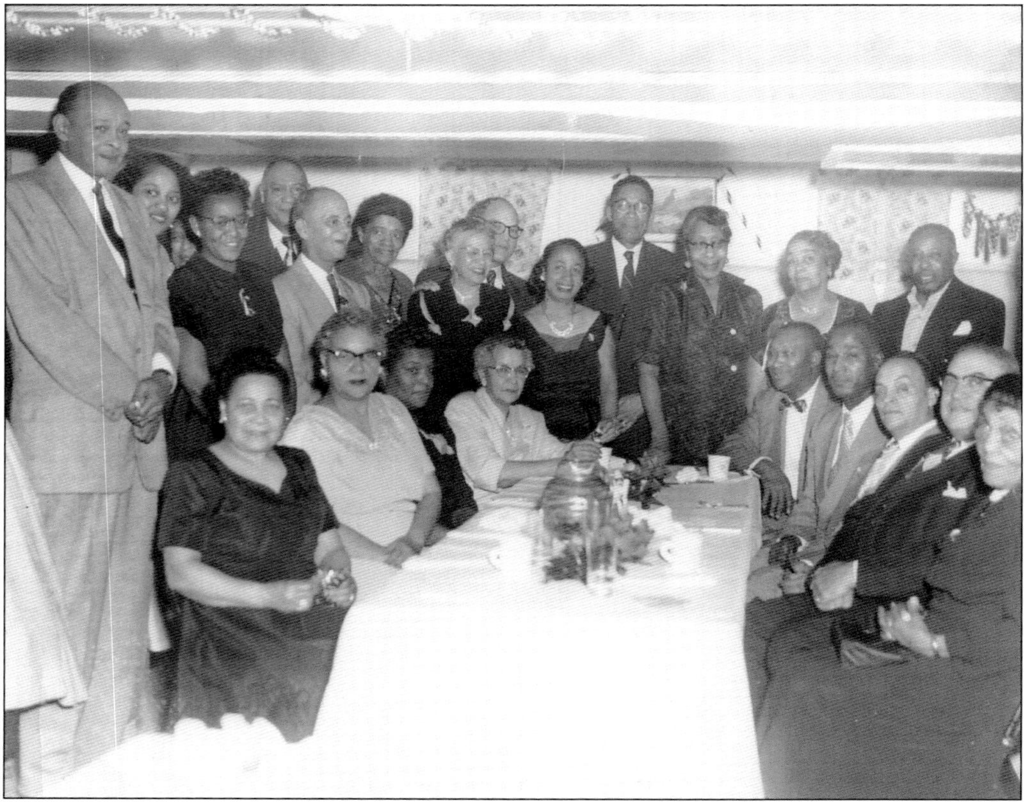

House parties were typical of this era. (Courtesy of the Rutherford Family Collection and PSU Library.)

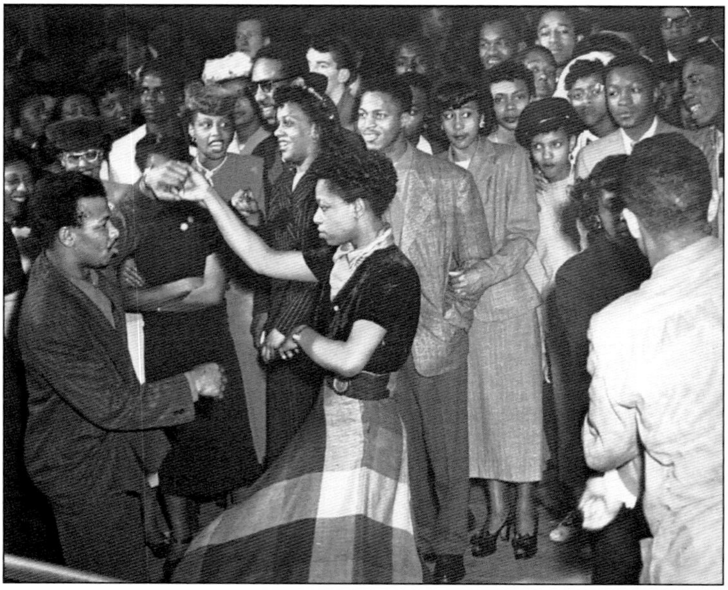

This picture appeared in the *Oregon Journal* in December 1949 with a caption that read, "Cognoscenti capered and listened appreciatively to be-bop but Dixieland jazz is gaining popularity fast." (Courtesy of the Oregon Historical Society.)

Portlander Mel Renfro attended the University of Oregon, where he was a track star and an All-American halfback and defensive back. The Dallas Cowboys drafted Renfro in the 1964 NFL Draft, and he played in three Super Bowls, VI, X, and XII. Renfro is enshrined in the College Football Hall of Fame and the Pro Football Hall of Fame. (Courtesy of Special Collections and University Archives, UO libraries.)

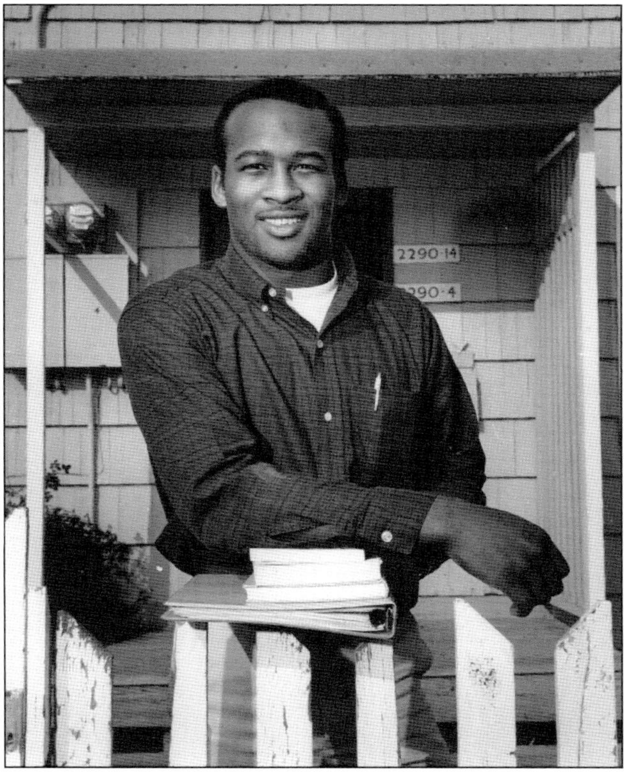

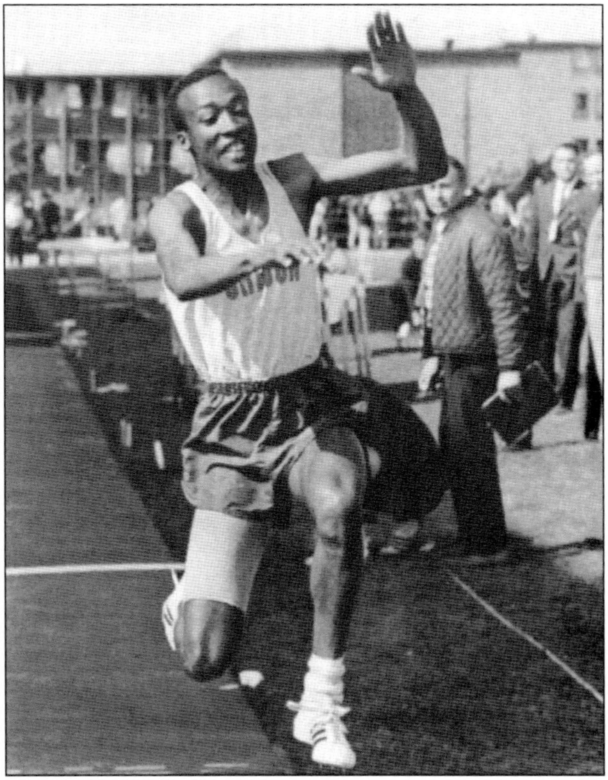

Several Portland youths excelled in collegiate athletics and attended Oregon colleges and universities. Herman Brame, pictured here, attended Jefferson High and ran track for the University of Oregon. Brame later became a sportswriter and historian of black athletes. He authored a history document entitled *African American Athletes in Oregon History from 1904 to 1950.* (Courtesy of Special Collections and University Archives, UO libraries.)

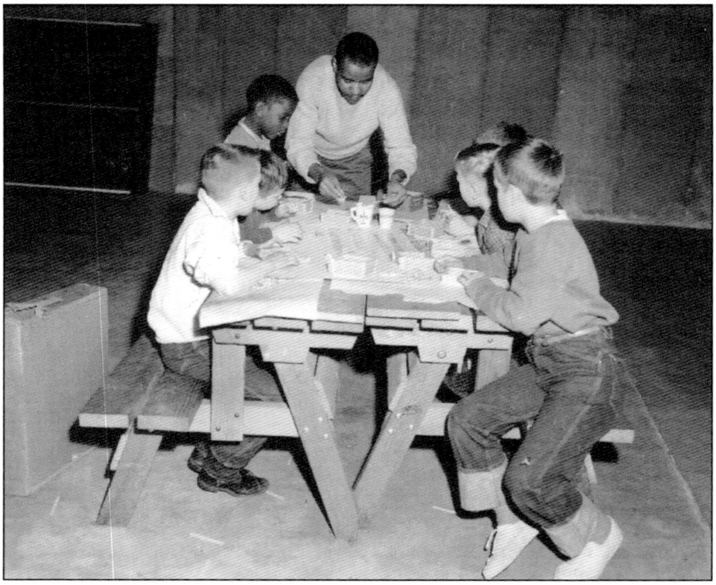

Social reform resulted in the policy and the practice of no discrimination in Portland's social agencies. Integrated facilities and social outings became more common. In this 1961 image, an African American male with the North Branch YMCA Adventure Club teaches young boys how to build structures out of popsicle sticks. (Courtesy of Urban League of Portland and OSU Special Collection and Archive Research Center.)

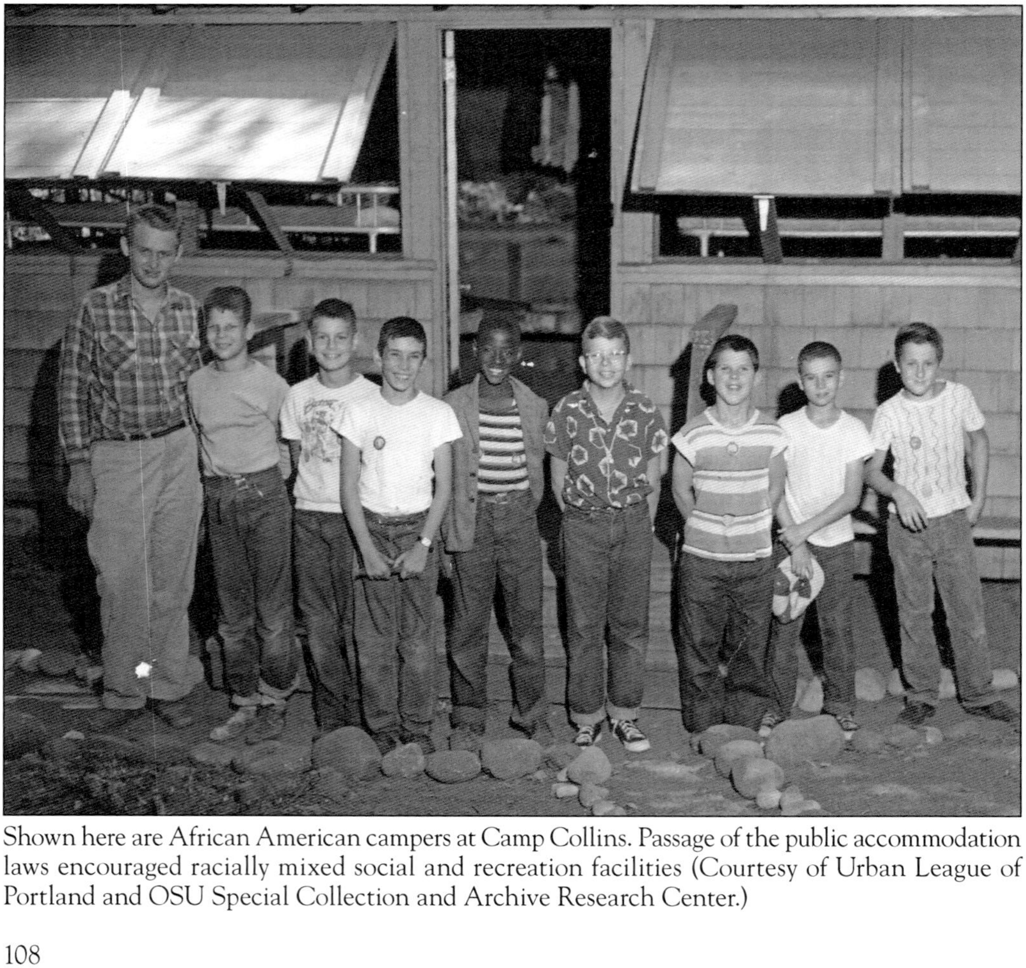

Shown here are African American campers at Camp Collins. Passage of the public accommodation laws encouraged racially mixed social and recreation facilities (Courtesy of Urban League of Portland and OSU Special Collection and Archive Research Center.)

Seven

REMAKING OF ALBINA

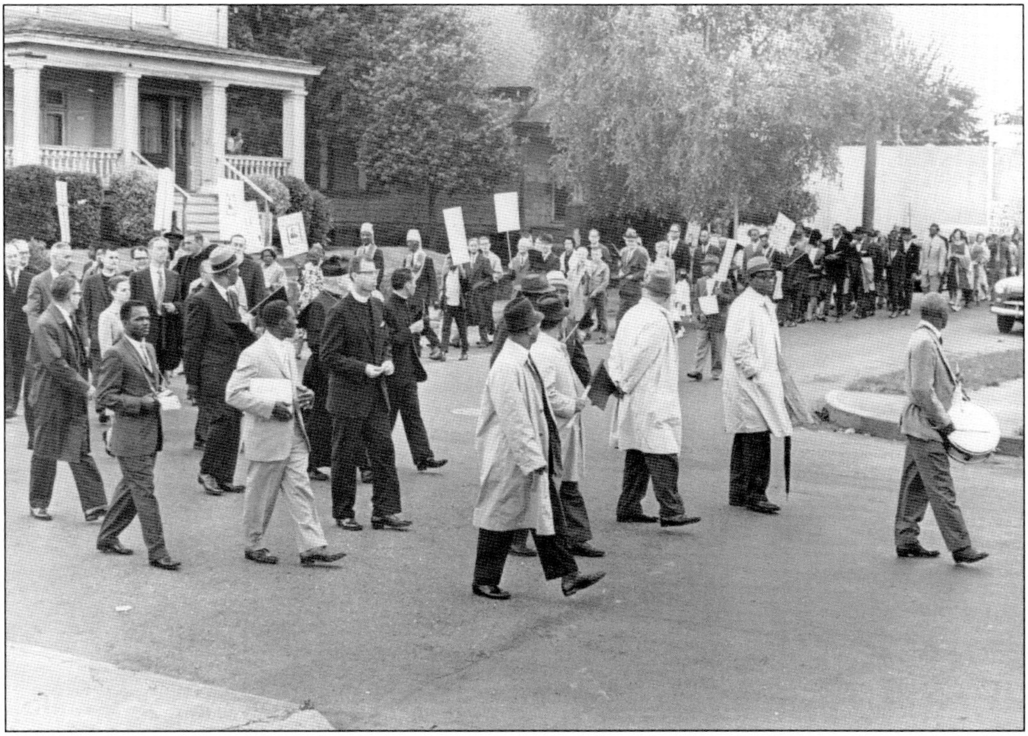

In June 1963, nearly 400 Portland mourners participated in the March of Mourning on behalf of Medgar Evers, the murdered civil rights activist and Mississippi field secretary for the NAACP. His death inspired protests throughout the United States, and the Portland march, led by Mayfield K. Webb, president of the Portland Branch of the NAACP, provided opportunity for Portland's leaders to address discriminatory practices in housing, schools, and labor unions. (Courtesy of the Oregon Historical Society.)

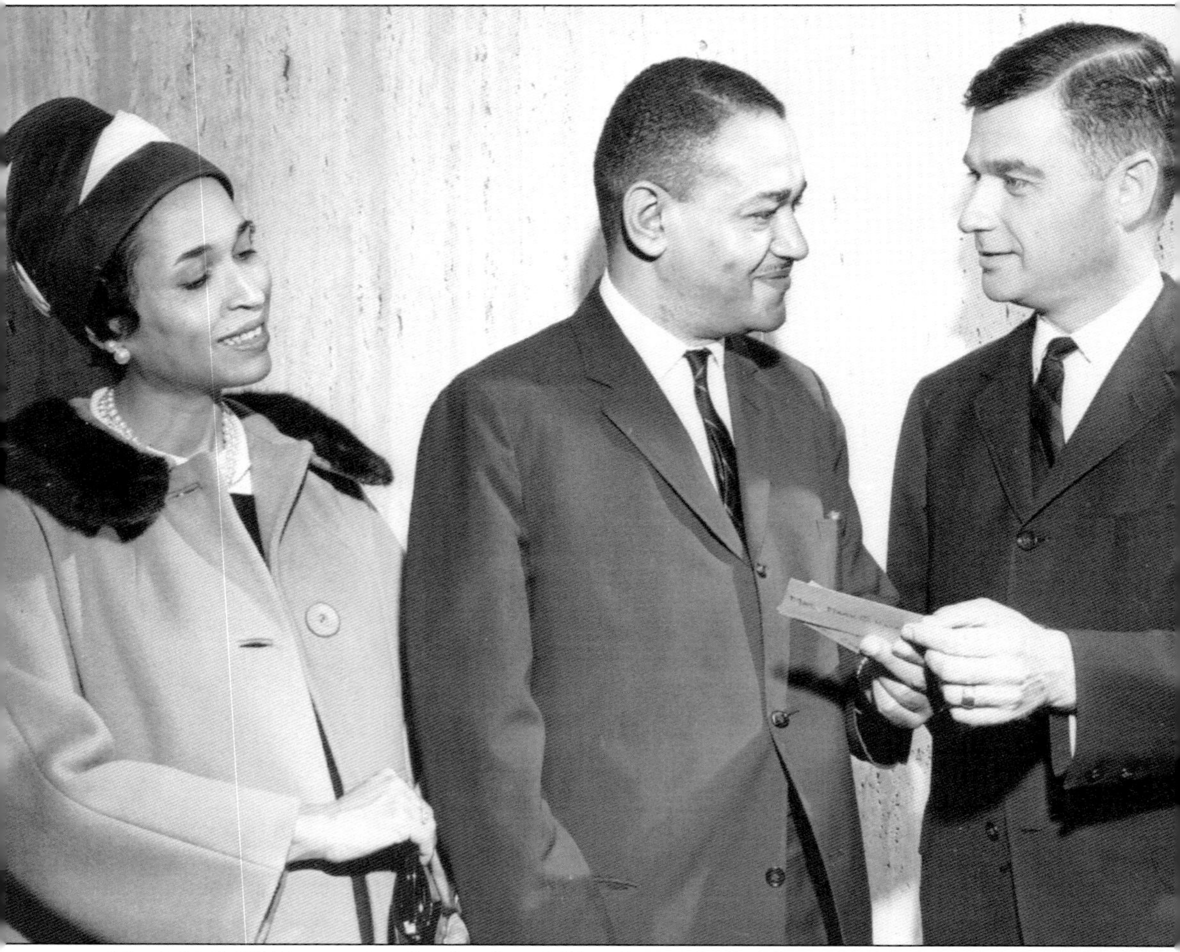

Mayfield K. Webb moved to Portland in 1955 and earned a law degree from Northwestern School of Law at Lewis & Clark College. After the War on Poverty was launched in 1965, Webb was appointed director for the Metropolitan Steering Committee. As director, he worked to improve the Model Cities Initiative. Disillusioned with federally funded programs, Webb left the Metropolitan Steering Committee to work as the executive director of the Albina Corporation, an industrial corporation that provided jobs to unemployed citizens from Albina. He married Juretta Lillian Oliver, a Portland native, who became the first Africa American graduate of Providence School of Nursing in Portland in 1950. In 1936, she participated in the Junior Rose Festival princess court. She worked for many years at Emanuel Hospital (now Legacy Emanuel Medical Center). She later joined Mariah Taylor to establish the Nurse Practitioner Community Health Clinic at Phil Reynolds Clinic. Pictured here from left to right are Juretta Lillian Webb, Mayfield Webb, and Gov. Mark O. Hatfield. (Courtesy of the Oregon Historical Society.)

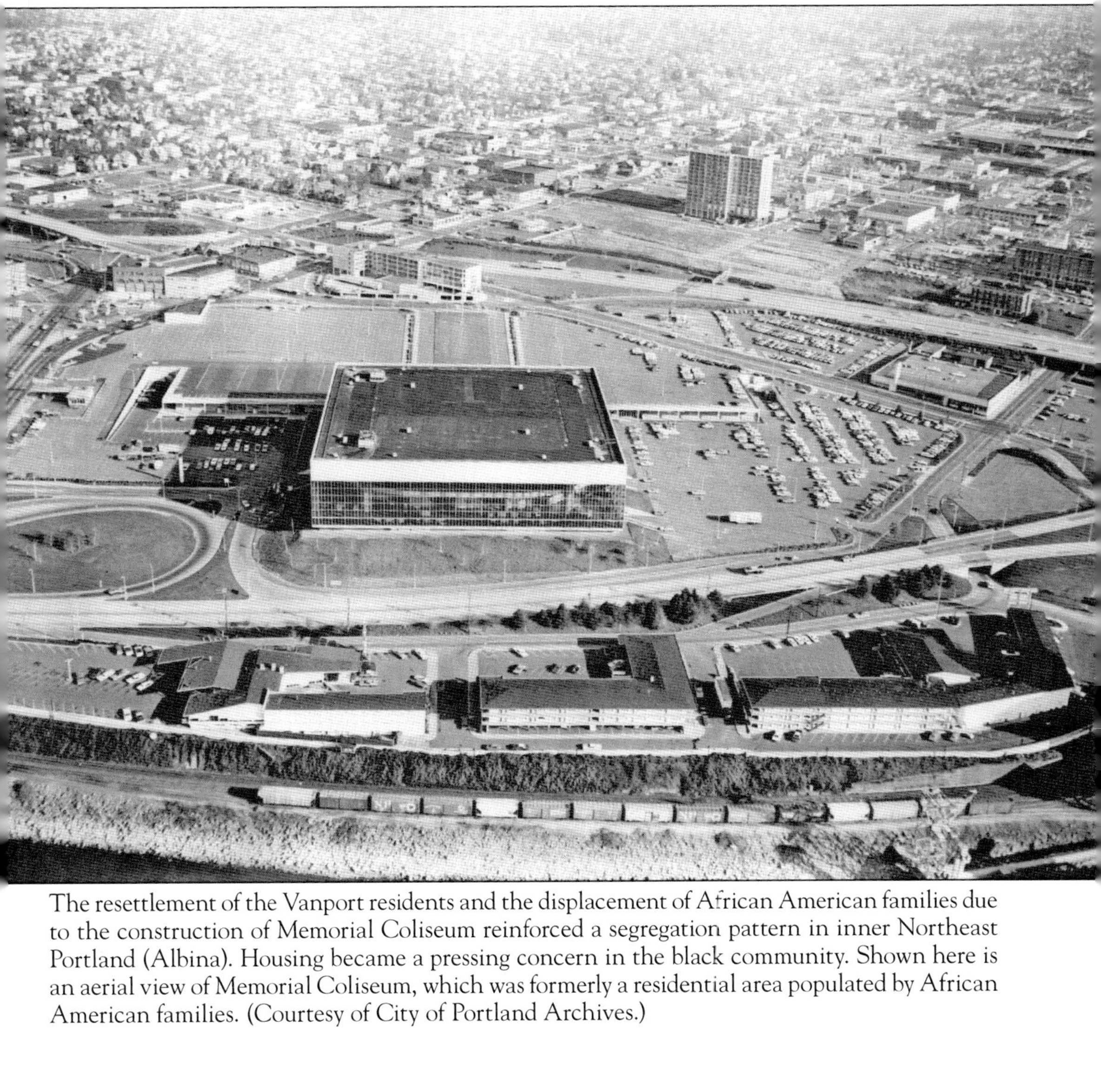

The resettlement of the Vanport residents and the displacement of African American families due to the construction of Memorial Coliseum reinforced a segregation pattern in inner Northeast Portland (Albina). Housing became a pressing concern in the black community. Shown here is an aerial view of Memorial Coliseum, which was formerly a residential area populated by African American families. (Courtesy of City of Portland Archives.)

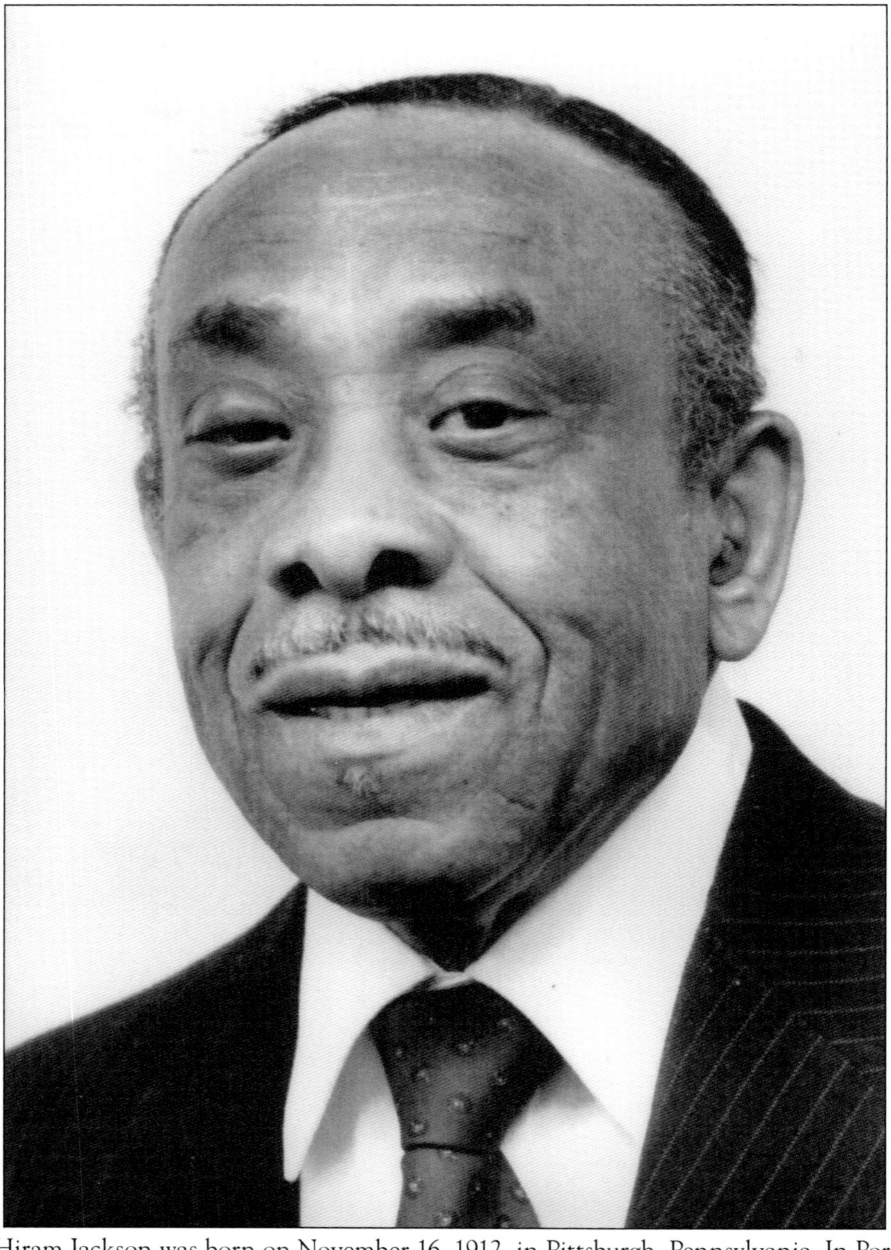

John Hiram Jackson was born on November 16, 1912, in Pittsburgh, Pennsylvania. In Portland, Jackson played a leading role in the civil rights struggle. In 1940, Jackson graduated from the University of Pittsburgh. He earned a bachelor of divinity degree from Union Theological Seminary in New York in 1945 and a master of education degree from the University of Pittsburgh in 1957. In 1959, Jackson moved to the Northwest, settling first in Seattle before moving to Portland in 1964, where he served as pastor of Mount Olivet Baptist Church until his retirement in 1987. Pastor Jackson was active in the Albina Ministerial Alliance, the Black United Front, the Urban League, One Church One Child, the NAACP, and many other organizations. He died in Portland in 1997. Herb Cawthorne, a fellow activist, remarked after Jackson's death, "I never met anybody in my life like him who could combine the pastoral sentimentality with the hard, raw political facts of a community trying to get out of the hole." (Courtesy of Mount Olivet Baptist Church.)

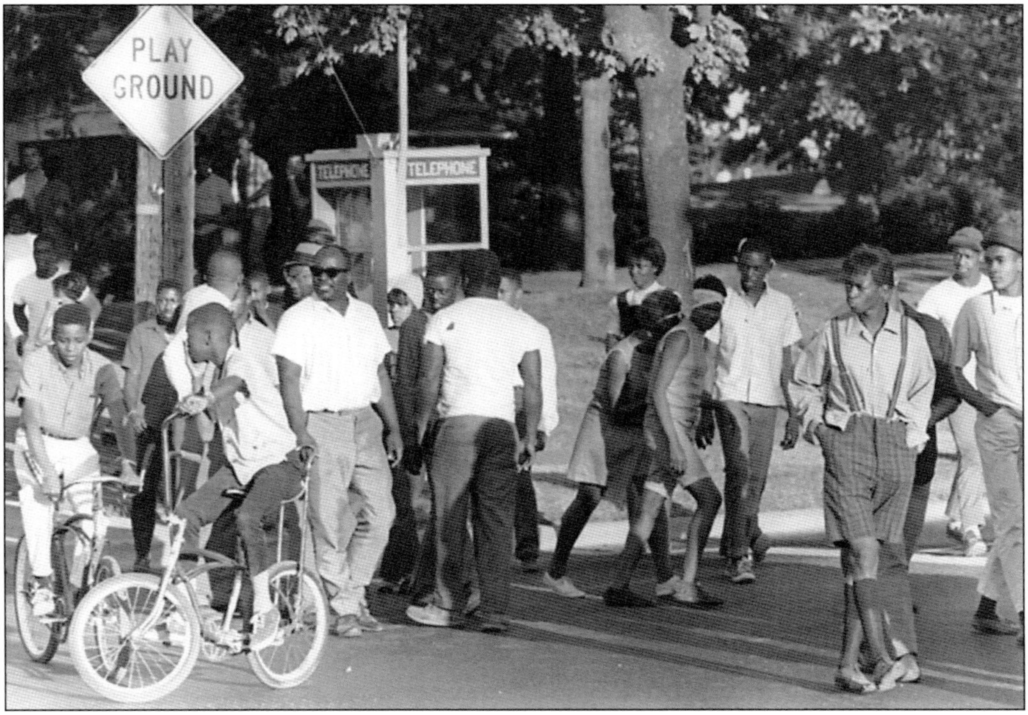

When African American youth took to the streets in 1967 and 1969, the traditional institutions like the churches, the Urban League, and the NAACP acted as calming influences. According to a CORE representative, nearly 200 African Americans gathered at Irving Park and endorsed a list of demands that included employment of more blacks, creation of more recreation facilities, and the inclusion of a black curriculum at Jefferson High School. (Courtesy of the Oregonian.)

Historian Dr. Darrell Millner commented that new voices emerging during the 1960s took a more confrontational and militant approach toward effecting changes. The members of the Congress of Racial Equality (CORE) were accused of inciting racial violence in the form of mini-riots that took place on Union Avenue in 1967 and 1969. In August 1967, the Portland Police surrounded a home near Northeast Union Avenue and Fremont Street and took one leader of the disturbance into custody. The *Oregonian* reported that the "mob" stoned a police car. (Courtesy of the *Oregonian*.)

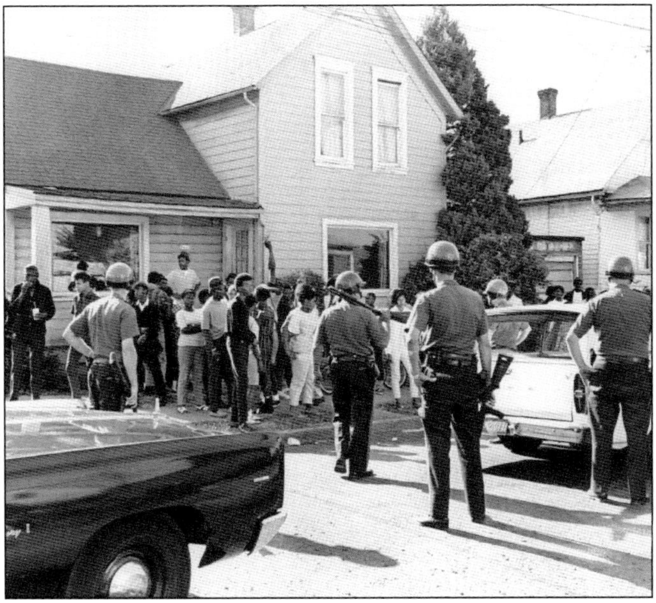

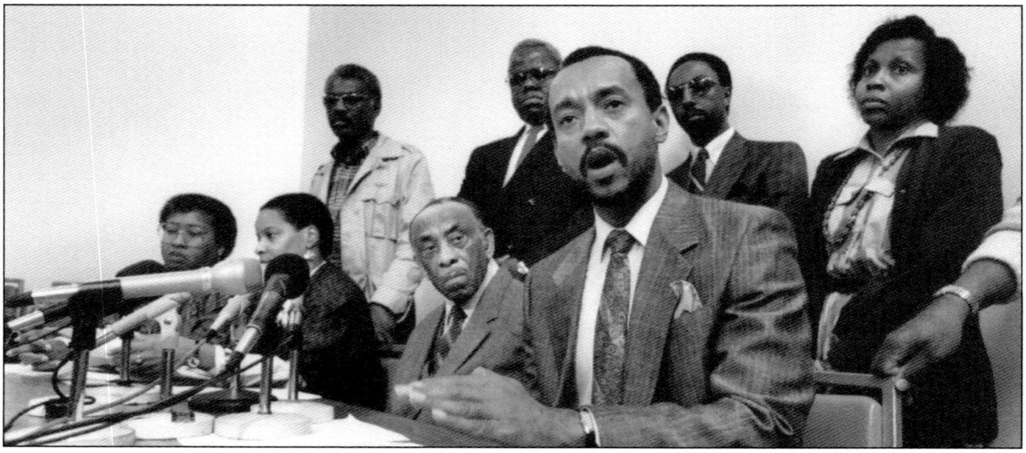

Ron Herndon arrived in Portland in 1968 to attend Reed College and helped lobby Reed College administrators to establish a Black Studies program. The civic leader and activist established a bookstore and the now-defunct Black Education Center, an independent school, in 1970. He later cofounded the Portland chapter of the Black United Front (BUF) to advocate the improvement of substandard Northeast Portland schools. As of 2012, Ron Herndon serves as the chairman of the National Head Start program. Since 1975, he has served as the director of the Albina Head Start program in Portland. Members of the BUF are pictured here, from left to right: (seated at table) Joyce Harris, Avel Gordly, Pastor John Jackson, and Ron Herndon; (standing) Richard Brown, Harold Williams, unidentified, and Cornetta Smith. (Courtesy of the *Oregonian*.)

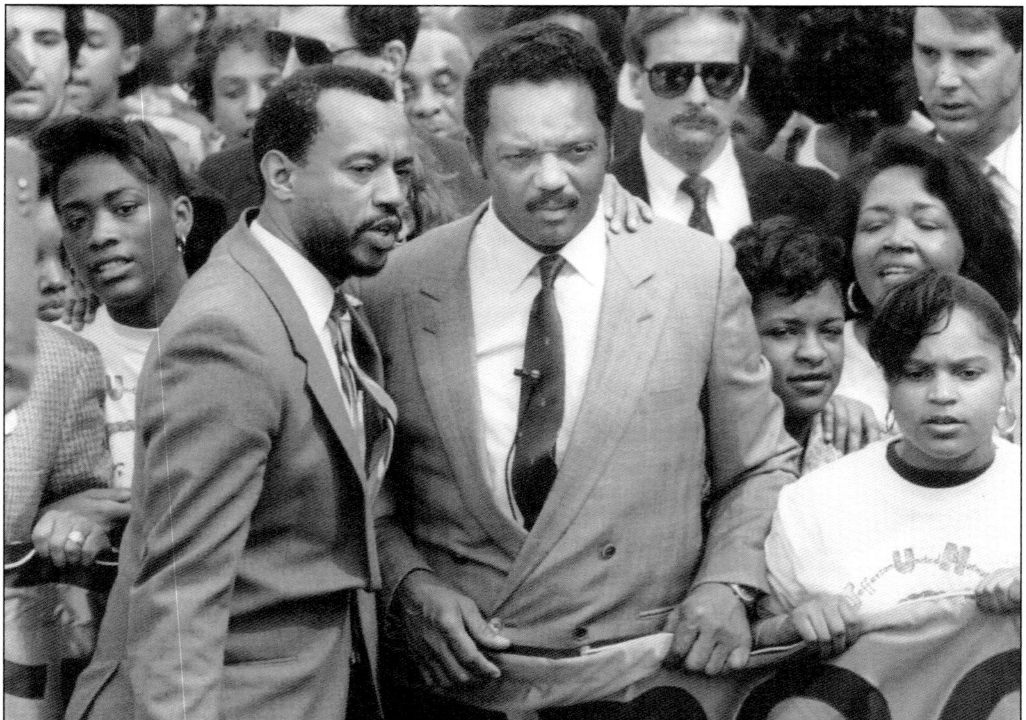

Ron Herndon, coleader of Portland's Black United Front, joins Jesse Jackson on an anti-drug march in Northeast Portland during a May campaign stop in one of Jackson's unsuccessful bids for the presidency. (Courtesy of the *Oregonian*.)

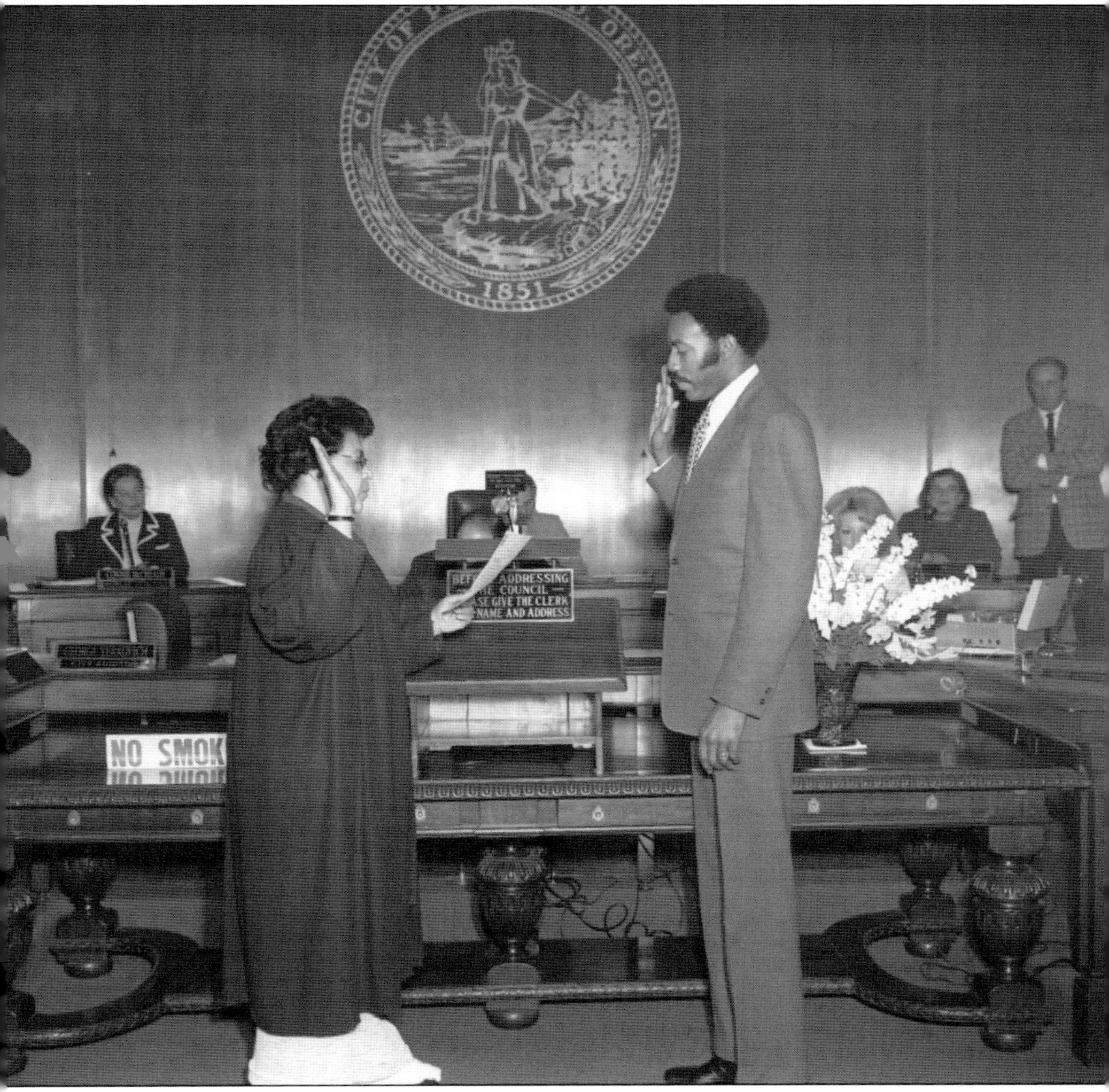

In 1974, Charles Jordan became Portland's first African American city commissioner. In this photograph, Judge Mercedes Deiz performs the swearing-in ceremony for Charles Jordan. He was elected twice as city commissioner and served 14 years as Portland Park & Recreation director; he also served in many national leadership roles for parks and conservation. Jordan's visionary leadership changed Portland's landscape. As city commissioner, Jordan created Portland's first police accountability body: the Police Internal Investigations Auditing Committee (PIIAC). He brought police into schools to create positive relationships, pushed for equity in city recruitment, and championed citizen involvement. (Courtesy of City of Portland Archives.)

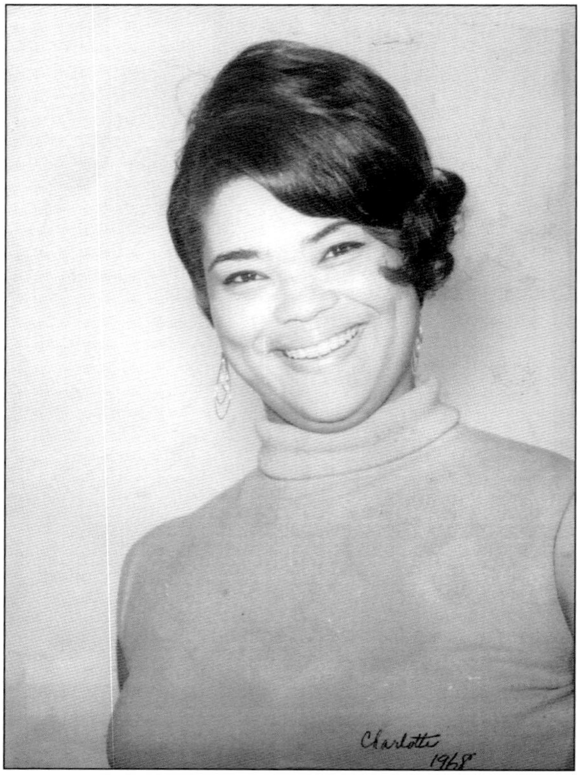

Charlotte Rutherford, a third-generation Portlander, is the daughter of Otto and Verdell Rutherford. Inspired by her parent's activism, she worked as an Oregon civil rights investigator and as a civil rights attorney for the NAACP Legal Defense and Educational Fund. She retired as an administrative judge for Oregon's Office of Administrative Hearings. She is a past president of the Oregon Association of Administrative Law Judges and Board of Governors of the National Association of Administrative Law Judges, as well as a board member of the Black United Fund of Oregon and the Oregon Black Pioneers. In 2012, the Portland State University Black Studies and History Departments celebrated Charlotte's donation of the Verdell Burdine and Otto G. Rutherford Family Collection to the PSU Special Collections Library. (Courtesy of the Rutherford Family Collection and PSU Library.)

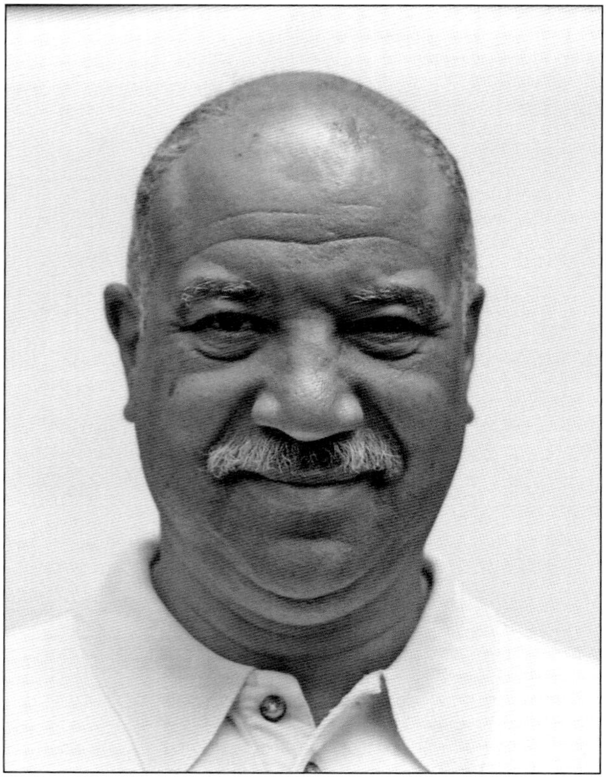

Civic leader and Portland native Carl Talton has a 40-year legacy of community service focused on economic development, housing development, health issues, and education. Talton's local community experiences include serving on the board of the Portland Urban League and being a founding member of the Northeast Community Development Corporation and the North/Northeast Economic Development Alliance. He is the former vice president of governmental affairs, economic, community, and business development for Portland General Electric, from which he retired in 2003. As of 2012, he serves as the executive chair of the Portland Family Funds and its affiliates and has facilitated more than $2 billion in investment in communities from Portland to New York through the placement of New Markets Tax Credits. (Courtesy of Carl Talton.)

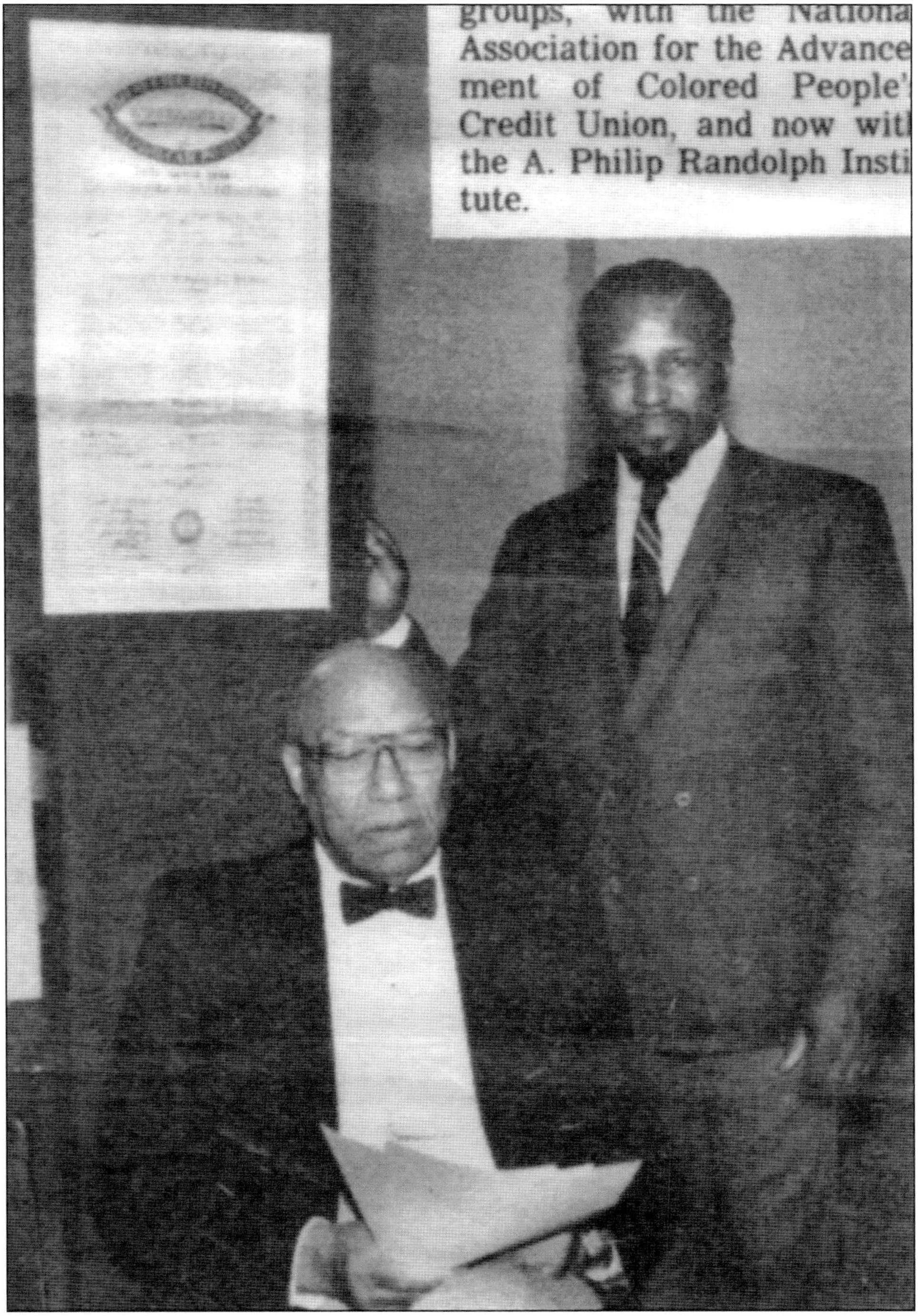

In 1979, the Portland Chapter of the A. Philip Randolph Institute (APRI) was dedicated and endorsed by the Oregon AFL-CIO. Pictured here are the late Eddie Butler (seated), former Pullman Porter and former president of the Railroad Senior Citizen Association, and Bob Boyer, former brakeman and former president of the Portland Chapter of the APRI. At the APRI dedication, Butler provided Boyer with the charter of defunct Portland branch of the Brotherhood of Sleeping Car Porters. (Courtesy of Bob and Judy Knawles Boyer.)

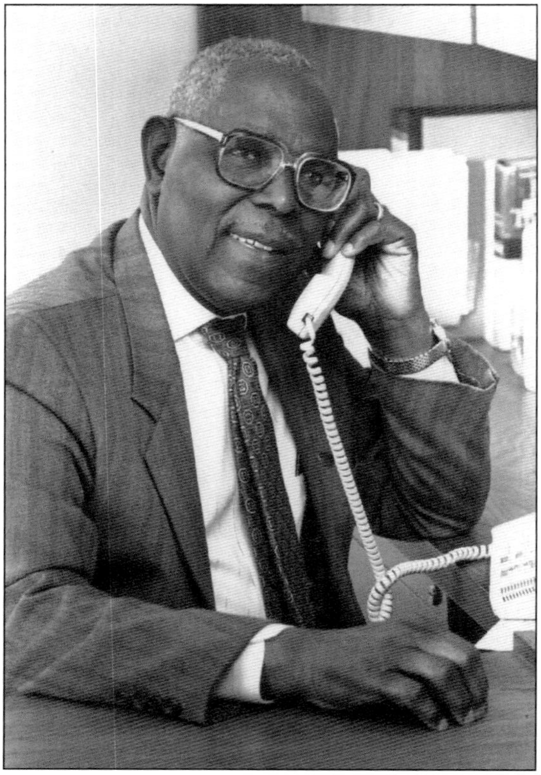

Sen. Bill McCoy was the first African American to serve in the Oregon Legislative Assembly. He was elected to the Oregon House of Representatives in 1973 and appointed to a vacant Oregon State Senate seat the following year. Senator McCoy championed civil rights, social services, and Oregon's working families. His wife, Gladys McCoy, was the first African American to serve on both the Portland School Board and the Multnomah County Board of Commissioners. (Courtesy of the McCoy family.)

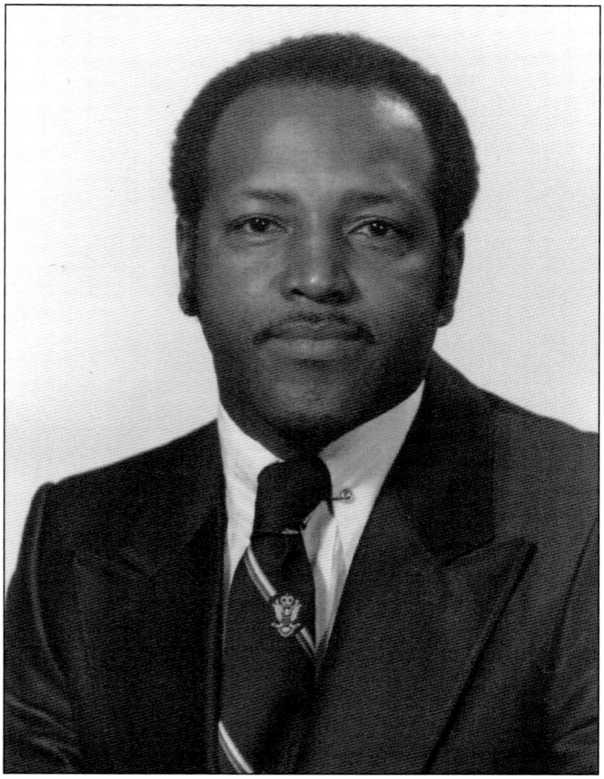

Robert "Bob" Boyer, known as "the senator of the waterfront," became the first African American to gain a major position in his union. In 1982, after 24 years of union work, he was elected as the chairman of the executive board of the Columbia River region of the Inlandboatmen's Union of the Pacific. In 1996, upon the death of Sen. Bill McCoy, Boyer was appointed to complete McCoy's term. (Courtesy of Bob and Judy Knawles Boyer.)

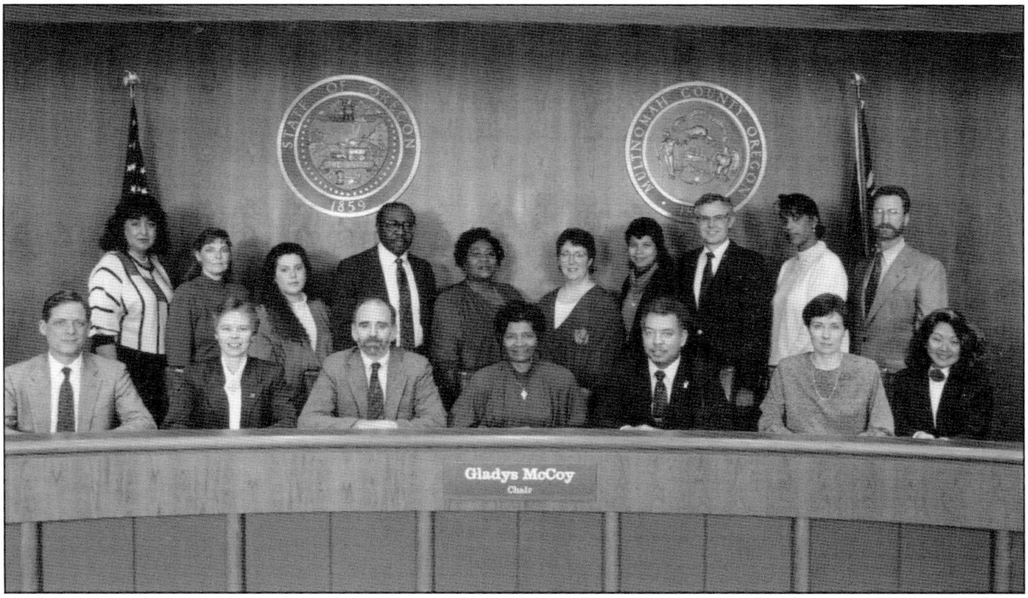

In 1970, Gladys McCoy became the first African American to serve in a local office when she was elected to the Portland School Board. In 1979, she served on the Multnomah County Board of Commissioners, and in 1986, she successfully ran for Multnomah County chair. She served as chairwoman until her death in 1993. She was married to state senator Bill McCoy. (Courtesy of the McCoy family.)

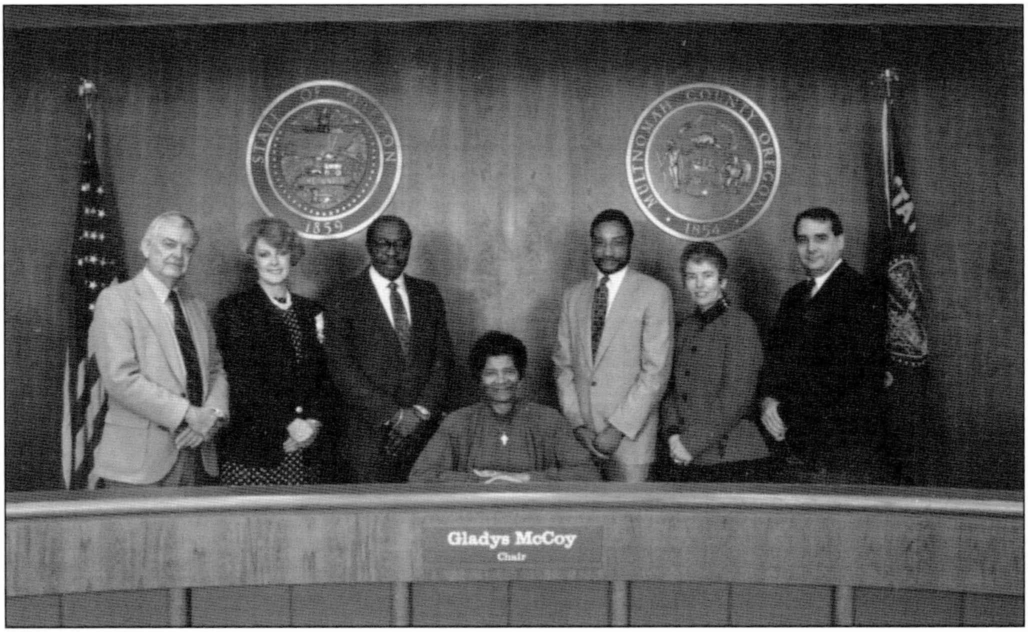

Gladys McCoy, pictured here with her multicultural staff, received many accolades for her outstanding service. In 1985, she was the first woman elected president of the Oregon Association of Counties. In 1997, during the 69th Oregon Legislative Assembly, Rep. Mike Fahey and Rep. Margaret Carter sponsored a bill declaring state senator Bill McCoy and Multnomah County chair Gladys McCoy the first African American political family of Oregon. (Courtesy of Bob and Judy Knawles Boyer.)

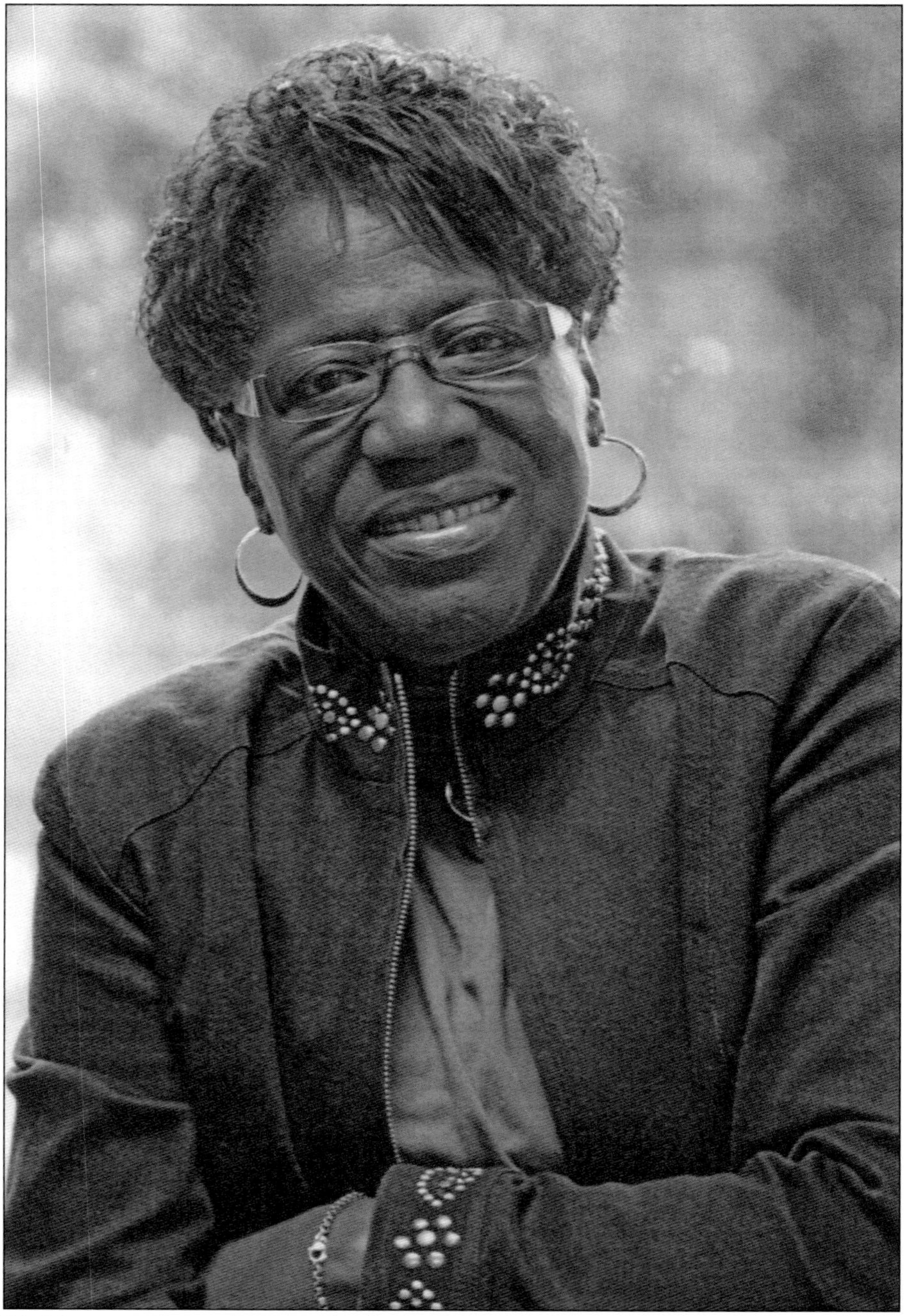

In 1984, Margaret Carter became the first African American women elected to the Oregon House of Representatives, and she was later elected to the Oregon State Senate in 2000. In the House of Representatives, she worked to pass legislation that ended state-controlled investments in South Africa and sponsored legislation to observe Martin Luther King Jr.'s birthday as a state holiday. In 2009, she was appointed by Gov. Ted Kuglongski as deputy director for human services programs at the Oregon Department of Human Services. Due to her long-standing commitment to education, the Portland Community College (PCC) Skill Center and Technology Education Building was renamed in her honor. (Courtesy of Portland Community College.)

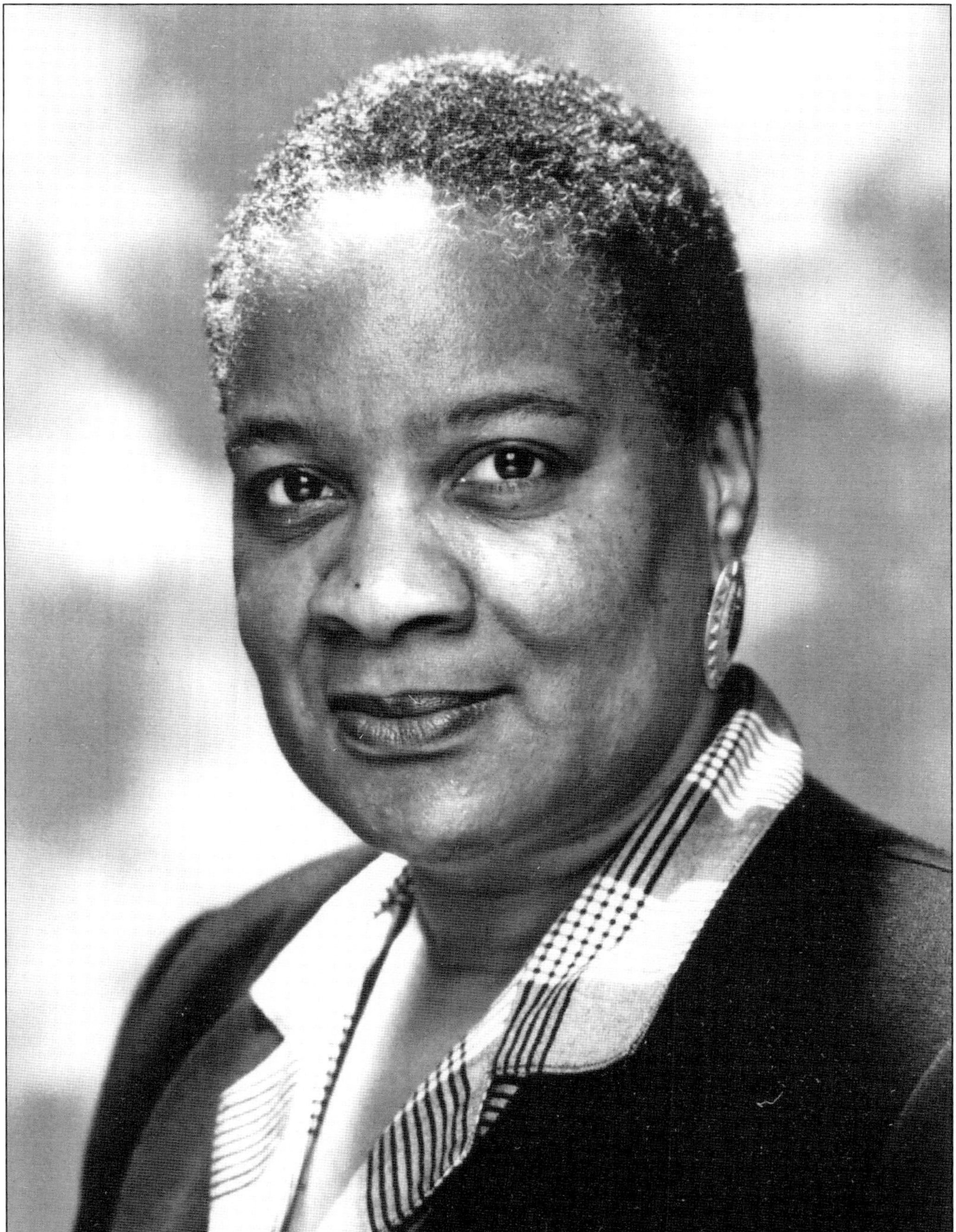

Avel Gordly served in the Oregon State Legislature from 1991 to 2008. After serving three terms in the House, she was elected as Oregon's first African American state senator in 1996. In 2002, Senator Gordly was the chief petitioner for a constitutional amendment that removed racist language from Oregon's constitution. Other legislation she sponsored included creating the Governor's Environmental Justice Task Force and creating the statewide Office of Multicultural Health. She retired from the position in 2008. (Courtesy of Avel Gordly.)

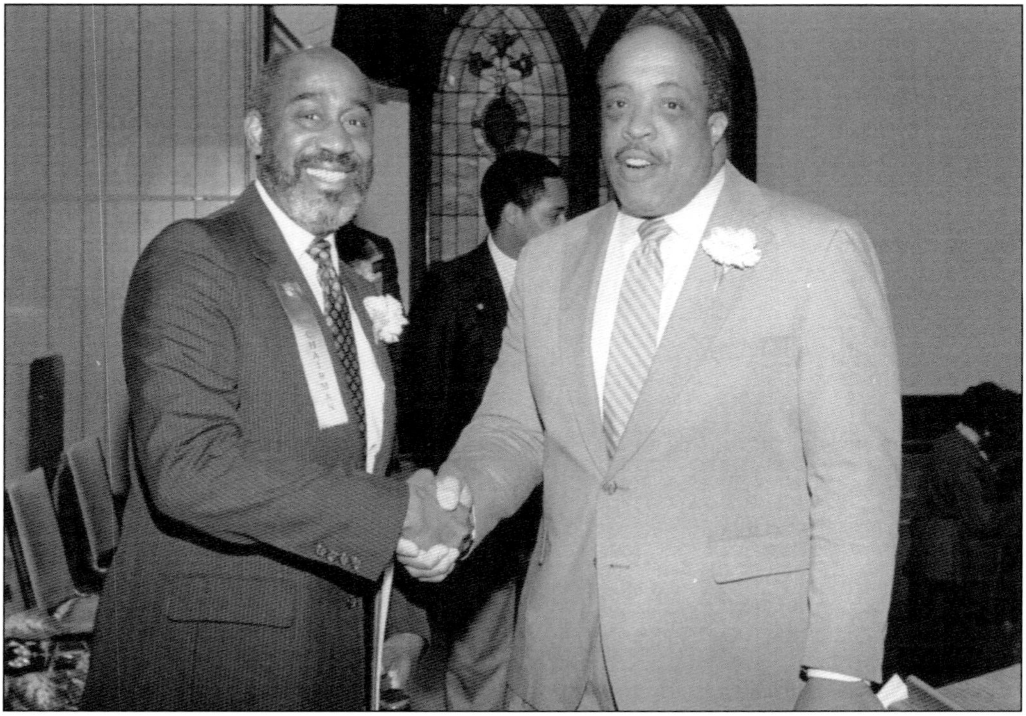

Judge Ancer Lee Haggerty (right) was born in Vanport and raised in inner Northeast Portland. He was appointed to the federal bench in November 1993 by President Clinton. In October 1990, Judge Haggerty presided over the notorious Multnomah County Circuit Court trial against Tom Metzger and the White Aryan Resistance. This trial upheld the civil action that a racist group and its individual leaders were liable for the death of Mulugeta Seraw, an Ethiopian-born student, and the Portland jury awarded $12.5 million to the Seraw family. (Courtesy of Ed Washington.)

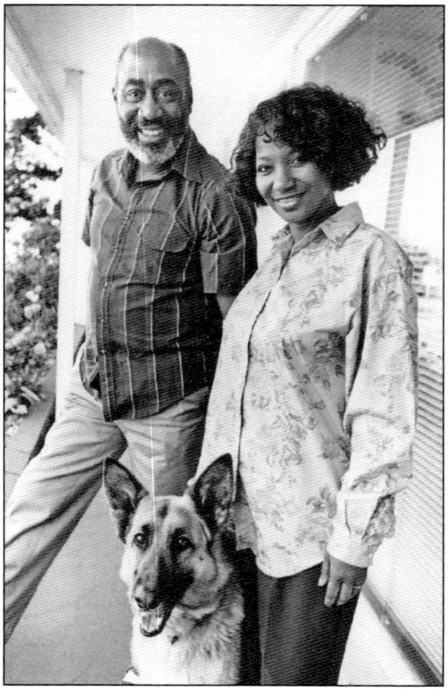

In 1992, Ed Washington, a former Vanport resident, became the first African American appointed and later elected as councilor for Metro, a regional government of Portland's metropolitan area. He currently serves as the community liaison for Diversity Initiatives & Inclusion for Portland State University and adjunct professor at Portland Community College. Ed Washington is pictured here with his late wife, Jean Nova, a former music teacher at Alameda elementary school and the first black chairwoman of Portland Music Educators. (Courtesy of Ed Washington.)

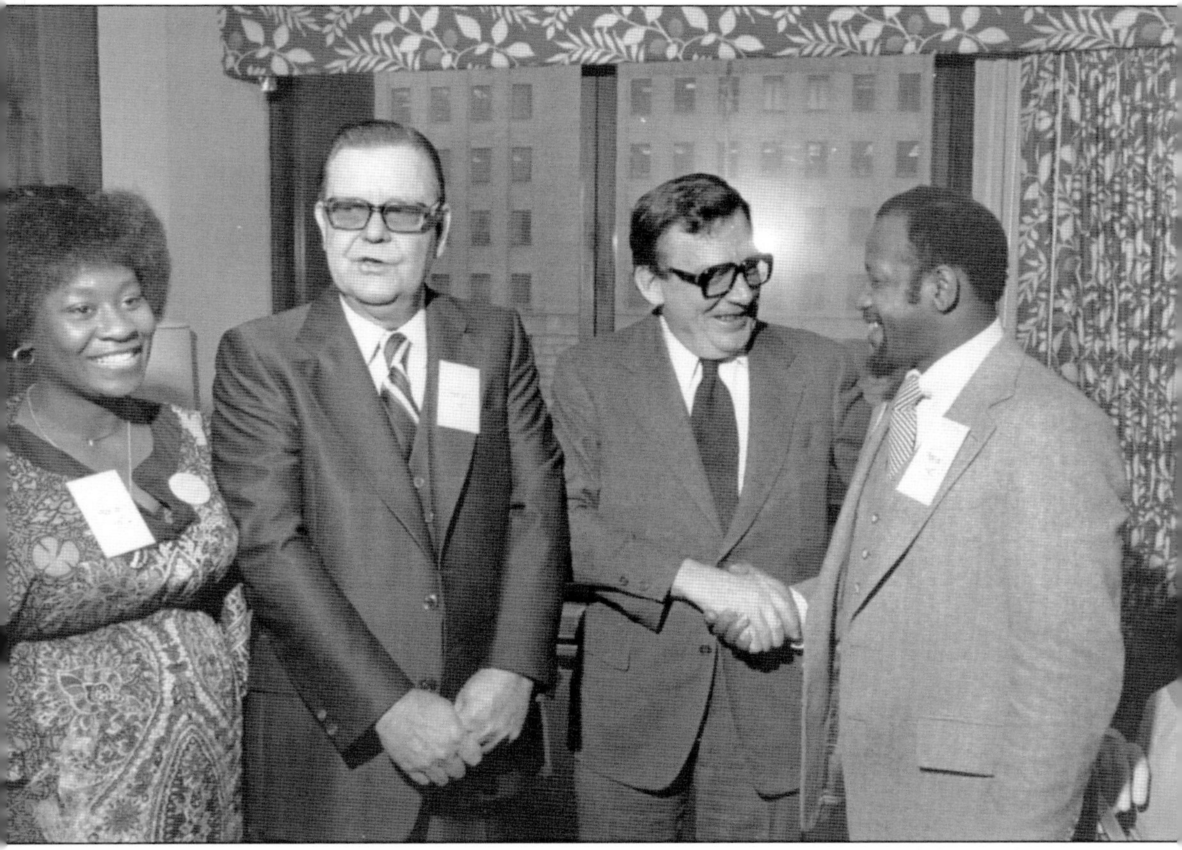

Union labor leaders continue to address job access for African Americans. From left to right are Judy (Knawles) Boyer, Walter Gray, Lane Kirkland (president of the AFL-CIO) and Bob Boyer. Judy was the office secretary in the AFL-CIO regional subdistrict office in Portland and served as an educational committee chairperson for the Portland Chapter of APRI. (Courtesy of Bob and Judy Knawles Boyer.)

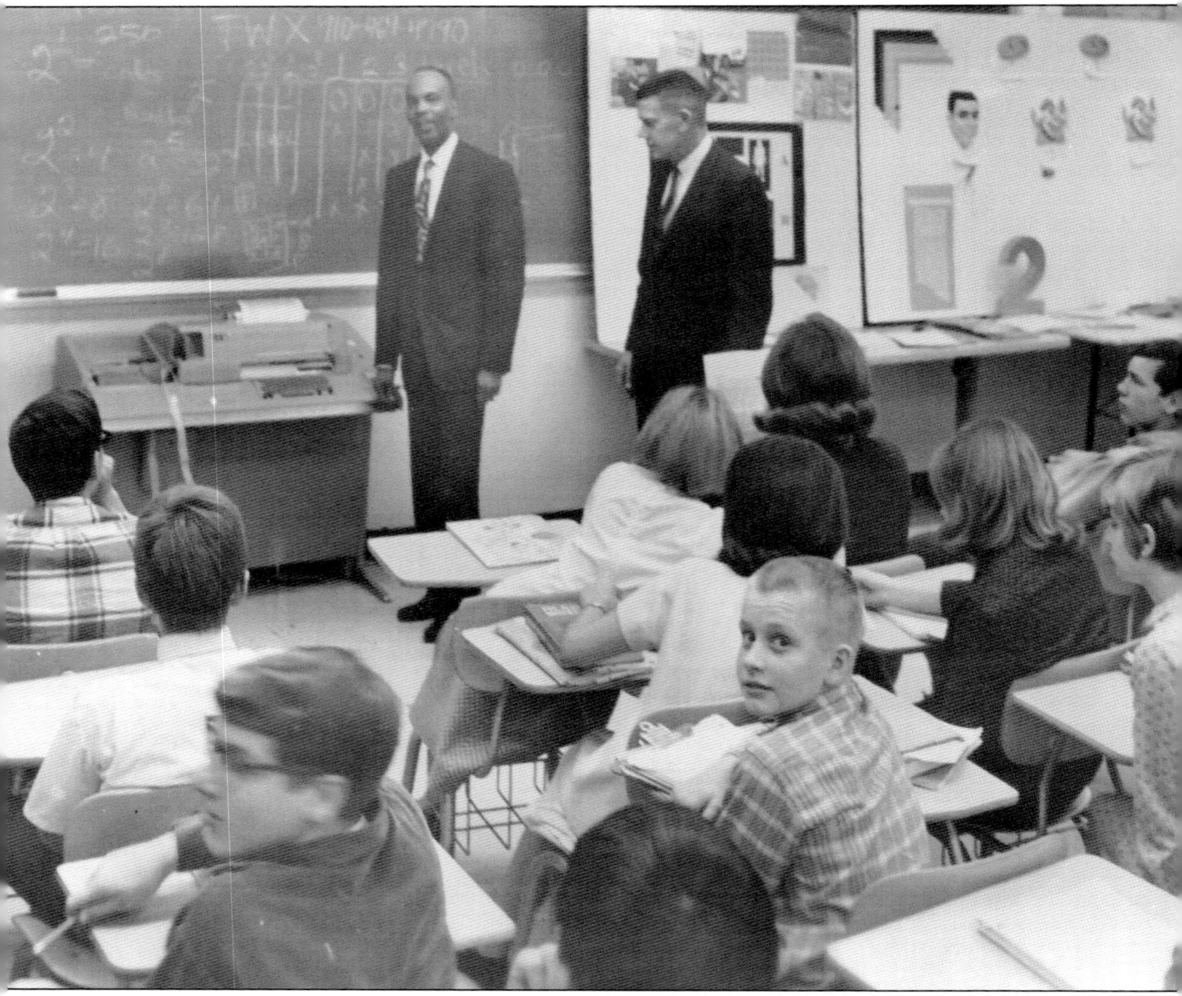

McKinley Burt, nicknamed "the Professor," was the author of *Black Inventors of America*, which detailed African American contributions to US industry. He came to Oregon in 1943 and went to work in the Vancouver, Washington, shipyards. In 1947, he became Oregon's first licensed African American accountant. In 1964, he worked as the chief accountant for the Albina Corporation, a manufacturing company. He wrote "Perspectives," a twice-weekly column for the *Portland Observer*, from 1987 to January 1999. A critic of the public education system, he called attention to the plight of African American youth. Burt is pictured here instructing children in The Dalles, Oregon, about computer technology. (Courtesy of the Oregon Historical Society.)

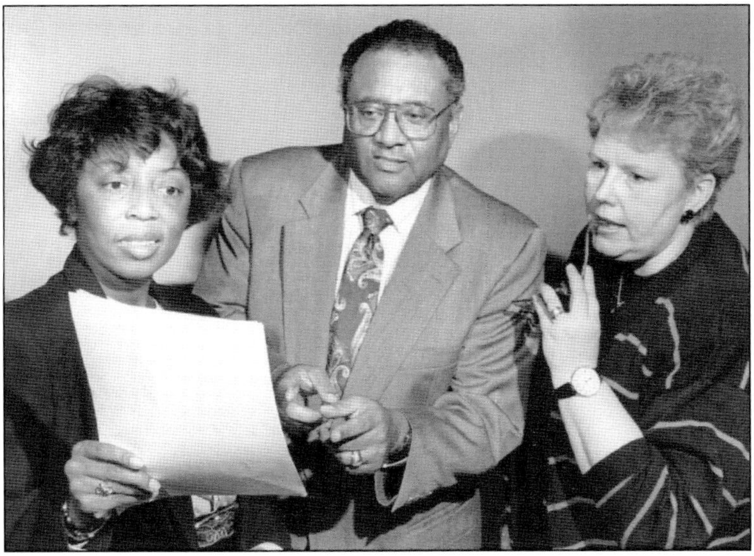

Commissioner Dick Bogle, Portland's second African American city commissioner, is pictured with members of the Contracting Equity Committee. Shirley Minor, a community activist and advocate for minority contractors, is seen to the left. (Courtesy of City of Portland Archives.)

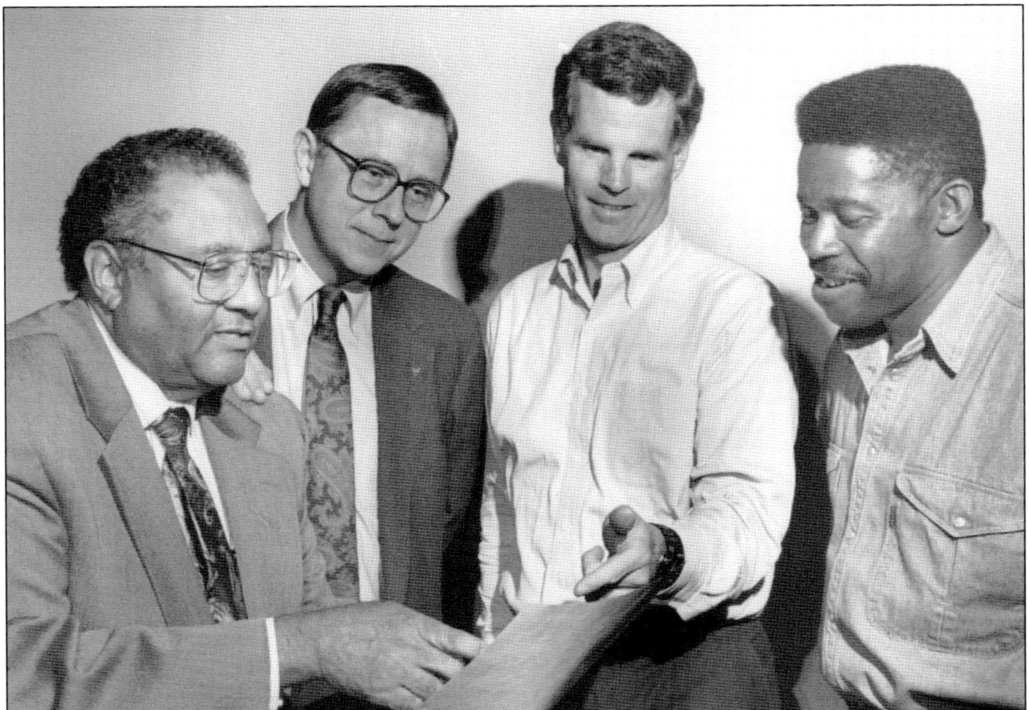

Portland city commissioner Dick Bogle (left) is pictured with additional members of the Contracting Equity Committee. James Posey, a recently retired construction contractor and longtime advocate for minority contractors, is pictured to the far right. (Courtesy of City of Portland Archives.)

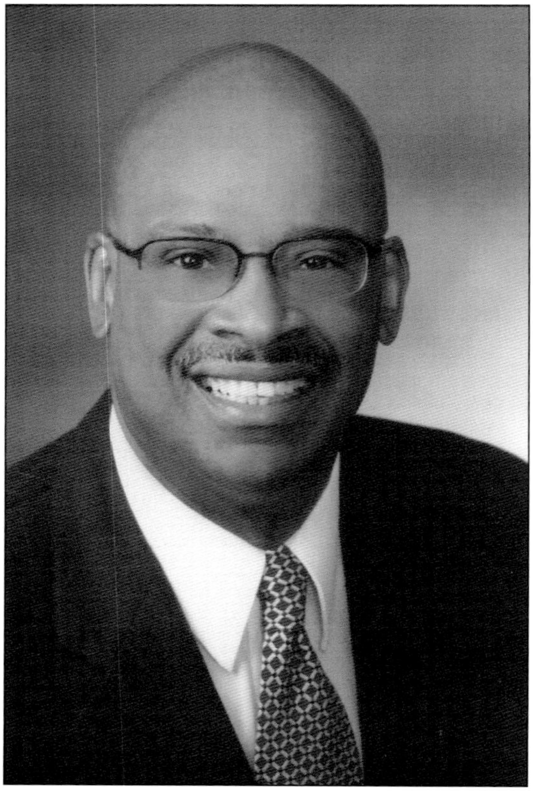

Dr. Preston Pulliams was Portland Community College's fifth president and the first African American to serve in that role. Dr. Pulliams's personal experience as a community college graduate and his commitment to connecting all people to college contributed to his success as PCC president. During his nine years as president, he helped boost the enrollment, endowment doubled, scholarships tripled, the foundations funds increased five-fold, and voters approved a $374-million bond measure. (Courtesy of Portland Community College.)

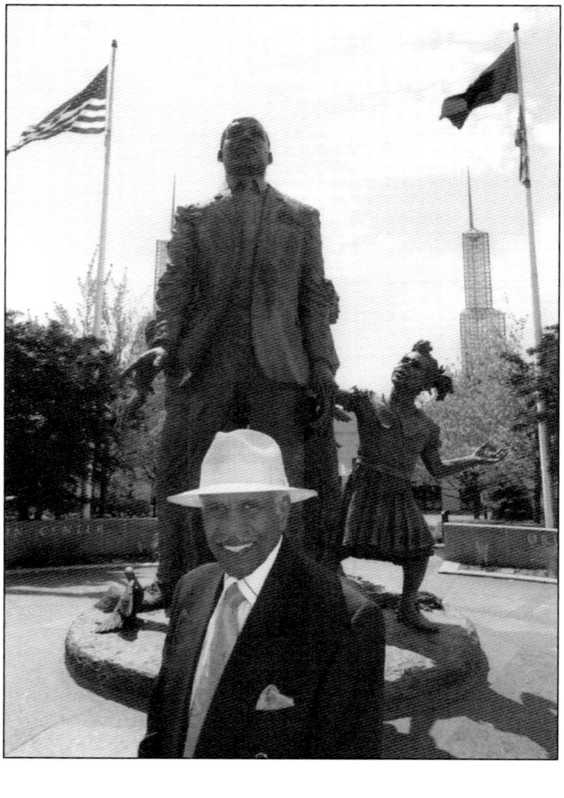

Paul Knauls, a longtime Portland resident and entrepreneur, was the former owner of the Cotton Club nightclub and Geneva hair salon. He was instrumental in obtaining a commission for the design of a bronze statue of Dr. Martin Luther King erected outside of the Oregon Convention Center. (Courtesy of Avel Gordly.)

Oregon Black Pioneers

The Oregon Black Pioneers (OBP) is an all-volunteer nonprofit organization based in Salem, Oregon. It was founded in 1993 with the mission of recognizing and commemorating the contributions of African Americans in the historical development of Oregon and educating all Oregonians about that history. Led by an active board of directors, the Oregon Black Pioneers works with community volunteers and confers with academic consultants and historical organizations in researching and compiling historical information and presenting its findings through oral presentations, exhibits, and publications. The proceeds from book sales will support the OBP's effort to establish an Oregon African American Museum.

Bibliography

Abbott, Carl. *Portland in Three Centuries: The Place and the People.* Corvallis: OSU Press, 2011.

Bosco-Milligan Foundation, Architectural Heritage Center. *Cornerstone of Community: Buildings of Portland's African American History, Revised and Expanded.* Portland: Architectural Heritage Center, 1997.

Gordly, Avel Louise and Patricia A. Schechter. *Remembering the Power of Words: The Life of an Oregon Activist, Legislator, and Community Leader.* Corvallis: OSU Press, 2011.

McLagan, Elizabeth. *A Peculiar Paradise: A History of Blacks in Oregon, 1788–1940.* Portland: Georgian Press Company, 1980.

Millner, Darrell. *The Urban League of Portland: On the Road to Equality, a 50 Year Retrospective.* Portland: Great Impression, 1995.

———. *York of the Corps of Discovery.* Portland: Oregon Historical Society Press, 2004.

Perseverance: A History of African Americans in Oregon's Marion and Polk Counties. Salem: Oregon Northwest Black Pioneers, 2011.

Portland Bureau of Planning and Kimberly S. Moreland. *The History of Portland's African American Community: 1805 to the Present.* Portland: City of Portland, 1993.

Pearson, Rudy. "A Menace to the Neighborhood: Housing and African Americans in 1941–1945." *Oregon Historical Quarterly*, Summer 2001.

Consistent with our mission to preserve history on a local level, this book was printed in South Carolina on American-made paper and manufactured entirely in the United States. Products carrying the accredited Forest Stewardship Council (FSC) label are printed on 100 percent FSC-certified paper.